THE
EXTRA
MILE

A TWENTIETH CENTURY FUND BOOK

THE
EXTRA
MILE

Rethinking Energy Policy for
Automotive Transportation

Pietro S. Nivola
Robert W. Crandall

THE BROOKINGS INSTITUTION
Washington, D.C.

BAW 5637-2/3

About Brookings

The Brookings Institution is a private nonprofit organization devoted to research, education, and publication on important issues of domestic and foreign policy. Its principal purpose is to bring knowledge to bear on current and emerging policy problems. The Institution was founded on December 8, 1927, to merge the activities of the Institute for Government Research, founded in 1916, the Institute of Economics, founded in 1922, and the Robert Brookings Graduate School of Economics, founded in 1924.

The Institution maintains a position of neutrality on issues of public policy. Interpretations or conclusions in Brookings publications should be understood to be solely those of the authors.

Copyright © 1995
THE BROOKINGS INSTITUTION
1775 Massachusetts Avenue, N.W., Washington, D.C. 20036

THE TWENTIETH CENTURY FUND, INC.
41 East 70th Street, New York, NY 10021

Library of Congress Cataloging-in-Publication data

Nivola, Pietro S.
The extra mile : rethinking energy policy for automotive transportation / Pietro S. Nivola, Robert W. Crandall.
    p.   cm.
Includes bibliographical references and index.
ISBN 0-8157-6092-2. — ISBN 0-8157-6091-4 (pbk.)
1. Energy consumption—Taxation—United States.   2. Gasoline—Taxation—United States.   3. Automobile industry and trade—United States—Energy consumption.   I. Crandall, Robert W.   II. Title.
HD9502.U52N58   1995
333.79'6816'0973—dc20   94–34675
                                                                                              CIP

9 8 7 6 5 4 3 2 1

The paper used in this publication meets the minimum requirements of the American National Standard for Information Sciences—Permanence of paper for Printed Library Materials, ANSI Z39.48–1984.

Set in Sabon
Composition by Graphic Composition, Inc.
Athens, Georgia

Printed by R. R. Donnelley and Sons Co.
Harrisonburg, Virginia

The Twentieth Century Fund sponsors and supervises timely analyses of economic policy, foreign affairs, and domestic political issues. Not-for-profit and nonpartisan, the Fund was founded in 1919 and endowed by Edward A. Filene.

For our families

Foreword

Popular political discussion in the United States usually drifts between economic issues and subjects that are loosely called "values." Energy policy, particularly when it concerns automobiles, deals in both. While the analysis of energy issues often involves very sophisticated economic calculations, the realities of energy politics often seem to be at variance with a world theoretically composed of rational consumers making rational economic decisions.

At the heart of this dissonance is the American romance with the automobile. It is no accident that the political power of the "road lobby" is legendary. At the state level, for example, dedicated taxes ensure a steady flow of revenue for highway expansion and improvement. The national government has "trust funds" for highways. These mechanisms, whatever their other merits, have the overwhelming virtue (from the standpoint of highway interests) of insulating support for automobile travel from the desperate competition for public dollars that is a routine part of budgetary politics today. Indeed, our public debates on the subject give little hint that the subsidy for drivers is larger than that for users of mass transit. Transit is a poor second when competing against a culture subsidized by government spending and celebrated by immense advertising campaigns from companies with a stake in the automobile.

Only in the years following the Arab oil embargo, which coincided with the rise of powerful environmental concerns, has the issue of measuring the true costs and benefits of auto use become a subject of serious political discussion. Serious yes, but still constrained by the very real fear elected officials have of the wrath of Americans who feel denied the God-given right to drive as far and as fast and as often as they wish.

After a bitter and politically costly battle in 1993, for example, a 4.3 cent increase in the gasoline tax was finally enacted. More successful has been the twenty-year struggle to require that auto manufacturers increase the miles per gallon consumed by the fleets they produce. None of these measures, however, has left anyone very satisfied with the results. The larger issue of how to price auto usage efficiently and fairly simmers in the background during those periods between crises about oil supply or a spike in concern about environmental degradation. It may well be that part of the reason is that the arguments about what works, and at what cost, remain too controversial.

With the persistent and unresolved nature of the public policy problems in mind, the Twentieth Century Fund saw the need to support a study of energy policy, especially as it relates to automobile use. We were fortunate that Pietro Nivola, senior fellow in the Governmental Studies program at the Brookings Institution, and Robert Crandall, senior fellow in the Economic Studies program at Brookings, were eager to take on further work in this field.

In the pages that follow, they explore the evidence available about the impact of existing policies, the merits of various alternatives under active consideration, and the case for their own approach to these issues at the national level. The authors recognize the profound differences in political culture that shape the differing paths on energy policy taken by Western democracies. Bear in mind one recent example.

During the Persian Gulf War in 1991, Germany, after agreeing to foot $11 billion of the cost of the conflict, swiftly enacted a 67 cents-a-gallon increase in gasoline taxes. For the Germans, committing troops was politically impossible, raising the already high cost of fuel was, well, in political terms, easy money.

This is not the first time the Fund has explored some of the issues addressed here. The oil shocks of the 1970s and 1980s led to the creation of two Fund task forces that examined the problems of maintaining an adequate national energy supply, and our interest in cities and the quality of life in them led to the book *Autos, Transit, and Cities* by John R. Meyer and Jose A. Gómez-Ibáñez. But changes occur so rapidly in our world that the policy recommendations put forth then—and the conditions facing those who would implement them—clearly needed revisiting. We are grateful to Pietro Nivola and Robert Crandall for their thorough exploration of this important issue.

Richard C. Leone, *President*
The Twentieth Century Fund

December 1994

Authors' Acknowledgments

This project received valuable advice and support from several individuals and organizations. Greg Anrig, Jr., John M. DeCicco, Anthony Downs, John Samples, Susan F. Tierney, and Joseph White contributed insights at various stages. James A. Dunn, Jr., Thomas E. Mann, Lee Schipper, Richard F. Winters, and David Vogel made helpful comments on earlier drafts of the manuscript. Ingeborg K. Lockwood, Eric Messick, Jason D. Rhoades, Jeffrey D. Santos, Ardith A. Spence, Susan A. Stewart, and Stephanie Wilshusen provided research and administrative assistance. Theresa B. Walker edited the manuscript, and Mary Ann Noyer and David H. Bearce checked it for accuracy. Patricia Ann Deminna prepared the appendix. Ivan Chermayeff and Thomas Geismar designed the cover. Funding for the book was generously provided by the Lynde and Harry Bradley Foundation, Inc., and the Twentieth Century Fund.

Contents

Figures

CHAPTER ONE

The Policy Problem

"IT'S HARD TO TAKE SERIOUSLY that a nation has deep problems if they can be fixed with a 50-cent-a-gallon gasoline tax."[1]

This witticism, directed at the United States by a former foreign minister of France, cannot be shrugged off. Obviously, stiffer taxation of gasoline cannot "fix" a deteriorating system of education, costs of health care, crime rates, or self-destructive litigiousness. Americans, moreover, are skeptical of advice from Europe, where traffic congestion, fuel combustion, and pollution have increased despite vehicular energy taxes far higher than 50 cents a gallon. Still, one has to wonder whether the U.S. government would be closer today to accomplishing professed national objectives if a higher levy on gasoline were in place.

A gasoline tax could alleviate the nation's chronic fiscal and trade deficits. Not least, it might restrain demand for oil more efficiently than do automotive fuel-use standards. Whatever the merits of the various rationales for energy conservation, the United States has explicitly sought for the past twenty years to moderate the consumption and importation of oil.[2] If the goal is serious, alternative means to achieve it must be assessed. The assessment needs to examine the work of other advanced countries. Have they had greater success with a mix of policies that include higher excise taxes than U.S. policy has achieved primarily by regulating the automobile industry?

In this book we evaluate in comparative perspective the U.S. reliance on an unusual regulatory program in lieu of tax measures to promote energy efficiency in automotive transportation. We also examine the comparative politics of this idiosyncratic policy preference.

Our conclusions are exhortative but also sobering. U.S. energy policy would indeed be more efficient if policymakers, instead of relying heavily on bureaucratic injunctions to save fuel in the transportation sector, had decided to tax gasoline. However, the political barriers to taxation have been, and are likely to remain, formidable. This is not because American politicians are less farsighted or imaginative than those in other governments, but because differing international tax rates and regulatory regimes are creatures of history and reflect basic differences among governmental institutions. The U.S. energy framework of mandatory fuel-mileage rules for vehicle manufacturers and low taxes for motorists is ultimately the outcome of public choices accreting over many decades, shaped and solidified by a unique political structure. The oil-saving excises that have evolved under fundamentally different political systems in Europe, Japan, Canada, and elsewhere are largely accidental energy programs that, despite considerable advantages, would be difficult to emulate in this country. Nonetheless, in the concluding chapter of this book, we suggest ways of increasing the feasibility of modest moves in that direction.

Concerns

American energy policy has made important progress in several areas.[3] Field prices of petroleum and natural gas have been fully decontrolled. The nation's primary heating fuel is being transported to markets with far fewer regulatory distortions. The electric utility industry is being restructured, promising significant gains in efficiency. The energy intensity of the U.S. economy as a whole has fallen substantially since the Arab oil embargo. Almost a third less primary energy is needed to produce a unit of national output today than in 1973, an improvement that compares favorably with the performance of other industrialized countries (figure 1-1). The use of oil has also declined in most parts of the economy (figure 1-2).

Most, but not all. In transportation, which runs almost entirely on refined petroleum products and which absorbs two-thirds of all the petroleum we consume, usage has grown.

This does not mean that America's transportation system as a whole is "wasteful." Most of the increased use of oil in transportation simply reflects economic growth and limited opportunities for fuel substitution: unlike utility boilers or home furnaces, the engines of cars, trucks, buses, and airplanes cannot run on chunks of coal or be hooked to natural gas

Figure 1-1. *Energy Intensity of Five OECD Countries, 1970-90*

Tons of oil equivalent per 1985 U.S. millions of dollars of GDP

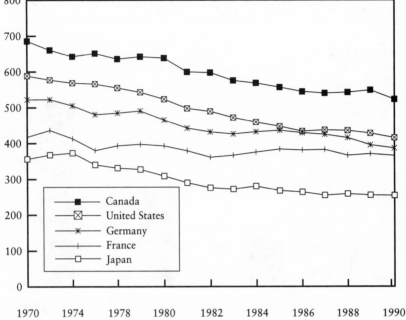

Source: International Energy Agency, *Energy Balances of OECD Countries* (Paris, 1993), pp. 90–170.

pipelines. (The engines can operate with methanol, ethanol, or compressed natural gas, but at much higher cost.)

The size of the country and the need to ship goods and bulk commodities over great distances inevitably adds to the energy requirements of commercial transport industries. Given the extent of the task, the freight modal mix, with its large component of rail, pipeline, and waterborne traffic, as well as an excellent highway network for trucking, makes comparatively efficient use of energy.[4] Similarly, air travel is a cost-effective way of moving passengers between distant cities. Turning as much as a tenth of each barrel of crude oil into jet fuel may be an optimal allocation of resources for American refineries.

Nonetheless, the oil appetite of private passenger vehicles has warranted scrutiny if only because it has been the object of prolonged government intervention. For here, on the premise that there is fat to cut, is

Figure 1-2. *U.S. Oil Consumption in Four Major Sectors, 1973, 1990*

Oil consumption in millions of barrels a day

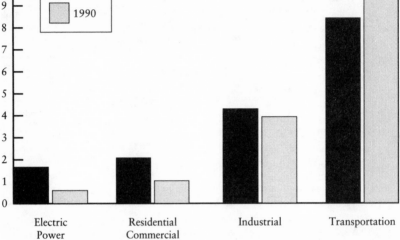

Source: Oak Ridge National Laboratory, *Transportation Energy Data Book, Edition 14* (Oak Ridge, Tenn.: Oak Ridge National Laboratory for the Department of Energy, 1994), pp. 2–7, 2–9, 2–10.

where regulators began intervening seventeen years ago to force a change. But changing the average mileage per gallon of vehicles, as required by federal law since 1978, has never addressed the main event: each year, Americans log about one and a half trillion miles in their cars—the equivalent of almost three million round trips to the moon (and counting). Most of this enormous amount of driving, as we discuss in chapter 4, does not simply derive from the natural geography of the United States.

The claim on oil by American automotive transportation is unlikely to abate in the foreseeable future, at least barring extended economic stagnation, a sudden reduction in the cost of alternative fuels or of new automobile technologies, a fundamental social transformation, or a major redirection of government policy. Hence, the Department of Energy has estimated that the oil required to power light-duty vehicles will increase at least 18 percent by the year 2010 compared with 1990.[5]

Does this anomaly matter?

Environmental and Security Issues

With less than 5 percent of the world's population, the United States still consumes annually more than a quarter of the world's crude oil output, mainly to propel some 200 million cars and trucks and to provide the extensive infrastructure they require.[6] Burning that much fuel contributes to the buildup of greenhouse gases and urban smog. Combined with a decline in domestic petroleum production, the magnitude of U.S. oil consumption also poses a potential security risk. Net petroleum imports now account for half of U.S. requirements, up from 35 percent in 1973, and are projected to reach nearly 60 percent by the end of the century.[7] While the United States had grown more dependent on imported oil by the end of the 1980s, Japan managed to reduce dependence on oil imports as a percentage of GNP to half of what it had been in 1973.[8] Increasing external dependency, especially on unstable sources, may leave the United States more vulnerable to future supply disruptions and price shocks.[9]

These dangers, and the efficacy of gasoline taxation in lessening them, can be debated. Following the UN Conference on Environment and Development (Rio Earth Summit) in 1992, the United States committed itself to lowering carbon dioxide emissions into the atmosphere. Additional taxes on automotive fuels would be a modest step, not a giant stride, toward honoring that commitment. Assuming that global warming is a threat (an open question), even quadrupling the present U.S. gasoline tax would have a small effect. If effluents from the U.S. transportation sector are adding approximately 7 percent to the earth's accumulation of carbon dioxide, and if a 50-cents-a-gallon tax brought about a 12 percent reduction in transport fuel combustion, the immediate worldwide reduction in CO_2 would be less than 1 percent.

The relentless growth of automotive travel and traffic appears to be largely responsible for the failure of several American cities to lower the levels of carbon monoxide and ozone in their air sheds.[10] A national gasoline tax, though helpful, is not the best solution to this problem. In theory, a combination of congestion pricing on urban roads and special pollution taxes would be more appropriate and equitable than a levy that charges motorists who drive in rural areas in the middle of the night the same fee as peak-hour users of congested facilities in a zone with polluted air.[11]

Nor is greater energy dependence necessarily perilous—provided the United States remains prepared to maintain an optimally managed strategic petroleum reserve (no simple matter, as we observe in a later chapter) and to defend the world's petroleum lifeline. When Iraq invaded Kuwait in 1990, no conservation measure, no matter how bold, could have afforded more energy security than did Operation Desert Storm.

Yet proponents of energy taxation to lower America's thirst for oil have a point. Almost one hundred U.S. metropolitan areas continue to violate federal clean air standards.[12] Some of those violations may be of minor consequence, but if the standards are to be enforced, emission controls (which have been tightened repeatedly) are not enough. Some important areas will not be brought into compliance without a policy that reduces vehicle miles traveled and traffic congestion.

A reliable flow of foreign energy supplies does depend, perhaps inordinately, on the ability and willingness of the U.S. government to use force if necessary to secure vital sources. That ability or willingness is hardly a foregone conclusion. If a less resolute president had been in office in the autumn of 1990, effective military action might have been postponed indefinitely. Recall that congressional support for the Bush administration's determination to go to war, rather than trust in porous economic sanctions against Iraq, was very much in doubt throughout the fall.[13]

Although boosting the federal excise on gasoline would represent only a partial and imperfect answer to such deficiencies and uncertainties, a central finding of this book is that an excise of 25 cents a gallon after 1985 would have conserved as much, if not more, oil than has the extant policy of administering gas mileage requirements for new passenger vehicles.

The CAFE Catch

The federal government's Corporate Average Fuel Economy (CAFE) regulations, in force since 1978, have required vehicle manufacturers to achieve specified sales-weighted fuel-intensity averages for fleets of new cars and light trucks. Mileage per gallon (mpg) in these fleets has improved, but the longevity of older vehicles and the volume of use contribute to a significant annual increase in petroleum consumption in transportation.[14] The CAFE system has had three serious shortcomings.

First of all, the regulatory scheme takes aim at motor vehicles, but does nothing to discourage their use. Indeed, amid stable or declining fuel prices, mandatory improvements in fuel efficiency may reduce the marginal cost of driving, perversely inducing increases in vehicle miles traveled (VMTs).[15] Figure 1-3 displays the growth of VMTs over the past half century. Save for an interlude during World War II and periods fol-

Figure 1-3. *Passenger Car and Truck Miles Traveled, 1936–92*[a]

Billions of vehicle miles traveled

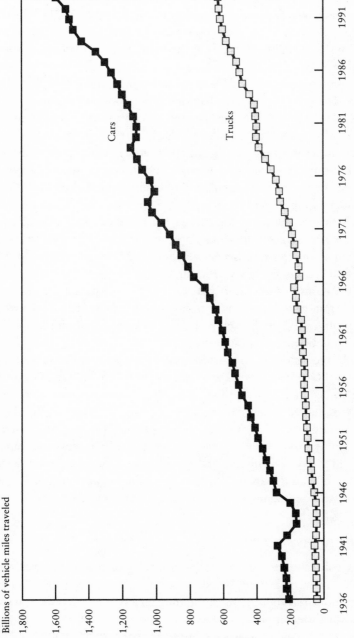

Cars

Trucks

Sources: Federal Highway Administration, *Highway Statistics, Summary to 1985* (Department of Transportation, 1987), pp. 229–32, table VM-201A, and *Highway Statistics*, 1987–1992 (Department of Transportation, 1989–93), annual editions, table VM-1, each year.
a. Because of a 1986 methodology change, data are recalculated starting in 1966.

lowing the two oil shocks of the 1970s, VMTs have risen without interruption. In the 1980s, with the CAFE standards applied to all new light-duty vehicles, VMTs climbed as steeply as ever, at almost four times the rate of population growth. An energy program that, unlike a gasoline tax, fails to make driving more costly at the margin inevitably forfeits potential fuel savings.

A second drawback of CAFE lies in its impact on the overall stock of vehicles. The program has an effect on the mpgs of *newly* manufactured automobiles, and they compare favorably, of course, with the poor performance of older cars. Automobiles produced in 1990 averaged 28 mpg—a far cry from the 14 mpg ratings of 1974 models.[16] The improvement in the average mpg, counting all passenger vehicles on the road, however, is a different story. The total population of light-duty vehicles in 1990 averaged under 19 mpg, a gain of fewer than 5 mpg over the average recorded ten years earlier.[17] Why has this change been so modest? Each year's generation of new vehicles, however improved, represents approximately 7 percent of all registered passenger vehicles. And that percentage has been falling over time as aging, less efficient models have remained on the road longer.[18] A conservation effort that focuses exclusively on redesigning a small fraction of the automotive fleet can only attain net energy savings over a protracted period. Each year, new vehicles account for less than 4 percent of national oil consumption.[19]

Finally, the changing composition of the vehicular stock has frustrated the goals of CAFE in another way: as sagging fuel prices lowered the operating costs of light trucks, vans, and recreational vehicles, sales of these products mounted to more than 30 percent of the market.[20] With lower mpg standards for this growing segment of the passenger fleet, average fuel economy, even for the newest vehicles, has not progressed as rapidly as it would have if a suitable fuel tax had been imposed. A tax would affect the operating expense (hence the VMTs) of all vehicles, old and new, but would discourage the use of gas guzzlers the most.

Nobody Does It Better?

Many observers recognize the inefficiencies of the U.S. conservation program in transportation, but some suggest that the transport systems of other industrial countries are becoming no less energy intensive in spite of radically different policies.

Some recent studies insist, for instance, that vehicular travel mileage has been leveling off in the United States while moving up rapidly elsewhere as incomes rise. The argument is that automobile ownership in this country is reaching saturation, whereas the automotive populations of other developed countries are growing faster. On the assumption that the intensity of use for a given stock of vehicles is relatively insensitive to fuel prices, the growth of VMTs (hence levels of motor fuel consumption) among industrial nations must converge steadily. And if that is the case, even the drastic fuel taxes and other "antiauto policies" of Europe and Japan will have proven ineffectual.[21]

There are at least two difficulties with this perspective, apart from the fact that fuel prices surely influence the use of automobiles. First, foreign rates of car ownership, though now increasing relative to those of the United States, have had to move from a much lower baseline. Hence, full convergence remains a distant prospect. If one extrapolates from rates of increase between 1970 and 1987, for instance, one finds that the number of cars per capita in France would not reach the U.S. level until the year 2032. The number of cars per person in Sweden, where living standards are commensurate with America's, would not equal the U.S. figure until the year 2073. Even to assume these linear extensions of 1970-87 rates over such long periods, however, may be highly questionable. The assumption rests on a host of debatable notions: that incomes will continue to rise as (or more) quickly abroad; that demographic trends (such as rates of female participation in the work force) will follow common national patterns over time; that the United States is nearing saturation at the level of two (as opposed to three or more) vehicles per household; and so on.[22]

Second, cross-national data on VMTs in the 1980s raise doubts about the convergence thesis. Compared with Americans, the French, Japanese, Germans, Italians, and others acquired automobiles at an accelerated rate—but they also continued to drive less. If anything, the difference as of 1991 was significantly greater than it was a decade earlier (figure 1-4).[23]

Maybe this gap will narrow again during the 1990s. No new baby-boom generation is poised to come of driving age in the United States. The number of women obtaining drivers' licenses may not increase as quickly as it did when women were first seeking jobs outside the home. Any stabilization in the number of vehicles per person of driving age, however, will be offset if average miles per vehicle continue to expand.[24] Such expansion is quite plausible. Although women still drive less than men, they are catching up. Households with working mothers, for example, do more driving (infants are delivered to and from day care centers, for instance). The percentage of women who work and choose to

Figure 1-4. *Comparison of Average Vehicle Miles Traveled per Passenger Vehicle, 1976–91*

Thousands of passenger vehicle miles

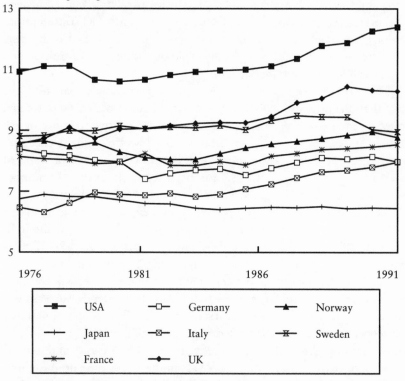

Sources: Data drawn from Lee Schipper and others, "Mind the Gap: The Vicious Circle of Measuring Automobile Fuel Use," *Energy Policy*, vol. 21 (December 1993), p. 1182; Lee Schipper and others, "Fuel Prices and Economy: Factors Affecting Land Travel," *Transport Policy*, vol. 1, no. 1 (1993), pp. 6–20; and more recent data provided by Lawrence Berkeley Laboratory, Berkeley, Calif.

have children has been increasing. Moreover, if, as expected, female workers reach nearly 48 percent of the labor force in the next ten years, more people will be living farther from their work places. Because two-income families often have difficulty finding housing within close proximity of both work places, one worker, or both, must commute over longer distances.

The fact is, the combined effect of fewer cars and fewer miles traveled per vehicle continues to mean that the amount of driving per capita in European countries and in Japan remains far less than in the United States

Figure 1-5. *Comparison of Passenger Vehicle Miles Traveled per Capita, 1976–91*

Thousands of passenger vehicle miles

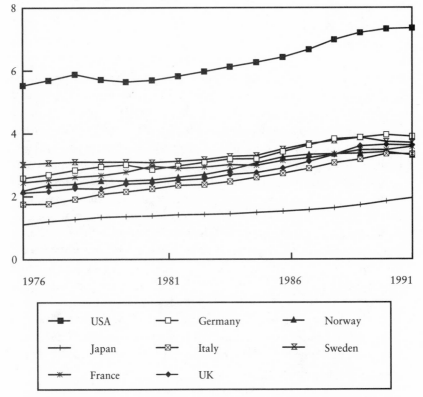

Sources: Data drawn from Schipper and others, "Mind the Gap"; Schipper and others, "Fuel Prices and Economy"; and more recent data provided by Lawrence Berkeley Laboratory. Population data drawn from International Monetary Fund, *Financial Statistics, Yearbook 1992* (Washington, 1993).

(figure 1-5). In energy usage, this travel behavior, compounded by the higher fuel intensity of the U.S. light vehicular fleet, has left the United States a distant outlier.[25] Average motor fuel consumption per vehicle here has remained approximately twice as high as the average in Europe and Japan.[26] On a per capita basis, Americans in 1990 were still consuming at least two to three times more motor fuel than the Europeans and Japanese, despite more than a decade of mandatory CAFE requirements for new vehicles in the United States and no similar regulatory strictures in the other countries. To put this into an economic perspective, at the close of the 1980s Germany still needed only about half as many gallons of motor fuel as the United States per dollar of gross domestic product; Japan needed a bit less than a third; and Holland needed less than a sixth.[27]

The Demand Response

How much of the difference in automotive fuel consumption among countries can be imputed to tax rates, rather than other variables, is hard to ascertain precisely. Variations in geography, incomes, population growth, auto ownership rates, and quality of mass transit services have a bearing. So do different environmental standards, safety regulations, and fees for vehicles. The automobiles in much of Europe may be consuming somewhat less fuel per mile partly because most European cars are not yet equipped with three-way catalytic converters.[28] The automotive fleets of some European countries are also more efficient partly because larger numbers of cars are diesel powered. In part, diesels have enjoyed a price advantage outside the United States because most other governments did not enforce particulate standards before 1990. Imposts on the acquisition and registration of vehicles vary widely and have differential effects. Many Dutch people and Danes ride bicycles to work, but not because they prefer the exercise or are inhabitants of third-world countries with flat terrains; the sales tax on a new, medium-sized car in the Netherlands is approximately nine times higher than in the United States; in Denmark, thirty-seven times higher![29]

Motor Fuel Taxation

Whatever else may explain the differing intensities of transport fuel use among nations, however, energy taxation seems to play an important part. Figure 1-6 plots the relationship between the annual quantity of motor fuel consumed per capita and the fuel taxes of countries in the Organization for Economic Cooperation and Development (OECD). The correlation is quite clear and systematic: national consumption varies inversely with tax rates. The pattern is also roughly consistent with consensus estimates of the price elasticity of demand for motor fuel: in the long run, each percentage point increase in real fuel prices reduces demand commensurately.

Proponents of the CAFE system may be underestimating the extent to which price (or tax) increases will depress consumption. They sometimes

Figure 1-6. *Relationship between Motor Fuel Consumption and Tax Rates, IEA Countries, 1990*

Motor fuel consumption by passenger vehicles (liters per capita)[a]

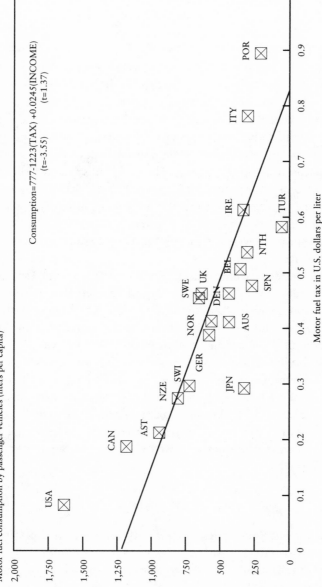

Consumption=777-1223(TAX) +0.0245(INCOME)
(t=-3.55)   (t=1.37)

Motor fuel tax in U.S. dollars per liter

Sources: Population data for countries drawn from International Monetary Fund, *International Financial Statistics Yearbook 1991* (Washington, 1992); International Energy Agency, *Energy Policies of IEA Countries* (Paris: OECD, 1992), p. 521, appendix A; Organization for Economic Cooperation and Development, *OECD Environmental Data: Compendium 1991* (Paris, 1991), p. 209.

a. Where consumption is equal to annual liters consumed per capita in 1990, TAX is the motor fuel tax in U.S. cents per liter at 1990 Purchasing Power Parity, and INCOME is 1990 income per capita in U.S. dollars. All data are deflated by purchasing power parity indexes from OECD. The estimated elasticity of consumption with respect to TAX at the point of means is -0.66.

seem to invoke a need for CAFE standards on the grounds that manufacturers are lethargic, stupid, or irresponsible in their choices of vehicle designs and technologies. Some also seem to assume that consumer preferences and driving habits are immutable.

Fewer Gas Guzzlers

The notion that rising prices do not suffice to induce automakers to alter mileage per gallon of individual models overlooks the fact that competition among automobile companies to optimize performance has intensified greatly since the 1970s. Even if no such competition existed, any sizable increase in fuel prices would inevitably reduce sales of large, low-mpg vehicles now in production, while boosting sales of smaller, high-mpg vehicles currently on the market. The problem is not that the auto manufacturers will not produce highly efficient cars. (They already do. General Motors' Geo Metro, for instance, averages 65 mpg.) The problem is that few of these cars can be sold at current energy prices.[30] Vehicular mpgs would improve in response to a higher fuel tax even if the automakers did nothing new.

Production strategies would almost certainly shift, however, especially in the United States. CAFE advocates are quick to stress that new vehicle fuel economy has not changed as markedly amid the high energy costs of Europe and Japan as in this country, where regulators rather than prices have forced manufacturers to make adjustments.[31] But the favorable comparison is misleading. There has been (and continues to be) wide scope for the U.S. automobile industry to show big strides in energy efficiency. The industries abroad had long taken fuel consumption into consideration, while the U.S. industry produced gas guzzlers. What might be asked about CAFE is why, after so many years, it still leaves the overall fuel intensity of American automobiles clearly above the averages of France, Japan, and Germany.[32]

Driving Less

The elasticity of vehicle miles traveled with respect to fuel prices has been extensively researched. Although a spread-out pattern of settlement severely limits the flexibility for adjustment in the United States, Americans, too, alter their behavior in response to relative prices. Figure 1-7 exhibits the changes in annual miles driven per automobile throughout the postwar period. Whenever prices rose sharply, as in 1974 or 1979, automotive mileage fell as motorists curtailed leisure trips and other dis-

Figure 1-7. *Real Gasoline Prices and Annual Miles Driven per Car, United States*

Thousands of miles traveled per car

1987 dollars per gallon

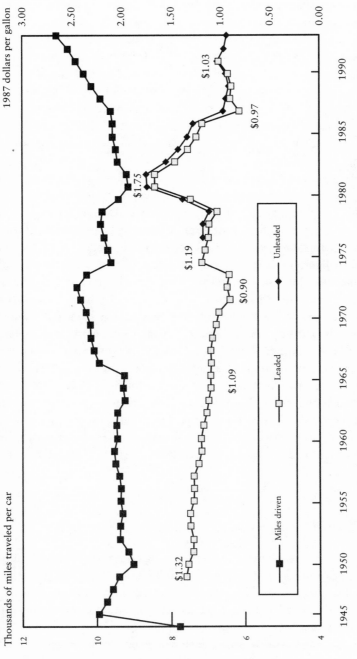

Sources: Energy Information Administration, "Motor Gasoline and Residential Heating Oil Retail Prices, 1949–1991," *Annual Energy Review 1991* (Department of Energy, 1992), p. 161; and Federal Highway Administration, *Highway Statistics, Summary to 1985* (Department of Transportation, 1987), table VM-201, and *Highway Statistics, 1986-1992* (Department of Transportation, 1987-93), annual editions, table VM-1 each year.

cretionary travel and even modified some entrenched commuting practices.[33] (Predictably, as prices softened in real terms in subsequent years,
mileage rebounded.)

Consumer sensitivity to prices has been equally evident in attitudinal
surveys. Time and again during the 1970s, large majorities indicated that
higher prices not only worked but worked better than anything else in
reducing gasoline consumption.[34] Pollsters found that consumers were
more likely to react to a general rise in energy prices by cutting back on
driving than by, say, turning off lights. Further, most drivers admitted they
could restrict the use of cars, at least one day a week, without extreme
sacrifice.[35]

Americans are exceptionally dependent on automobiles to get to and
from work. But even for commuters, effects of prices on gasoline consumption are discernible. In early 1991, unleaded regular gasoline was
selling in the United States for approximately $1.30 a gallon, including
taxes. On that base, a price increase of $0.35 would have caused just
under a 10 percent drop in gasoline used for work trips, or the equivalent
of triple the volume of oil imported from Kuwait, Iran, and Algeria combined.[36] How could this happen in the context of limited or nonexistent
public transportation in much of the country? The principal reason appears to be the appreciable latitude for altering vehicular load factors
through ride sharing. Shifts in the commuting pattern within the Washington, D.C., metropolitan area during the past decade illustrate the consequences of price fluctuations. At the end of the 1980s, after real fuel
prices had collapsed, only 15 percent of Washington's suburban commuters car-pooled.[37] The percentage of persons driving to work alone reached
69 percent, up from 60 percent in 1980. At the start of that decade, soar-
ing oil prices had prompted almost a quarter of the commuters to resort
to car and van pools.

Economic Effects

Almost no one recommends superimposing on North America a Europe-
an-style gasoline levy of $2.00 to $3.00 a gallon. The question is whether
the United States would suffer from an additional tax increase in the
range of $0.20 to $0.50 a gallon, a level of taxation more comparable to
that of Canada.

The case against this price adjustment, and for renewing CAFE controls instead, is often buttressed by pessimistic predictions of how a
higher fuel tax would affect the U.S. economy. In 1988, for instance, de-

fenders of the regulatory approach could point to a much-publicized study commissioned by the American Automobile Association. It concluded that a hypothetical 30-cent gas tax would promptly reduce gross national product by $30 billion, throw more than a half million persons out of work, raise the consumer price index by a full percentage point, and lower the nation's personal savings rate by nearly 8 percent.[38]

Apocalypse Not

Such forecasts paint a distorted picture of the tax option's macroeconomic impact. Their deficiency goes beyond the environmentalists' objection that motor fuels may be underpriced.[39] (A proper cost-benefit analysis of higher gasoline taxes ought to measure gains from potential reductions in congestion and pollution.)

Historically, incomes and savings have not simply moved in lockstep with the going rate for motor fuel. Households' expenditures for gasoline were larger as a percentage of total household expenditures in the 1950s and 1960s, yet incomes grew more rapidly than in the past decade. The costs of automotive travel (cents per mile in constant 1991 dollars) are now half of what they were in 1974, hence transportation's share of total personal consumption expenditures is significantly lower.[40] Yet savings rates were higher twenty years ago than today.

The consequences of proposed taxes differ, depending on one's time frame and on whether the added tax dollars might bring relief from other, more harmful, forms of taxation or will help contain the long-range federal deficit. Like any other deficit-controlling revenue measure of comparable magnitude, any increase in the gasoline tax above a dime a gallon would temporarily slow GNP growth slightly.[41] It would also cause a noticeable one-time increase in the consumer price index and an inevitable loss of private disposable income. But the near-term contractionary effects of higher fuel taxes could eventually be more than offset by the advantages of smaller government deficits in out-years or of lower taxes on capital gains and savings, which could result in higher aggregate rates of saving, lower long-term costs of capital, and additional productive investment.[42]

Trade Effects

The balance of trade would also be affected. This dimension deserves attention in light of frequent American complaints about "unfair" imbalances with the rest of the world. The United States has run a persistent deficit in international trade because its total expenditures on goods and services, including imports, exceed its domestic production. A tax hike (at least by a fiscally disciplined government) would reduce some of this excess spending.

In addition, by trimming oil imports, higher taxes on motor fuels would alter the trade flows directly. No commodity plays a larger role in the U.S. external deficit than does imported oil. In most of the years in which the United States experienced a trade shortfall since 1970, trade would have been either in surplus or virtually balanced but for the rate of oil importation.[43] Of course, energy taxation cannot (and should not) have the attainment of overall trade balances as its raison d'être. A gasoline tax of 25 cents a gallon would only dent the country's massive net oil import requirements by less than 5 percent, at least in the short run.[44] Over time, however, the influence on the volume and composition of trade could become more significant as firms and households adjusted their spending patterns to reflect the increase in the relative prices of motor fuels and of goods and services using these fuels.

Tax and Spend?

Net benefits from levying any energy tax are likely to be elusive if its revenues are matched by corresponding increases in government spending. If past is necessarily prologue, critics could understandably remain as skeptical as ever about the government's capacity for fiscal restraint. Certainly before 1990 the history of federal gasoline taxes seemed indicative of the problem. Only once, in 1932, had any part of the gas tax been used to reduce a fiscal imbalance rather than to support spending. The tax was reauthorized on a dozen separate occasions after its inception. Each extension was supposed to be "temporary," but every increase became permanent, proving, as the French say, that "*rien ne dure comme le provisoire*." And nearly every infusion of dollars was expended.

Nevertheless, ruling out a higher fuel tax (or, for that matter, additional revenue of any kind) on the premise that it will be squandered has become less convincing of late. For all their flaws, the budget agreements of recent years have demonstrated greater determination in Congress to restrain discretionary spending. In any event, antitax maximalism presupposes that Congress can somehow shrink deficits with spending cuts alone. That expectation is fanciful, if not dangerous. For all their abstract elegance, proposals to balance the budget by cutting deeply into social security and medical outlays, getting rid of farm subsidies, terminating all aid for small businesses, and so on are utopian.[45] In the real world, big budgetary reductions have not come in these categories, but have occurred preponderantly in defense. It is not too much to say that rigid adherence to "no new taxes" may be less of a guarantee against profligacy than of a larger national debt and an inadequate national defense, along with further retreat from America's global leadership responsibilities.

Distributional Issues

Proponents of regulatory techniques in place of fiscal incentives to promote automotive energy efficiency make a final argument: fuel taxation has uneven incidence.

Against an idealized standard in which every source of revenue for the federal government has to be structured progressively to reflect household incomes and geographic circumstances, a national gasoline tax looks inequitable. The costs of gasoline as a percent of estimated income might be three or four times higher for the lowest 10 percent of households than for the top 10 percent.[46] And the burden may fall more onerously on persons forced to drive long distances in sparsely populated states than on persons living in densely settled places. A resident of Wyoming might pay more than twice as much a year in taxes as an inhabitant of New York.[47]

But is gasoline taxation actually as regressive as its opponents ritually assert? Data on the energy burdens of income groups are notoriously unreliable. Income statistics do not normally include in-kind benefits, such as food stamps or medicaid. Moreover, people tend to move in and out of different income brackets depending on events, such as illness, unemployment, or retirement. Household spending levels, which reflect past and expected income streams, are likely to be a better guide to household well-being. By this measure, the lowest 10 percent of households have been estimated to spend under 4 percent of their outlays on gasoline, or roughly the same share as the top 10 percent spend.[48]

Middle-income motorists, not the poor or the rich, bear the brunt of gasoline tax increases. Of course, this incidence remains "unfair," if every federal tax needs to be based strictly on ability to pay throughout the income distribution. But there is little hope of managing federal fiscal imbalances without taxing the middle class. And in the context of a national tax system that relies massively on progressive income taxation, with regressive excise charges constituting a small and shrinking share of total revenue, taxing fuel consumption less timidly should not be considered egregiously unjust.

There is no getting around the somewhat disparate, though hardly drastic, regional impacts of a higher gasoline excise. Drivers in the low-density states of the West might feel overtaxed compared with many drivers in the denser states of the Northeast. Exactly how injurious this is to the westerners depends on a variety of factors, including the relative costs of other forms of energy and relative travel times. Many western states have long enjoyed comparatively low prices for natural gas and electricity, for instance.[49] Also, commuters in at least some of those states may drive long distances but in less time than it takes to make shorter trips on the congested northeast corridor. Motorists continually stuck in traffic can easily spend as much on fuel as long-distance drivers do.

Conclusion

It is not the purpose of this study to make another case for punitive taxation. The United States remains richly endowed with energy resources. Much of the economy employs those resources appropriately—increasingly so in most spheres. The need for an all-inclusive penalty on energy use (a "Btu tax," for example) is dubious at best: is it necessary or desirable to tax not only dirty or risky fossil fuels but also hydroelectric power, for example, and clean-burning natural gas? And what about an important source of comparative advantage for the American economy: access to low-cost energy inputs? Not only is indiscriminate taxation of "energy" difficult to justify on security or even environmental grounds; it could weaken the international competitiveness of key industries, thereby giving them reason to seek compensation through subsidies or trade protection. Even the professed goal of regaining fiscal equilibrium will not enhance the argument for such a tax if recent commitments to spending restraint prove illusory.

Targeted Taxation

However, a sales tax limited to fuel used in transportation, particularly gasoline, merits further consideration. This device would target a problematic sector, the one most clearly implicated in the growth of oil imports and the persistence of substandard urban air quality. Whether or not one agrees that these conditions—mounting oil dependency, persistent city smog—are serious matters, alleviating them has been a long-standing concern of policymakers. Government should not enshrine in law public ends that require means it is unwilling to adopt. But such a disjuncture between ends and means has characterized Congress's quest for energy savings in the oil-intensive transportation sector. The best way to maximize such savings over the past decade, we conclude, would have been to raise the price of gasoline, instead of engineering mileage codes for motor vehicles.

Plan of the Book

The first part of this book provides an economic analysis of the alternatives: fiscal instruments versus continued regulation. The second part examines their politics. Specifically, chapter 2 advances a detailed empirical critique of the U.S. automotive fuel economy standards. Chapter 3 scrutinizes the proposed substitute, a fuel tax, in terms of its energy-saving potential and its economic and distributional implications.

Chapter 4 examines the development of motor-fuel excises in several other industrialized nations, principally Great Britain, France, Germany, Japan, and Canada. Chapter 5 recounts the American policy experience. The aim in these pages is to compare the historical and political forces responsible for divergent national policy orientations.

A final chapter assesses the possibility of replacing the troubled enforcement of U.S. energy mandates with an adequate fuel excise. Although we conclude that a nontrivial increase in the federal gasoline tax remains a distant prospect, the case for it may become increasingly respectable as deficits persist and as policymakers try to promote new automotive technologies in the face of declining oil prices. Innovations in related fields, such as federal transportation programs and state land-use guidelines, could also nudge policy in a better direction.

CHAPTER TWO

The CAFE Conundrum

T WENTY-TWO YEARS after the Arab oil embargo, U.S. policy for conserving transportation fuels remains limited to the Corporate Average Fuel Economy (CAFE) program, which requires manufacturers to meet minimum fuel-efficiency standards on all passenger vehicles sold in the United States.[1] The program, enacted in 1975, persists despite great shifts in energy prices, changes in the geopolitics of world oil, and the mounting empirical evidence that casts doubt on CAFE's efficiency in achieving energy conservation.

Background

In 1975 Congress faced a dilemma. In response to the previous year's oil shock, the Federal Energy Administration had extended controls on domestic crude-oil and refined-product prices.[2] As a result, U.S. consumers faced fuel prices that were below world levels and far below prevailing estimates of future prices. The artificially low prices undercut conservation, but Congress was unwilling to allow them to rise for fear of the effects on the overall rate of inflation and on distributional equity.

A better decision would have been to allow energy prices to rise, and then perhaps to capture a large share of the increase through an import fee levied by all importing countries on imported oil, rebating some of the revenues to taxpayers through a cut in income taxes. Such a fee would have required a degree of cooperation among most OECD countries that was not easily orchestrated, however, and would have angered a number

Table 2-1. *Corporate Average Fuel Economy (CAFE) Standards for Passenger Cars and Light Trucks, 1978–93 Model Years*
Miles per gallon

Model year	Passenger cars	All light trucks	Two-wheel drive light trucks	Four-wheel drive light trucks
1978	18.0	...	...	...
1979	19.0	...	17.2	15.8
1980	20.0	...	16.0	14.0
1981	22.0	...	16.7	15.0
1982	24.0	17.5	18.0	16.0
1983	26.0	19.0	19.5	17.5
1984	27.0	20.0	20.3	18.5
1985	27.5	19.5	19.7	18.9
1986	26.0	20.0	20.5	19.5
1987	26.0	20.5	21.0	19.5
1988	26.0	20.5	21.0	19.5
1989	26.5	20.5	21.5	19.0
1990	27.5	20.0	20.5	19.0
1991	27.5	20.2	20.7	19.1
1992	27.5	20.2	...	...
1993	27.5	20.4	...	...

Source: National Highway Traffic Safety Administration, "Summary of Fuel Economy Performance" (Department of Transportation, September 1993).

of important U.S. allies among exporting countries—namely, Mexico, Saudi Arabia, the United Kingdom, Venezuela, and Norway.

The policy actually chosen was one that substituted fuel-economy standards for fuel-price incentives to influence automobile design. Beginning with the 1978 model year, all manufacturers of motor vehicles sold in the United States would be forced to meet a fleet-average fuel economy of 18 miles per gallon (mpg) for new passenger cars, as determined by the Environmental Protection Agency's (EPA) testing of new models under a standard driving cycle.[3] This CAFE standard was to rise to 27.5 mpg for passenger cars by the 1985 model year—the level at which it remains today (table 2-1). Thereafter, the Department of Transportation (DOT) would be empowered to set each model year's target based on technical practicability, economic feasibility, and the need for conservation. The DOT was also authorized to establish requirements for light trucks and vans.[4] These standards have generally been set 25 to 30 percent below the passenger-car standards (table 2-1).

The regulations have now been in force for seventeen years. Their goals must be met by each manufacturer for each of four annual model-year sales categories: domestic cars, domestic light trucks, imported cars, and imported light trucks. A separation of imports from domestic vehicles for compliance with the standards was designed to prevent domestic manufacturers from meeting the standards by simply importing smaller cars from Japan, Korea, or Mexico. While such an import strategy by the domestic auto industry might be efficient, it would have reduced domestic employment in the motor-vehicle industry and therefore was fervently opposed by the United Auto Workers.

Anticipation of CAFE's strictures may have influenced the major automobile producers for a short time in the latter 1970s, after the first oil shock. Real motor fuel prices fell by 6 percent between 1975 and 1978, in part because of government price controls (figure 2-1). In late 1978, however, the Iranian revolution set off a second surge of fuel prices that continued until 1981, when recession and the advent of decontrol caused a reversal. In the 1978-81 environment, therefore, CAFE was largely irrelevant as vehicle producers, racing to introduce new small front-wheel drive automobiles in response to consumer demand, routinely exceeded the standard.[5]

Lower fuel prices, particularly after OPEC's collapse in 1985, reversed the trend toward smaller passenger vehicles. The average weight of new passenger cars fell from about 4,000 pounds in 1974 to 3,100 pounds in 1985 through downsizing and materials substitution (table 2-2). After 1985, however, the average weight of new cars began to rise slowly again as consumers, luxuriating in cheap gasoline, began to demand larger, heavier, and more powerful vehicles.

The drop in energy prices after 1981 thus placed two of the major U.S. vehicle companies, Ford and General Motors, in a difficult position. They could meet a 27.5 mpg standard only by raising large-car and large-engine prices substantially, thereby losing market share to foreign nameplates or to Chrysler. As a result, they successfully petitioned the Department of Transportation to reduce the standard to 26.0 mpg for model year 1986, a level that was maintained through the 1988 model year. In 1989 the passenger-car standard was once again raised to 26.5 mpg, and the first major action of the Department of Transportation during the Bush administration was to reimpose a goal of 27.5 mpg.

Although real motor-fuel prices have stabilized since 1986, it seems doubtful that they will soon return to their lofty 1980-81 levels. Two federal gasoline tax increases have occurred since 1986, adding about 9 percent to the nominal price of fuel. Even with these modest increases,

Figure 2-1. *Real Fuel Prices, Actual Fuel Economy, and Passenger Car CAFE Standards, 1970–92*

Miles per gallon

CPI index for motor fuels (1982–84 = 100)

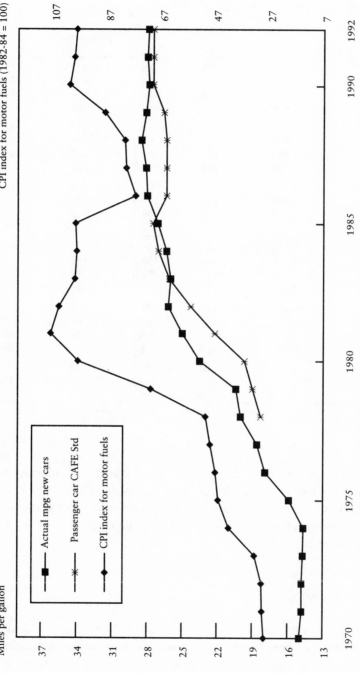

Sources: Actual mpg and passenger car CAFE from National Highway Traffic Safety Administration, "Survey of Fuel Economy Performance" (Department of Transportation, 1993); and CPI from *Economic Report of the President, February 1994*, p. 337.

Table 2-2. *Characteristics of the Average New Passenger Car Sold in the United States, 1970–92 Model Years*

Model year	Weight (lbs.)	Acceleration (sec, 0–60 mph)	Interior volume (cu. ft.)	Displacement (cu. in.)	MPG (harmonic average)
1970	3,877	n.a.	n.a.	297	14.8
1971	3,887	n.a.	n.a.	n.a.	14.4
1972	3,942	n.a.	n.a.	293	14.4
1973	3,969	n.a.	n.a.	286	14.2
1974	3,968	n.a.	n.a.	289	14.2
1975	4,058	14.2	n.a.	288	15.8
1976	4,059	14.4	n.a.	287	17.5
1977	3,944	14.0	110.9	279	18.3
1978	3,588	13.7	109.5	251	19.9
1979	3,485	13.8	109.4	238	20.3
1980	3,101	14.3	104.7	188	23.5
1981	3,076	14.4	107.0	182	25.1
1982	3,054	14.4	106.6	175	26.0
1983	3,112	14.0	109.2	182	25.9
1984	3,099	13.8	108.0	179	26.3
1985	3,093	13.3	108.6	177	27.0
1986	3,041	13.2	107.8	167	27.9
1987	3,031	13.0	107.1	162	28.1
1988	3,047	12.8	107.5	160	28.6
1989	3,099	12.5	108.2	163	28.1
1990	3,179	12.1	107.6	164	27.7
1991	3,153	11.8	107.3	163	28.0
1992	3,228	11.6	108.4	168	27.7

Source: J. Dillard Murrell, Karl H. Hellman, and Robert M. Heavenrich, "Light-Duty Automotive Technology and Fuel Economy Trends through 1993" (Ann Arbor, Mich.: Environmental Protection Agency, May 1993).
n.a. Not available.

the real price of gasoline is at its post–World War II low, inducing strong consumer demand for larger cars and increased vehicle miles of travel. Fuel prices in 1994 were about 10 percent lower than during the Korean War—when energy conservation and environmental concerns were not on the public agenda.[6]

The Case for CAFE

Proponents of fuel-economy regulation generally base their case on the existence of market failure. Of the two variants to this argument one focuses on consumer ignorance or lethargy, the other on the supposed lack of producer response to the demands of consumers. Neither is persuasive.

The thesis that consumers fail to understand the trade-offs among fuel costs, performance, and more expensive, fuel-efficient technology in new cars is implausible for several reasons. First, under federal law all new vehicles must carry labels that show their fuel-efficiency ratings as determined by EPA. Second, many popular consumer magazines provide detailed analyses of the performance characteristics of all new passenger vehicles, including their fuel efficiency under a variety of conditions. Third, strong evidence shows that consumers respond to changes in fuel prices by buying less or more fuel-intensive cars, and that this response varies with the longer-run expectations about the permanence of fuel-price changes.[7]

Producers may be slow to respond to market signals if the industry is organized as a stable, somnolent oligopoly. When there were only three major suppliers of passenger vehicles to the U.S. market in the 1960s and early 1970s,[8] producers were less likely to react vigorously to changing market conditions. In the late 1970s and 1980s, however, the Big Three American companies (Chrysler, Ford, General Motors) lost market power. Toyota, Nissan, Honda, Mitsubishi, Mazda, Hyundai, Subaru, Suzuki, and Isuzu not only became aggressive exporters to the United States but actually established production facilities in the United States and Canada. In this more competitive environment, it is difficult to believe that producers would not be responding to new market conditions, including changes in energy prices.

In truth, CAFE has more to do with politics than with economic "market failure." Legislators fear political retribution for tax increases, especially for highly visible excises such as a tax on motor fuels. Given the relatively low price elasticity of demand for fuel in the short run, a rather noticeable gasoline tax would be required to achieve a sudden reduction in fuel consumption. Such a tax is more difficult to impose than is a policy that seems to place the compliance burden on the vehicle producers, not the consumers.

Why CAFE Falters

There is an unfortunate tendency in policy discussions of fuel-economy regulation to assume that tougher standards will reduce fuel consumption proportionately. Mandated improvements in average new-vehicle fuel efficiency for each manufacturer do not necessarily translate into reductions in fuel use. One must examine consumer and producer responses to the regulatory program to gauge its full effect on consumption.

How Consumers Respond

To be sure, a binding CAFE requirement improves the fuel efficiency of some cars. If the government dictates an increase in the average fuel efficiency of new cars, new vehicles will consume less fuel for any given number of miles driven. Unfortunately, the full effect of such regulations is much more difficult to identify. Passenger vehicles enjoy a useful life that can stretch up to twenty years or more. When new vehicles become less attractive, more expensive, or both, consumers postpone their replacement decisions. When fuel prices fall and are expected to remain low, consumers demand less fuel-efficient cars. If the government enforces a tight regulatory constraint when fuel prices are falling, producers will be restrained in their ability to design and produce vehicles that consumers want.

For instance, at the end of the 1970s, before CAFE became binding, consumers began to shift to lighter vehicles with smaller engines in response to the first oil crisis (table 2-2). The average weight of a new passenger car began to decline in 1977 and continued to fall until the 1982 model year, just after fuel prices reached their post–World War II peak. As fuel prices declined, consumers began to demand larger, heavier cars. The vehicle companies were constrained by CAFE, however, in their ability to respond to this demand. Nevertheless, improvements in average fuel economy slowed dramatically after the 1982 model year as consumers began to move back to heavier cars. In the next decade, the average weight of new cars gradually rose to more than 3,180 pounds, an average not seen since 1979. The average time required to accelerate from 0 to 60 miles per hour fell from 14.4 seconds in 1981-82 to less than 12 seconds in 1991. With real motor-fuel prices in 1992 at their lowest level since 1974, consumers were clearly looking again for larger, more powerful cars. Given the continuing decline in real fuel prices through mid-1994, it is not difficult to predict that these shifts in product mix will continue, stimulating increases in the consumption of motor fuel.

With relatively low fuel prices and a government standard of 27.5 mpg, U.S. vehicle producers have faced a dilemma. If they were to price cars at the level that market conditions (without CAFE) currently dictate, they would find that sales of larger cars would rise and that sales of smaller, lighter cars would decline. As a result, to meet CAFE standards they must

Table 2-3. *U.S. Retail Sales of Passenger Cars and Light Trucks,*
1972–93

Thousands

Year	Passenger cars	Light trucks
1972	10,940	2,116
1973	11,424	2,513
1974	8,853	2,176
1975	8,624	2,054
1976	10,110	2,974
1977	11,183	3,440
1978	11,314	3,810
1979	10,673	3,211
1980	8,979	2,211
1981	8,536	2,032
1982	7,982	2,383
1983	9,182	2,942
1984	10,390	3,786
1985	11,042	4,403
1986	11,460	4,606
1987	10,277	4,596
1988	10,530	4,796
1989	9,772	4,621
1990	9,300	4,356
1991	8,175	3,917
1992	8,213	4,273
1993	8,518	4,987

Source: Passenger cars from AAMA, *Motor Vehicle Facts and Figures,* various issues. Light trucks, unpublished information from Department of Commerce, BEA.

raise the price of larger cars while investing in additional technology to achieve greater fuel economy than market conditions (including current state and federal excises) would otherwise induce. The net effect is likely to be a reduction in overall sales of new cars as persons preferring large cars are encouraged to keep their vehicles longer.

In addition, because regulatory standards for fuel economy, safety, and emissions for new light trucks[9] are less onerous than are the standards for passenger cars, the price-quality combinations for pickup trucks, sport-utility vehicles, and vans improve relative to the combinations offered by domestic passenger cars. It is no surprise that the shift from passenger cars to light trucks accelerated markedly in the late 1970s and 1980s (table 2-3), reducing the conservation benefits of CAFE because light trucks are generally less fuel efficient than the cars they replace.

These regulation-induced price-quality outcomes clearly diminish the attractiveness of new cars, suppressing their sales as consumers hold onto older vehicles longer. This reduces the average fuel economy of all vehicles on the road for two reasons: older cars degrade with use, thereby lowering their efficiency; and many of the older vehicles were less energy efficient than current models when they were built.

Last but not least, improving the fuel economy of vehicles while keeping fuel prices low reduces the marginal cost of driving for those consumers who purchase new vehicles.

How Producers Respond

Regulating mileage per gallon through the CAFE regime results in a number of other surprising side effects. First, any policy that requires firms to raise prices of large cars in order to minimize their penalties under the regime clearly benefits those companies that produce these vehicles. In essence, CAFE is a cartelizing device for the large-car producers over some range of miles per gallon. Ford and General Motors have dominated the U.S. market for large automobiles since 1978, except for the luxury-car niche. Chrysler was essentially absent from this segment of the market from the time of its brush with bankruptcy in the late 1970s until the recent introduction of its LH sedans.

Thus, when CAFE binds amid soft energy prices, it may actually increase the profits of large-car producers, as it did for Ford and GM throughout the 1980s. Of course, it is possible that raising fuel-economy requirements too high will force prices above the cartel-maximizing level. For this reason, GM and Ford (which were not vocal opponents of CAFE in the 1980s)[10] began to mount a strong campaign against proposals to raise the program's targets to 33 or 40 mpg.[11]

Despite frequently expressed concerns about the U.S. bilateral trade deficit with Japan, the CAFE system has, if anything, contributed to the problem by rewarding producers of small autos, largely Japanese, with substantial excess "credits" that they may carry forward for future years. These credits have allowed the Japanese companies to introduce powerful new luxury cars in the U.S. market without worrying about complying with CAFE requirements. Since each producer must meet CAFE criteria for its imported and domestic fleets separately, the Japanese import some small cars and luxury cars while often producing midsized cars in the United States.[12] Notice the large difference between the Japanese producers' actual mpg ratings and the CAFE standard through the late 1980s (table 2-4). During the mid-1980s the American companies, particularly Ford and General Motors, struggled to meet CAFE's goals with their do-

Table 2-4. *CAFE Ratings for Big Three and Major Japanese Passenger-Car Manufacturers, 1978–91 Model Years (domestic cars for Big Three; imported cars for Japanese)*

Miles per gallon

Manufacturer	1978	1979	1980	1981	1982	1983	1984	1985	1986	1987	1988	1989	1990	1991
Chrysler	18.4	20.5	22.3	26.8	27.6	26.9	27.8	27.8	27.8	27.5	28.5	28.0	27.4	27.5
Ford	18.4	19.2	22.9	24.1	25.0	24.3	25.8	26.6	27.0	26.9	26.6	26.6	26.3	27.7
GM	19.0	19.1	22.6	23.8	24.6	24.0	24.9	25.8	26.6	26.9	27.6	27.3	27.1	27.2
Honda	33.7	29.0	30.1	31.6	33.9	36.0	35.8	34.5	33.3	33.2	32.1	31.6	30.8	30.7
Toyota	26.8	24.0	28.3	31.8	30.9	33.3	33.5	33.5	32.7	33.4	33.0	32.1	30.8	30.9
Mazda	35.5	25.6	26.8	30.9	29.8	29.4	30.6	30.3	29.7	29.6	28.7	29.8	30.2	30.5
Nissan	26.8	26.8	32.2	31.4	31.2	33.4	32.5	30.1	30.3	29.7	30.8	30.4	30.8	29.2
CAFE standard	18.0	19.0	20.0	22.0	24.0	26.0	27.0	27.5	26.0	26.0	26.0	26.5	27.5	27.5

Source: Authors' calculations based on National Highway Traffic Safety Administration, "Summary of Fuel Economy Performance."

mestic passenger-car sales. In the late 1980s, Japanese manufacturers began to introduce luxury cars while their U.S. competitors were hampered by CAFE from attempting to expand their luxury-car output.

The U.S. companies were also given an incentive to shift part of their large-car production abroad to reduce their domestic CAFE ratings while raising their ratings for imports, which were already above the standard. Alternatively, they can produce cars in U.S. joint ventures with Japanese companies, importing sufficient parts to qualify the vehicles as imports for CAFE purposes.[13] (Any vehicle with less than 75 percent domestic content is defined as an "import" under the CAFE legislation.)

None of these arguments suggests that CAFE has no impact on the fuel economy of new vehicles. Government policy has clearly succeeded in promoting smaller, lighter, less fuel-hungry automobiles than would have been produced without a binding regulatory constraint. Given that CAFE has certainly been binding after fuel prices plummeted in the mid-1980s, it has induced some improvement in the fuel economy of new vehicles. Still, the effect even on new vehicles has been partly offset by shifts in consumer demand among new vehicles. CAFE's effect on total fuel consumption has been attenuated by the increase in driving and in the average age of vehicles on the road that the regulations have partly encouraged.

Existing Research

Several studies have explored the effects of the Corporate Average Fuel Economy experiment, but only two have attempted to estimate the full economic impacts. Several economists have shown that CAFE could, under reasonable assumptions, lead to no improvement in overall fuel consumption.[14] For example, Andrew Kleit concludes that the program led to increased fuel consumption in the 1989 model year (table 2-5). This result flows from economic models that focus on the choice of large-car and small-car production levels by profit-maximizing manufacturers. Possibly, these manufacturers increase their output of small cars only to maintain a high volume of large cars, so that the vehicle stock and the fuel it consumes actually increase in response to CAFE. These economic models, however, do not account for changes in weight, engine size, or technical energy efficiency. Others have examined the effect of CAFE regulation on weight, engine displacement, and technology and have found that at least half of CAFE's effect is registered through reductions in vehicle weight and in engine size.[15]

Table 2-5. *Estimates of the Welfare Costs of CAFE and Fuel Taxes (private producer and consumer surplus)*

Costs	Optimistic (Greene)	Pessimistic (Kleit)	Mid-range (Leone and Parkinson)
Discounted fuel savings due to CAFE (billions of gallons a year)	14.8	−0.4	0.6
Annual welfare cost of CAFE (producer and consumer surplus in billions of 1990 dollars)	4.4	1.0	0.4
Welfare cost of CAFE per gallon of fuel saved (1990 dollars per gallon)	0.30	No fuel saved	0.59
Welfare cost of CAFE-equivalent fuel tax increase per gallon saved (1990 dollars per gallon)	n.a.	No fuel saved	0.08

Source: Adapted from Robert W. Crandall, "Policy Watch: Corporate Average Fuel Economy Standards," *Journal of Economic Perspectives,*" vol. 6 (Spring 1992), p. 177.

Unfortunately, the two most comprehensive analyses were commissioned by motor-vehicle manufacturers, who obviously have a stake in the issue. Nevertheless, they provide the only current estimates of the overall consequences of the CAFE program for fuel consumption, societal costs, and economic welfare. Both studies conclude that CAFE is far less efficient than a fuel tax in achieving conservation.

Robert A. Leone and Thomas Parkinson, for instance, conclude that a gasoline tax increase of between 2.4 cents and 6.0 cents would have provided the same fuel saving as did CAFE over the 1978-89 period.[16] This remarkable result is partly an artifact of the time frame investigated; CAFE had little or no effect from 1978 through 1981 because of high market prices for oil. Were the authors to examine only the period after 1981, the tax needed to save an equivalent amount of fuel would clearly have had to be substantially greater. However, Leone and Parkinson's conclusion that CAFE is a very expensive energy-conservation policy remains valid. The authors estimate that the gasoline tax required to match CAFE's conservation effect would have reduced producer and consumer welfare by 8 cents a gallon saved while the regulatory alternative actually reduced welfare by around 60 cents a gallon saved (table 2-5).[17]

The other major study, by Charles River Associates, demonstrates that a gasoline tax would be far superior for purposes of conserving petroleum or reducing emissions of CO_2.[18] This study examines alternatives for future reductions of fuel consumption. Its most optimistic scenario concludes that a tax that begins at 3 cents a gallon in 1996 and rises to 25 cents a gallon by 2006 would be equivalent to raising CAFE standards to 34 mpg in 1996 and to 40 mpg by 2006. But the gasoline tax would be far more efficient, exacting a loss of producer and consumer welfare that is only a fraction of that caused by the CAFE strategy.

The studies that have lent the most support to CAFE have been undertaken by David Greene and associates for the Department of Energy.[19] Greene finds that CAFE, not fuel prices, drove fuel-economy improvements between 1978 and 1989 and that the improvements ultimately were worth the loss in vehicular performance from the standpoint of consumers. However, Crandall has shown that even Greene's results suggest a consumer welfare loss of 30 cents a gallon saved, far above the welfare cost of a modest gasoline tax.[20]

The Mechanics of Fuel Conservation

By definition, fuel consumption is equal to vehicle miles traveled divided by average fuel economy. To reduce consumption, we must either drive less or drive more fuel-efficient cars, or both. More efficiency can be delivered by manufacturers through size reductions, performance reductions (such as reductions in acceleration), or technical improvements. In this section, we provide new evidence of how CAFE regulation and fuel prices influence each of these determinants of fuel use.

Vehicle Miles Traveled

In chapter 1, we showed that the total miles of passenger-car and truck travel have risen sharply since the end of the second oil shock, associated with the Iranian revolution. Clearly, low fuel prices are responsible for much of this rise, as was the long economic expansion after the 1982 recession. CAFE's contribution was twofold. It increased the efficiency of the new-car fleet, other things being equal, lowering the cost of driving and thereby increasing the miles of vehicle travel. It also extended the life of older gas guzzlers.

Recent research by Greene suggests that the "snap-back" effect of CAFE on vehicle miles traveled has been relatively small, but his results depend on a measure of the cost per mile of driving that does not accurately represent the incremental cost of driving.[21] Less controversial, and perhaps more important, is the effect of fuel prices on miles of travel. If higher fuel prices are substituted for CAFE as a conservation method, they will induce less driving, particularly for noncommuting trips. By contrast, the current policy of allowing fuel prices to decline to historically low levels while maintaining a binding CAFE standard facilitates motoring. The increases in vehicle miles of travel vitiate much of the energy savings sought by CAFE's administrators. The empirical evidence on the price elasticity of demand for motor fuel is very convincing on this point, pointing to approximately a 5 percent increase in miles driven for every 10 percent decline in real gasoline prices in the short run if the fuel efficiency of the vehicle fleet is held constant.

Weight

Cars can come in all shapes and sizes. To the consumer, weight is a correlate of size, comfort, ride, and safety. Reducing weight may improve fuel economy, but such a reduction may also make for a rougher ride. Consumers, depending on their tastes, transportation requirements, and income, purchase a variety of vehicles. Vehicle manufacturers deliver a variety of vehicles of different sizes, pricing them to maximize profits subject to the various regulatory constraints, including those of CAFE.

As already noted, in the early 1970s the average new passenger car weighed almost 4,000 pounds, as did the average new light truck. As fuel-economy standards were tightened and energy prices rose in the late 1970s, the average weight of new automobiles fell sharply, but the average weight of light trucks fell much more slowly (figure 2-2). These trucks are used for both passenger and commercial purposes; hence, it is difficult to sort out the determinants of their various attributes.

For automobiles, the problem is more straightforward. One would expect the demand for them to reflect demographic measures, such as the age of the driver and family size, as well as the price of complementary factors such as fuel. The mix of cars actually sold will reflect the pricing decisions of manufacturers for each model, constrained by various regulations. The average weight of cars sold should fall with increases in actual and expected gasoline prices and with increases in the prices of essential materials such as steel. Other things being equal, a rising CAFE standard should also lead to lower average weight. The latter effect is likely to be the combination of the effects of lower vehicle design weights and higher

Figure 2-2. *Average Weight of New Passenger Cars and Light Trucks, 1970–93*

Weight in pounds

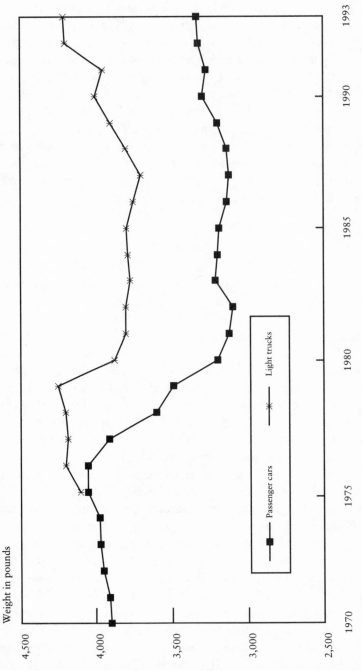

Source: Authors' calculations with data from J. Dillard Murrell, Karl H. Hellman, and Robert M. Heavenrich, "Light-Duty Automotive Technology and Fuel Economy Trends through 1993" (Ann Arbor, Mich.: Environmental Protection Agency, May 1993).

prices for large cars relative to the prices of smaller cars in years in which CAFE is binding.

An econometric (time-series) investigation of the effects of all of these various influences shows that real fuel prices and fuel-economy rules have had significant impacts on average passenger-car weight for new vehicles sold in the 1968-92 model years. The estimated equation indicates that the decline in fuel prices after 1981 has fully offset the effect of the increase in CAFE standards since 1981. The regulatory program has reduced the weight of an average new passenger car by about 400 pounds, but the decline in real fuel prices increases average weight by 400 pounds once a four-year design lag is allowed to run its course.[22]

Performance

The performance of a vehicle may be measured along many dimensions: handling, ride, cornering, passing on a two-lane highway, or accelerating from a stopped position onto a freeway. Fuel prices and CAFE mandates have their greatest impact on those performance measures related to fuel consumption, namely, acceleration or its (inverse) correlate, engine displacement. Over time, the size of engine required to deliver a given performance has declined because of technical progress. However, neither displacement nor acceleration is significantly related to CAFE or to real fuel prices for a given average weight of car in a time-series econometric analysis of data for 1970 through 1992. Apparently, vehicle weight drives the choice of engine by producers and consumers alike. Thus CAFE has not appeared to reduce engine size for a given weight of vehicle.

Technical Fuel Efficiency

Automobile technology is not constant. Enormous improvements have been made in safety, handling, engine performance, transmissions, tires, fit and finish, and reliability of motor vehicles over the past several decades. Improvements in these various dimensions of vehicle quality occur even if government policy toward the automobile creates disincentives. Only the rate of progress seems to be reduced or enhanced by government intervention.

Incorporating new fuel-saving technology will make vehicles more attractive to prospective buyers, especially when fuel prices are high. One might expect vehicle producers to invest more heavily in such technology when real fuel prices rise or when CAFE requirements become more se-

Figure 2-3. *The Increase in Technical Fuel Efficiency in New U.S. Passenger Cars, Model Years 1971–93*

Percentage change from 1970

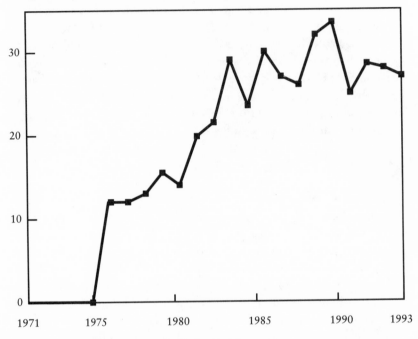

Source: Authors' calculations. See appendix A, table A-2.

vere, but no one has documented a clear effect of fuel-economy mandates on technological innovation. This is largely because most empirical analyses of CAFE focus on a manufacturer's fleet-average fuel economy, not the fuel economy of *individual* vehicles. Changes in fleet averages reflect the mix of cars sold as well as changes in the design of the individual models. Thus average fuel efficiency can increase if consumers shift to smaller, energy-sparing cars even when the technology built into the vehicles does not change.

To overcome this inadequacy, we analyzed the determinants of fuel efficiency for 268 individual passenger-car models produced by U.S. companies in the 1970-93 model years. After accounting for the effects of weight and displacement, we obtained estimates of the rate of progress in efficiency over time.[23] The pattern of estimated progress is shown in figure 2-3. There is no significant progress between the 1970 and the 1975 model years. The 1976 model-year automobiles were introduced two years after the Arab oil embargo, and these vehicles exhibit a sizable increase of more than 12 percent in technical efficiency over their 1970-75 predecessors. The progress would continue through the late 1980s, but the data suggest a mild retrogression beginning with the 1990 model year, slightly less than four years after the collapse of oil prices in the spring of 1986.

Given that CAFE was clearly a binding constraint on the automobile industry only after energy prices began to decline in the 1981-86 period, these results do not augur well for the theory that ambitious mandatory standards force technological improvements in fuel efficiency above those induced by expectations of rising fuel prices. Indeed, a regression analysis of our 268-car database finds that real fuel prices, lagged four years to reflect the vehicle design cycle, are significantly related to fuel efficiency, but that the addition of the CAFE standard adds nothing to the explanatory power of the equation.[24]

These results convince us that the technology for fuel economy built into new vehicles reflects the anticipation of real fuel prices rather than CAFE pressure. The current value or the next year's value of the CAFE standard affects the weight of cars sold, but it seems to have little influence on the vehicle producer's choice of fuel-efficient technologies. The decided slowdown and even retrogression in technical progress in achieving efficiency exhibited in the 1990s is strongly correlated with declining fuel prices over the late 1980s. Apparently, vehicle producers are unwilling to commit to expensive new technology to save fuel in an environment of falling gasoline prices.

Shifts in the Mix of Cars Sold

We have demonstrated that the CAFE program has its principal impact through the average weight of cars purchased by U.S. consumers. This does not mean that all vehicles are downsized to achieve this effect, but, rather, that downsizing and a shift of vehicle mix combine to reduce the average weight of vehicles sold. Before 1984, CAFE was for all practical purposes inoperative, and, therefore, vehicle producers did not need to shift buyers from their larger cars to their smaller vehicles to meet the regulatory standard. After 1983, however, the U.S. vehicle producers were faced with sharply declining fuel prices and a consequent shift in consumer demand toward larger cars. The firms would be expected to respond immediately by raising the prices of large cars and reducing the prices of small cars.

The pricing behavior of the domestic passenger-car producers conforms to this expectation. An analysis of the 268-car sample of 1970-93 model-year cars described above demonstrates that vehicle manufacturers greatly increased the price of large cars and large engines after the 1983 model year. Using a hedonic model of the list prices of these vehicles that relates price to measures of ride, acceleration, and weight as well as the presence of power steering, power brakes, automatic transmission, air conditioning, air bags, and antilock brakes, we find that the price charged for additional weight doubled after 1983. At the same time, the price of acceleration more than tripled.[25]

Possibly, something other than regulation accounts for this dramatic increase in the price of weight and acceleration, but it is difficult to suggest what else might be responsible. The real price of steel was falling in the 1980s after rising in the 1970s. Competition in the larger-car segments of the market was increasing, not declining. The average weight of cars sold by the Japanese and Korean companies had remained about 2,500 pounds over the 1977-83 model years but then began to rise steadily to nearly 3,000 pounds by the 1993 model year as new, heavier models were introduced by virtually every Asian producer. Thus, exogenous forces other than CAFE standards should have been inducing price reductions on larger, more powerful domestic cars, not price increases. It is difficult to resist the conclusion that CAFE regulations accounted for a dramatic change in the pricing behavior of U.S. companies.

The Effects on Vehicle Safety

Perhaps the most intensely debated consequence of U.S. fuel-economy requirements has been their alleged effect on vehicular occupant safety. As we have demonstrated, there is no doubt that CAFE spurs producers to lower vehicle weight and to reduce the relative prices of smaller cars.[26] While smaller, lighter vehicles can be made as safe as larger cars with additional engineering expense, the reduction of size reduces occupant safety, other things equal.

The 1990 model-year CAFE standards were raised by EPA from 26.5 mpg to 27.5 mpg, provoking a court challenge from two public interest groups, who based their complaint in large part on the results of research into safety issues. The U.S. Court of Appeals for the D.C. Circuit remanded the standard to the Department of Transportation on the grounds that DOT had not adequately addressed these issues.[27] Since that challenge, new evidence has confirmed the effect of size on crashworthiness.[28]

We do not intend to delve at length into the question of highway safety in this book, but this much is clear: problems of safety can further reduce the net social benefits of CAFE regulation. Indeed, some critics have dubbed the continued pursuit of government-mandated fuel economy as the sacrifice of "blood for oil." Earlier studies by Leonard Evans and by Crandall and John Graham suggest that by the late 1980s, CAFE may have been indirectly responsible for about 2,200 to 3,900 additional deaths for each model year's passenger cars over a ten-year period following their introduction.[29] Even without the feedback effects of keeping older cars on the road longer and inducing additional vehicle miles of travel, CAFE would save only about 500 million gallons of fuel a year in these cars, or about 6 billion gallons over twelve years. Thus the program could be said to "cost" about one additional fatality per 2 million gallons saved. In short, at the value of $4 million per statistical life saved that is used in most public-safety calculations, the entire value of the fuel saved by CAFE may be squandered in additional highway fatalities.

Note that the fuel taxes required to reduce fuel consumption would not have as deleterious an effect on motor-vehicle safety as does the CAFE system. Higher fuel prices would reduce vehicle miles traveled, thereby reducing the need for as much downsizing as the CAFE law requires to obtain a given decrement of fuel consumption. Lower VMT and somewhat larger cars would combine to provide fewer fatalities than the current regulatory apparatus permits.

Conclusion

This chapter has reviewed the developing evidence about the effect of the Corporate Average Fuel Economy program on energy consumption. The evidence supports the theory that CAFE is clearly less efficient than fuel taxes as an energy-saving policy because CAFE distorts the new-car market far more than would be necessary with a tax. A tax would make vehicles more energy efficient and would moderate their use.

Additional evidence shows that technical change in fuel economy is driven primarily by higher fuel prices. Because of the declining price of oil, there has been no appreciable progress in the technical fuel efficiency of new passenger cars since the mid-1980s despite the intervention of CAFE during this period. Moreover, although the regulations cause a reduction in vehicle weight, so do high fuel prices after a lag. Higher fuel prices, unlike the CAFE approach, would curb discretionary driving in all vehicles. All told, the full economic cost of reducing fuel consumption through the CAFE policy is several times as great as the cost of achieving similar reductions from an increase in fuel taxes.

CHAPTER THREE

The Fuel Tax Option

T HE FEDERAL Corporate Average Fuel Economy regulatory program
has had a measurable impact on the fuel economy of new vehicles. This
effect is principally the result of downsizing and a shift in the mix of large
and small cars. CAFE could not alter the fuel economy of older vehicles,
but it has undoubtedly kept older cars on the road longer, thereby nulli-
fying some of the program's conservation benefits. Nor has fuel-economy
regulation effected noticeable improvements in the technical efficiency of
new vehicles. Most important, the program has not been able to slow the
growth in vehicle miles of travel. Indeed, it has probably increased VMTs
through the "rebound" effect of higher-mpg new cars.

In view of these flaws, would higher fuel prices be a better mechanism
for conserving fuel? Would they not lead to greater economic welfare,
greater use of newer cars, and reduced fuel consumption relative to the
current CAFE standards?

In this chapter we review the empirical evidence on the price elasticity
of demand for motor fuel. We then estimate the fuel tax that would be
necessary to yield the energy savings now obtained through regulation
and assess its effects on income distribution and overall economic performance.

The Price Elasticity of Demand for Motor Fuel

The demand for fuel can be broken down into two components, the demand for travel (VMT) and the choice of fuel efficiency (MPG):

(3-1) $$Q_f = VMT / MPG,$$

where Q_f is the quantity of fuel consumed, *VMT* is miles driven, and *MPG* is fuel efficiency in miles per gallon. The price elasticity of demand for fuel, ε_f, may be written as the difference between the elasticity of *VMT* with respect to the price of fuel, ε_{vmt}, and the elasticity of MPG with respect to the fuel price, ε_{mpg}:

(3-2) $$\varepsilon_f = \varepsilon_{vmt} - \varepsilon_{mpg}.$$

Carol Dahl and Thomas Sterner have surveyed the literature and found that estimates vary with the type of model estimated and with the lag structure assumed.[1] Estimates of short-run (that is, one month or one quarter) price elasticity of demand cluster in the range of –0.1 to –0.4, and the long-term estimates are generally between –0.6 and –1.1. These elasticities mean that, for instance, a 10 percent price increase is likely to reduce fuel consumption by 1 to 4 percent in the first few months, but by 6 to 11 percent once consumers have had the opportunity to replace their existing vehicles with more fuel-efficient models.

The "average" estimate is about –0.3 for the short-term price elasticity and between –0.8 and –1.0 for the long-term elasticity. The more recent estimates seem somewhat larger in absolute value than do those from earlier studies, suggesting that the price sensitivity of demand is increasing over time or that improved empirical techniques reduce the downward bias of earlier estimates. For instance, a 1993 analysis by Margaret A. Walls, Alan J. Krupnick, and H. Carter Hood of more than 20,000 respondents to the National Personal Transportation Survey of 1990 concluded that the weighted, short-term price elasticity of gasoline was –0.51.[2]

If the general policy concern is the long-term growth of energy consumption, one should focus on the long-run price elasticities of fuel demand in assessing the effect of using fuel prices to achieve conservation goals. These elasticities are higher than the short-term elasticities because households and businesses need time to adjust their choices of transportation modes, their vehicle stocks, and their travel patterns (*VMT*) in response to changes in relative prices. In her 1986 survey, Dahl concluded that the empirical literature provided average estimates of the long-run elasticities in equation 3-2 of –0.55 for *VMT* and 0.57 for MPG, summing to an overall long-run price elasticity of –1.12.[3] The average of the direct estimates of the long-run price elasticity was –1.02. These figures provide a benchmark for our own estimates.

The Adjustment to Changing Fuel Prices

Given that fuel-economy mandates have prevailed since 1978, it is difficult to separate their impact on vehicle fuel efficiency and utilization from those of relative prices. However, given that these regulations were not generally binding until world oil prices began falling in the 1980s, it is possible to disentangle the effects of fuel prices from those of CAFE for a period that ends in the early to mid-1980s.

Before 1984, U.S. vehicle manufacturers had been amassing substantial CAFE credits because high fuel prices had generated a consumer demand for even greater fuel efficiency than the law required.[4] It was not until 1984 that the U.S. manufacturers found themselves producing passenger cars whose fuel economy averaged below the extant CAFE standard.[5] Given the predictions of $50 to $100 a barrel of oil that were common in the late 1970s and early 1980s, it is reasonable to assume that the U.S. companies did not view CAFE regulations as a constraint until fuel prices began to fall in earnest in the early 1980s.

Earlier we showed that the automobile companies adjusted to higher fuel prices by reducing the weight of their cars. This adjustment was accompanied by reductions in engine size. In this chapter, we investigate the effects of fuel prices on vehicle fuel economy and vehicle miles traveled. Our analysis utilizes time-series data on fuel economy, fuel prices, real output, and vehicle miles traveled.

Vehicle Miles

Previous research by David Greene and Dermot Gately has attempted to explain vehicle miles traveled of light-duty vehicles (passenger cars, small pickups, vans, and sport-utility vehicles) by estimating a single-equation model that includes the average cost per mile traveled, *GDP,* and the number of drivers as independent variables.[6] But the cost per mile traveled is simply the price of fuel divided by average miles per gallon for the light-vehicle fleet. We proceed with a formulation that includes both *MPG* and the real price of fuel, p_f, but is otherwise similar to the methodology of Greene and Gately.

A time-series analysis of the determinants of VMT for passenger cars and for light trucks using data for 1966–92 results in surprisingly low estimates of the effects of real fuel prices (appendix B, table B-1).[7] The average *MPG* of all vehicles on the road has no explanatory value, probably because of measurement error. If the mpg variable is dropped and a distributed-lag formulation is used for real gasoline prices, the estimated (long-run) price elasticity of *VMT* for fuel prices is between −0.2 and −0.3. When the period of a binding CAFE constraint, 1984–92, is eliminated, the estimated elasticity is −0.31 for passenger cars. In the simulations below, we use both our 1966–92 estimate and the average estimate of −0.55 from the literature reported by Dahl.

Miles per Gallon

There are two measures of fuel efficiency that are often confused in discussions of fuel economy: mpg for new vehicles and mpg for the fleet of vehicles on the road. Obviously, the latter responds more slowly than the former to shocks in exogenous variables, such as fuel prices.

Chapter 2 showed that fuel economy in a given new car is a function of vehicle weight and engine displacement and that technical fuel efficiency in a new model responds to lagged gasoline prices but not to CAFE standards. Here, we examine the responses of the average fuel efficiency of cars sold in a given model year and of the average fuel efficiency of all vehicles on the road to changes in real fuel prices and in the standards. The difference between the analysis in the previous chapter and this one is subtle but important. Higher fuel prices or CAFE requirements may have major impacts on the design of a new Chevrolet, for example, but may have very different effects on overall fuel efficiency if consumers shift their purchase decisions toward Geo Metros or Toyota Corollas or simply decide to keep driving their 1980 Buicks. If policymakers are truly interested in conserving fuel, they should be less interested in forcing producers to design exotic electric cars that few consumers may want than in inducing motorists to purchase and operate more fuel-efficient cars and to drive fewer miles. Higher fuel taxes do both.

Higher prices of fuel induce improvements in technical fuel efficiency in the design of a vehicle after about a four-year lag because manufacturers require this time to adjust their vehicle designs. Consumers, however, may respond much more quickly, by shifting from larger to smaller, less powerful cars. This shift can be accelerated by CAFE-constrained vehicle companies through changes in the relative prices of large and small cars.

We examined the changes in average new-vehicle fuel economy since 1968, the first year for which consistent data are available. The essence of the results is in table 3-1 (for the complete results, see table B-2 of appendix B). In the period of generally rising fuel prices, 1968–83, the long-run elasticity of new-car mpg for fuel prices is estimated to be 0.43.

Table 3-1. *Estimated Elasticities of Average New-Car Fuel Efficiency with Respect to Real Fuel Prices and CAFE Standards, 1968–92*

Variable	1968–83	1968–92
Real fuel price (distributed 4-year lag)	0.43	0.39
CAFE (2-year lag)	0	0.25
Time	0.024	0.026

Source: Authors' calculations based on sources described in appendix B.

In other words, consumers and manufacturers combined to produce a 4.3 percent increase in average fuel efficiency of new cars for each 10 percent rise in fuel prices. During this period, there was no statistically detectable effect of CAFE on average mpg.

When we extend the period of estimation to 1968–92, the importance of real fuel prices declines somewhat, and CAFE becomes statistically significant. After a lag of two years, each 10 percent increase in CAFE requirements induces a 2.5 percent increase in mpg. The lag may be the response of the manufacturers to the realization that their CAFE credits were being exhausted, requiring the companies to raise large-car prices relative to those of smaller models. Note that the exogenous time trend in the improvement of mpg, about 2.5 percent, is somewhat above the estimate for individual-model data in chapter 2. This result should not be surprising, given that consumers may have switched to smaller cars over time.

The effects of fuel prices and regulatory standards on each Big Three manufacturer's fuel economy may be estimated for only 1978–92, the limited period for which individual-firm mpg ratings are available from the Department of Transportation, an approach that deprives us of information on how producers responded to market signals before government regulators began to instruct producers on the "optimal" level of fuel economy. Once again, the results show that fuel prices appear to be much more important than CAFE mandates in explaining the average mpg, either for the entire period or just since 1983 (table 3-2). The fuel-price elasticities are highest for Chrysler and lowest for General Motors, probably reflecting the fact that Chrysler essentially abandoned large-car production in the early 1980s while General Motors continued to produce big cars. The CAFE variable is not statistically significant in the Chrysler equation, but is significant (after a two-year lag) for both General Motors and Ford, the two large-car producers. For the latter companies, the estimated effect of the fuel-economy regulations is to increase the average energy efficiency of their fleet by about 5 mpg.

Table 3-2. *The Estimated Elasticity of the Big Three's Annual New-Car Fuel Economy, 1978–92*

Manufacturer	Real fuel price (distributed four-year lag)	CAFE (two-year lag)
Chrysler	0.65	0
Ford	0.30	0.24
General Motors	0.15	0.28

Sources: Authors' calculations based on sources described in appendix B.

Interestingly, the response of the individual Big Three producers' mpg to changes in fuel prices is less than the response of the overall fleet of new cars to such changes. This suggests that consumers react to changes in real fuel prices by migrating between, say, GM's large cars and Chrysler's smaller cars.

For new light trucks, average fuel economy responds to fuel prices with an elasticity of about 0.5 (in the equation that excludes CAFE). The estimated elasticity is somewhat lower for all light trucks on the road and much less statistically significant. The rate of technical progress is similar for light trucks and passenger cars, but steel prices appear to have no effect. CAFE once again has no statistically significant effect when included with energy prices.

These results clearly show that both consumers and producers respond to higher prices of energy by adjusting the fuel efficiency of the cars they purchase or offer for sale. These findings are not entirely new, but they offer more timely corroboration of the results of the earlier studies summarized by Dahl. With no CAFE standards, higher prices would induce greater automotive fuel efficiency and less driving.

Substituting a Fuel Tax

Assume that no fuel-efficiency mandates had ever been implemented. Had gasoline taxes been raised after 1981 to offset some of the decline in the real price of oil that occurred in the mid-1980s, energy consumption could have been restrained. But how high would the tax have had to be to yield fuel savings equivalent to those induced by CAFE? To answer this question for passenger cars, we use the results from estimating the determinants of VMT and of mpg for new cars described in this chapter and in chapter 2 to simulate the effect of various gasoline taxes.[8]

Table 3-3. *The Effects of Increased Fuel Taxes on Fuel Economy, Vehicle Miles, and Fuel Consumption for Passenger Cars, 1992*

Year	Vehicle miles (billions)	MPG, new cars	MPG, all cars on the road	Fuel consumed (billions of gallons)
	Levels with CAFE			
1980	1,111.2	23.5	15.5	71.9
1992	1,595.4	27.7	21.6	73.8
	Estimated Levels without CAFE			
1992 with 1981 real gas price (reduction)	1,286.7	28.4	21.0	61.4 (−16.8%)
1992 with 25-cent additional tax after 1985 (reduction)	1,400.4	24.7	19.6	71.4 (−3.3%)

Source: Authors' calculations based on sources described in appendix B.

The results of this simulation exercise are shown in table 3-3 for two scenarios: (1) an additional tax that keeps real U.S. fuel prices at their 1981 level for every year thereafter, and (2) an additional 25-cent tax imposed in 1986, after oil prices crashed, and remaining in effect every year thereafter. This last tax amounts to about 20 percent of 1991–92 prices. Note that these simulations involve an increase in fuel taxes over the current average national level.

For each scenario, we show the trend in passenger-car miles of travel, *new*-car fuel economy, average fuel economy for all passenger cars on the road, and fuel consumption. For example, the perpetuation of 1981 real fuel prices (approximately 75 percent above 1992 real prices) would have pushed new-car fuel economy to 28.4 mpg by 1992, or slightly above the level mandated by CAFE. But because 1981 real prices would also have reduced VMT sharply, this option would have reduced fuel consumption by more than 16 percent from the actual 1992 levels achieved under the CAFE regime.

Interestingly, a 25-cent tax imposed in 1986 is sufficient to induce at least as much conservation as was achieved by government regulation. Using our equations, which include a conservative price elasticity of vehicle miles for fuel prices of just −0.3, we estimate that this tax would have resulted in 3.3 percent less fuel consumption in 1992 than was actually accomplished under CAFE. If the elasticity of travel with respect to fuel prices is assumed to be −0.55, a less cautious estimate in line with recent research, the 25-cent option results in appreciably less passenger-car energy consumption than was actually registered in 1992 (about 5 percent). Note that because the higher gasoline prices reduce VMT, overall energy savings are achieved with new-car fuel efficiency rising to only 24.7 mpg. As a result, conservation is attained at far lower social costs.

This assessment of the beneficial effects of a 25-cent increase in the fuel tax is clearly conservative. All of the above simulations assume that new-car sales are unaffected by the abandonment of CAFE. But if vehicle manufacturers are no longer forced to provide high fuel efficiency in the teeth of falling gas prices, consumers might be more receptive to purchasing new passenger cars rather than holding on to older vehicles or buying vans, pickups, or sports-utility vehicles. Thus, if anything, we have underestimated the efficacy of a fuel tax. The tax hike required to emulate CAFE's effect on conservation is almost certainly even less than 25 cents.

Is a Higher Gas Tax Fair?

There has been considerable academic debate about the distributional impact of energy taxes. As with most excise taxes on nonluxury goods, a gasoline tax is regressive, but this regressivity is modest because gasoline expenditures are a relatively modest share of total consumer expenditures, even in the lowest income brackets.

A recent paper by James M. Poterba argued that although the excise on gasoline is regressive in terms of family income, it is not in terms of consumption expenditures.[9] Incomes vary over time, and reported current incomes for relatively comfortable households can understate their purchasing power. Poterba's results, based on an analysis of the 1985 Consumer Expenditure Survey, are shown in table 3-4. Note that the share of income spent on gasoline and motor oil falls from 6.7 percent for the lowest current-income decile to 2.4 percent for the highest current-income decile (table 3-4, column 2).[10] However, the distribution of gasoline and motor oil expenditures as a share of total expenditure exhibits a very different pattern, rising from the first to second decile and remaining relatively flat until the ninth decile and then falling off in the last decile (table 3-4, column 3).[11] Poterba concludes from this analysis that the incidence of gasoline taxes is not generally regressive over time because current consumption expenditures are likely to be more closely related to permanent income than is current income.

A more recent paper by Howard Chernick and Andrew Reschovsky questions Poterba's finding that the gasoline tax is proportional over

Table 3-4. *The Distribution of Gasoline Expenditures across Income Groups*

1985 family income decile (1)	Gasoline expenditures as share of income (2)	Gasoline expenditures as share of total consumption[a] (3)	Average 1976–86 family income decile (4)	Gasoline expenditures as share of average 1976–86 family income (5)
1	0.067	0.039	1	0.042
2	0.065	0.057	2	0.051
3	0.064	0.058	3	0.051
4	0.061	0.061	4	0.052
5	0.050	0.056	5	0.048
6	0.047	0.056	6	0.045
7	0.044	0.054	7	0.043
8	0.038	0.049	8	0.042
9	0.036	0.048	9	0.037
10	0.024	0.034	10	0.031

Sources: Columns 2 and 3 from James W. Poterba, "Is the Gasoline Tax Regressive?" in David Bradford, ed., *Tax Policy and the Economy 5* (National Bureau of Economic Research and MIT Press, 1991), pp. 151–52; Column 5 from Howard Chernick and Andrew Reschovsky, "Is the Gasoline Tax Regressive?" Discussion Paper 980–92 (University of Wisconsin-Madison Institute for Research on Poverty, August 1992), p. 8.

a. Total consumption expenditures include imputed rent but exclude automobile purchases.

much of the income distribution.[12] Using longitudinal data from the Panel Study of Income Dynamics for 1976–86, Chernick and Reschovsky show that the share of gasoline and motor oil expenditures in average 1976–86 income for lower-income families is about one-third higher than the share for the highest decile in the income distribution (table 3-4, column 5).

The Chernick-Reschovsky study centers on the high point of real oil prices in the past fifty years, 1981. Since that year, motor-fuel prices have declined substantially while real incomes have risen. As a result, the share of personal consumption expenditures on gasoline and oil has declined from an average of 5.1 percent in 1981 to just 2.3 percent in 1993.[13] Assuming that this decline is proportional across income groups, this means that the share of income spent by families in the three or four lowest deciles has fallen from less than 5 percent to less than 3 percent. For families in the top three or four deciles, the share has declined to about 1.8 percent.

These data suggest that a gasoline tax is likely to be regressive, much as municipal water charges or garbage tipping fees are regressive, but that this regressivity is likely to have only a small effect on income distribution because gasoline expenditures account for a small share of consumption.[14] Further, as Poterba points out, even this moderate regressivity may

Table 3-5. *The Burden of Gasoline Expenditures after Indexation of Transfer Payments*

Family income decile, 1985 (1)	Unindexed gasoline expenditures as share of family income (2)	Average 1976–86 family income decile (3)	Unindexed gasoline expenditures as share of average 1976–86 family income (4)
1	0.007	1	0.026
2	0.028	2	0.048
3	0.047	3	0.047
4	0.047	4	0.048
5	0.050	5	0.047
6	0.043	6	0.045
7	0.052	7	0.041
8	0.045	8	0.040
9	0.057	9	0.037
10	0.050	10	0.028

Sources: Column 2 from Poterba, "Is the Gasoline Tax Regressive?" p. 158; column 4 from Chernick and Reschovsky, "Is the Gasoline Tax Regressive?" p. 26.

be offset by the indexation of transfer payments.[15] Poterba found that the lowest four family expenditure deciles received 40 percent of their income from indexed transfer payments in 1985; the top four deciles received only 4 percent of their income in this form. Chernick and Reschovsky found that the lowest four average income deciles received only 18 percent of their income in the form of indexed transfer payments in 1976–86 while the top four deciles received just 1.4 percent of their incomes in indexed form.[16] Whatever the magnitude, indexation substantially reduces the inequitable effect of any increase in gasoline taxes that is passed through to consumers. Indeed, Chernick and Reschovsky's results show a rough proportionality of gasoline expenditure burdens from the second through the eighth income deciles (table 3-5, column 4). Their results show at worst mild regressivity until the ninth or tenth income deciles. Poterba's results show that, after accounting for the effects of indexation, a gasoline tax increase is not regressive at all (table 3-5, column 2).[17]

Estimating from Chernick and Reschovsky's results, a gasoline tax of 25 cents would raise gasoline expenditures by an average of about 0.6 percent of family income, assuming full pass-through of the tax and no reduction in VMT.[18] The lowest two average family income deciles would experience a direct expenditure increase of about 0.9 percent of income; the next two deciles would experience an increase of about 0.7 percent of income. Such a tax increase would not seem particularly burdensome, or unfair, given the indexation of transfer payments.

Nor is there much reason to believe that a federal gasoline tax has drastically different effects across geographic regions. Chernick and Reschovsky calculate that the average family in the West, where people drive the most, would have to pay $82.00 more a year if a $0.075 a gallon (in 1994 dollars) gasoline tax were passed; the average family in the Northeast, where people drive fewer miles, would pay $76.00 more. Our 20 percent gasoline tax increase would be slightly more than three times this $0.075 increase; hence, the average difference annually would be about $20.00 per family between these regions.

Finally, it must be recognized that a substantial share of motor fuel is used in commerce. This commercial use increases the average direct cost of the tax increases calculated above by about 43 percent according to Chernick and Reschovsky. If these costs are passed on to consumers in proportional increases in the cost of consumption, and if consumption rises proportionately with permanent income, these expenditures should be roughly proportional to permanent income. Thus the overall distributional consequence of an increase in gasoline taxes is at worst moderately regressive in the upper ranges of income and nonregressive at lower income levels.

Economic Costs

The economic costs of a fuel tax may be divided conceptually into two components. First, such a tax distorts relative prices by raising the price of motor fuel above its incremental cost, thereby inducing inefficient consumption decisions. The costs of these shifts in consumption patterns at full employment are referred to as the "economic welfare costs" of the tax. Second, any tax increase may have a depressing macroeconomic effect on the nation's employment and output. If the tax increase is not offset by other monetary or fiscal actions, a short-term reduction in national output could result.

Welfare Losses

What would be the losses in consumer welfare occasioned by a $0.25 tax on motor fuel for passenger cars—a tax that would have conserved as much oil as CAFE? We ignore the effects of an adjustment to 1992 prices over time and simply calculate the static welfare costs at long-run equilibrium. For this purpose, we assume that the long-run price elasticity of demand for fuel is –1.0. Given average fuel prices of $1.20 a gallon in

1992, gasoline prices would have been $1.45 with the $0.25 additional tax. At these price and demand elasticities, consumers would have purchased 71 billion gallons of fuel for passenger cars. At the $1.20 price, absent CAFE, consumption would have been 86 billion gallons. The deadweight loss of the $0.25 tax may be calculated as $1.88 billion, or about $0.125 per gallon saved. This compares favorably with the social costs of CAFE, which have been estimated to reach as high as $5 billion.[19]

Macroeconomic Implications

Opponents of higher gasoline taxation generally presume that such a tax is not only inequitable but likely to depress overall economic activity. Advocates of a higher gas tax, however, argue that increased federal energy taxation would not only reduce harmful environmental externalities but could also help reduce the federal budget deficit. Both are correct: a higher fuel tax is likely to reduce economic growth rates; it may also help close budget deficits if it is not negated by other fiscal or monetary policy initiatives. But our point is not that higher fuel taxes are necessarily welfare enhancing, only that they are a superior substitute for the socially inefficient policy of mandating automotive fuel efficiency.

An increase in the tax on motor fuels, particularly the 25-cents-a-gallon levy that would be required to replace the CAFE policy, might be accompanied by compensatory fiscal or monetary actions. Proposals for higher energy taxation have often assumed, for instance, offsetting decreases in taxes on lower-income households, perhaps through higher earned-income credits. Fuel tax increases can also be cushioned by, say, payroll tax reductions or even by lower levies on telephone service.

We do not wish to explore the many possibilities for changing the mix in monetary and fiscal measures, but it is obvious that the contractionary consequence of higher energy taxes can be blunted by more expansive monetary policy. Indeed, through much of the 1980s, Chairman Paul Volcker would periodically invite Congress to "do the right thing" (tighten fiscal policy) with the implicit understanding that he would reciprocate by easing the monetary supply.

But assume that Congress, in a fit of clairvoyance, would pass the 25-cent fuel excise, end the CAFE program, and not enact any new tax preferences for rich, poor, or middle-class households. What would be the macroeconomic impact of such forthrightness? Existing studies suggest that the fuel tax by itself would reduce gross domestic product by 0.1 to 0.2 percent a year for about three years. Thereafter, the economy would return to its original growth path.[20] This is not a large impact—and it is surely one that can be softened by appropriate fiscal or monetary offsets.

The Strategic Petroleum Reserve

Although the politics of gasoline taxation tend to exaggerate its economic downside, the cost of defaulting to other policies seldom receives equal attention. The other programs purporting to enhance U.S. energy security include, besides CAFE requirements, an expensive Strategic Petroleum Reserve (SPR). The SPR warrants brief discussion because some critics of both fuel-economy regulations and fuel taxes have suggested that it may afford sufficient, indeed optimal, protection against possible supply disruptions.

Between 1977 and 1990, the U.S. government built the world's largest public stockpile of oil, accumulating nearly 600 million barrels in salt domes in Louisiana and Texas. In theory, a well-timed drawdown from the reserve during an energy crisis might have a moderating influence on spot prices. In practice, regrettably, the effectiveness of this device is questionable.

To begin with, it has not been clear that the government's existing stockpile adds to total inventories, public and private. Private inventories have actually fallen since 1977 when the SPR began to fill.[21] If government inventories simply displace private stocks, releasing oil from the SPR would have little net effect during a shortage.

Moreover, the reserve, huge as it is, may still be too small to dampen prices in so large a market. The SPR's maximum rate of drawdown is 3.5 million barrels a day, or just over one-fifth of total U.S. average daily consumption.

Finally, apart from the still unanswered question of whether the government can orchestrate releases from the reserve in a timely and efficient manner, the cost of the reserve seems surprisingly high.[22] This is partly because the annual additions to SPR rise in periods of high oil prices and decline when oil prices fall.[23] One possible explanation for the seemingly perverse inventory management is elastic expectations: when oil prices move up, Congress authorizes increases in SPR purchases of oil in anticipation of further price increases. Conversely, when prices drop, expectations of a continuing decline may lead to less acquisition.[24]

Whatever the case, serious doubts arise as to whether the SPR can be managed cost effectively. Its limitations suggest that supplemental measures are probably necessary to cushion potential disruptions. But to slacken marginal demand by regulating the fuel economy of autos, rather than by levying a straightforward tax on fuel consumption, adds yet another layer of undesirable consequences. A full evaluation of the economic penalties, if any, from fuel taxation should also take account of this administrative context.

Conclusion

A tax that raised the price of motor fuel by 25 cents after 1985 would have conserved as much energy as the federal regulation of passenger-car fuel efficiency over the fourteen-year period 1978–92. If anything, this analysis understates the beneficial effects of a fuel tax on the mix of passenger cars and trucks and thus somewhat overstates the necessary increase in prices.

Even with this 20 percent increase in fuel prices, however, the cost to the economy would have been much less than the cost of the regulatory alternative. A tax that bolstered gasoline prices by 20 percent would cost the economy approximately $1.9 billion a year, but existing estimates of the economic cost of CAFE regulations suggest their costs may have run as high as $5 billion a year.[25] Whatever the political feasibility of gasoline taxes, their economic net benefits as a replacement for CAFE loom large.

The distributional effects of a 20 percent increase in gasoline taxes turn out to be surprisingly modest when one takes into account the indexation of transfer payments that form an important share of the incomes of poorer families. Even the regional inequities are less dramatic than often supposed because western drivers do not log many more miles than northeastern drivers on average, nor do they endure much longer travel times. Of course, no tax change is without some distributional implications. Those individuals who choose or are forced to drive very long distances to work each day will be more affected than those who can use mass transit. Nevertheless, these issues of tax equity seem much less fundamental than the fact that a gasoline tax is highly visible, ubiquitously unpopular, and beset by institutional obstacles in the United States. Hence it is to the politics of energy taxation that the next chapters of this book now turn.

CHAPTER FOUR

What Other Countries Do

H OW HAVE GOVERNMENTS in Europe, Japan, and Canada contributed
to the comparatively frugal levels of energy use in their national transportation sectors? Instead of ordering manufacturers to produce fuel-efficient
vehicles, the governments have, intentionally or not, taxed motor fuel
much more heavily than the United States has.

Some Hypotheses about Energy Taxes

To say that foreign capacity to tax fuel simply reflects natural circumstances—geographic conditions, for example, or national energy needs—
does not suffice. The fuel-tax policies abroad also evolved within governmental frameworks unlike America's. The importance of the historical
and institutional context of energy taxation becomes apparent after con-
sidering a variety of other explanations.

Greener Pastures?

It is sometimes posited that the steep foreign taxes reflect superior environmental consciousness. This impression is largely false. Environmental
protection, especially for air quality, in Europe has generally lagged behind efforts in the United States. Whereas U.S. manufacturers began
equipping new cars with three-way catalytic converters as early as 1981,
the European Community did not adopt a similar standard for its automobile manufacturers until 1989. The EC's emission controls will not

come into effect until the mid-1990s. The use of leaded gasoline had been virtually eliminated in the U.S. market by the mid-1970s, but leaded gasoline is still in use abroad.[1] Unleaded petrol constituted only 3 percent of total fuel deliveries in Britain as recently as 1988.[2] The 1990 amendments to the U.S. Clean Air Act require gasoline to be reformulated, sharply limiting hazardous contents such as benzene; no comparable requirements have been set in recent EC directives.[3] And although concern in Europe over global warming seems especially vocal, only two European governments currently penalize the use of coal, while six continue to subsidize their coal industries.[4]

Until the European Union completes its process of regulatory harmonization, of course, it is not easy to generalize about European environmental guidelines. National policies differ, sometimes drastically. Unique tax incentives to promote cleaner and quieter vehicles have been at work in the Netherlands since the mid-1980s.[5] By 1989 more than 70 percent of new cars sold there were fitted with state-of-the-art catalytic converters.[6] Germany's automotive fleet is cleaner than most others in Europe as well because Germany's mandatory standards predated the EC's by five years. Nowhere in Europe, however, did efforts to encourage clean-burning cars commence as early as in the United States.

The same cannot be said of Japan. To comply with strict air quality criteria set in 1978, Japanese auto manufacturers began fitting cars with three-way catalyzers at about the same time as U.S. producers.[7] Leaded gasoline was phased out soon after 1975, when the Ministry of International Trade and Industry "guided" petroleum refiners and refined-product importers into marketing unleaded fuel.[8] Like the United States (but unlike Europe, except for Sweden and Norway), Japan has also promulgated limits on evaporative hydrocarbon emissions for automobiles.[9]

But although Japan seemed to keep pace with U.S. initiatives in the 1970s, studies comparing the environmental movements in the two countries note that Japanese pollution control efforts began to flag during the past decade, whereas the U.S. commitment (to wit, the recent Clean Air Act amendments and the interventions of several American states) intensified.[10]

The higher gas tax rates in Europe and Japan generate environmental side benefits. Increasingly in recent years, environmentalism has provided a helpful pretext for those rates. But that does not mean it accounts for them.

Coherent Energy Strategies?

Most of western Europe and especially Japan are heavily dependent on imported petroleum. It stands to reason that these nations would restrain their energy requirements much more aggressively than does the United States, which still produces about as much oil as it imports. Forceful taxation of petroleum-based fuels, in other words, can be part of a deliberate strategy to conserve energy.

Granted, oil security considerations have been among the explicit reasons for raising fuel taxes in some instances. In France, for instance, the first general consumption tax on petroleum products was imposed shortly after the disruptions of the First World War, partly to prepare the economy for the possibility of similar emergencies in the future. As the threat of international conflict loomed again in the late 1930s, the internal petroleum tax was supplemented by much higher tariffs on imports.[11] In more recent years, however, the hallmark of French energy policy has not been conservation but rather a monomaniacal commitment to nuclear-sourced electricity, partly on the theory that *l'économie "toute électrique"* strengthens the nation's balance of payments.[12]

Americans may believe that the relatively low energy intensity of the Japanese economy is a deliberate consequence of clever tax policies in Japan. In truth, Japan's taxes are not meant to advance energy goals. Demand for fuel in Japan is suppressed by higher costs than in all but six countries in the Organization for Economic Cooperation and Development (figure 4-1). But Japan's high fuel costs have more to do with cartel pricing by refineries and an extraordinarily inefficient distribution system than with fiscal measures. Among the several different taxes levied on petroleum refined-products, just one of the levies (accounting for only 12 percent of the revenue from all the petroleum-related taxes) serves an energy purpose.[13] The lion's share of Japan's energy taxes pays for wasteful programs, such as support of domestic coal mining, or for activities such as road and airport construction that, if anything, facilitate fuel consumption.

Precious few countries have attempted to use fuel taxation primarily as an instrument to save energy, but Sweden and Denmark have been notable exceptions.[14] In 1983 Sweden's Parliament decreed as a matter of national policy that declining oil prices should be bolstered by taxes to promote conservation.

In general, though, national fuel tax levels are not neatly a function of

Figure 4-1. *Gasoline Prices and Taxes in OECD Countries, Fourth Quarter, 1992*

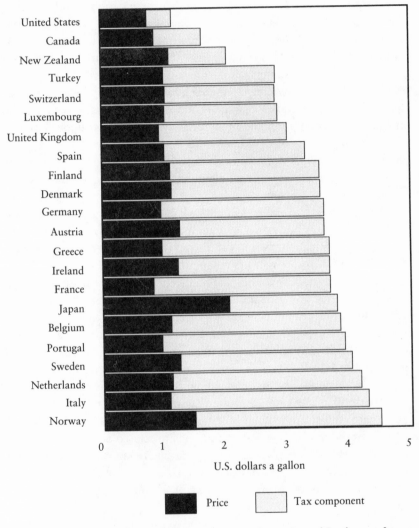

U.S. dollars a gallon

Price ▪   Tax component ☐

Source: Organization for Economic Cooperation and Development, International Energy Agency, *Energy Prices and Taxes, Fourth Quarter, 1992* (Paris, 1993), pp. xxii, 291.

relative energy dependency. The prices and tax rates for gasoline in the OECD countries are exhibited in figure 4-1. Italy has the highest tax, which is consistent with Italy's very low level of energy self-sufficiency (only 17 percent).[15] Yet taxes as a share of the retail price in Japan, whose self-sufficiency (15 percent) is even less than Italy's, are half as high. Germany and France are almost the same in their degree of self-sufficiency (48 percent and 47 percent, respectively), but as recently as 1988 Germany's tax amounted to about $1.50 a gallon while the tax in France was closer to $2.50 a gallon.[16] Only after 1991 did the tax levels of these countries become comparable, owing to a sharp increase in Germany. Norway is a net exporter of energy, but Norway's tax rate is higher than Germany's. Canada is completely energy self-sufficient, while the United States is now in a somewhat less auspicious position (85 percent self-sufficient). Yet Canadian taxes on gasoline in 1992 were at least twice as high as U.S. taxes.

The International Energy Agency (IEA) concludes that "there is no country where taxation and energy objectives are brought together in a systematic and well-balanced fashion."[17] This may be an overstatement. At least one country, the Netherlands, has mounted a coordinated assault on the use of automobiles. In the past few years, the Dutch have, among other things, subjected cars to a half-dozen special tax penalties; capped income-tax relief for automotive commuting costs; enforced a rule of no more than twenty parking spaces per one hundred employees in urban work centers; and imposed draconian restrictions on the development of new industrial, commercial, and residential real estate along highways.[18]

Nevertheless, the IEA is basically right: most developed nations have not formulated coherent "antiauto policies" to enhance energy independence. The special tax treatment of company cars illustrates the continuing inconsistencies, even in various energy-sensitive European countries.[19] Up to 60 percent of all new cars in Great Britain, and nearly one-third in Sweden and Germany, are vehicles purchased by employers for use by employees. The latter typically pay a flat fee on their income taxes in exchange for this major fringe benefit, and many pay little or nothing for operating expenses. This subsidy effectively blunts some of the impact of high petrol levies—so much so in England that VMTs per passenger car soared in the 1980s, approaching the U.S. level by 1990 even though personal ownership of automobiles is still barely half as common as in the United States.[20]

Geography

Perhaps the average American consumes far more motor fuel than the average west European or Japanese because America, in Antoine de Saint-Exupéry's words, "is a continent, not merely a nation." Presumably, Americans have to drive much longer distances—a powerful motive to resist onerous increases in gasoline prices.

But this idea, too, is an oversimplification. Two-thirds of all vehicle miles traveled in the United States are on urban roads, not "open plains."[21] Ninety percent of the trips are fewer than ten miles long, and the average length of the trips appears to be virtually the same as or shorter than in some other countries, including Germany and Britain.[22] "Americans," as Lee Schipper and his associates have recently observed, "do not necessarily have farther to go or go farther."[23] They mainly go more frequently, whereas Europeans more often stay put, walk, or use other modes of transportation.

PUBLIC TRANSPORTATION. The other modes include extensive systems of passenger rail and bus service in and between many large cities abroad. Mass transit (local and intercity) carries approximately 15 percent of total travel in Europe, compared with about 3 percent in the United States.[24]

Europe's 15 percent, however, overstates the margin of international difference between the automotive and nonautomotive modal mix. The higher utilization of intercity rail transportation in Europe, for instance, is partly offset by America's much more intensive air travel.[25] In any event, Europe's mass transit systems obviously do not suffice to explain the enormous disparity in fuel consumption on opposite sides of the Atlantic.[26] Automotive travel accounts for at least 80 percent of all domestic travel in virtually every developed country except Japan, where it represents less than 60 percent.[27] Again, a key distinction seems to be that, on a daily basis, more people in the United States take more motorized trips.

DENSITY. The oft-cited reason for this anomalous travel pattern is the low population density of the United States. To be sure, in decentralized communities, characteristic of many U.S. metropolitan areas, cars are often the only practical way to get from "here" to "there," not only when people are commuting to work but for shopping, recreation, and virtually every other activity.[28] The result is a rising volume of automobile journeys, burning more gasoline.

But only in this sense—namely, the influence of the built environment—can American driving habits, energy demand, and a keen preference for cheap fuel be attributed substantially to density. The population per square mile in Canada and in Australia is approximately one-tenth that of the United States. Yet taxation of gasoline is considerably lower in the United States, and per capita consumption is significantly higher.[29] Sweden has the same density as the United States, but the Swedes tax gasoline at many times the U.S. rate and consume far less fuel per head. America is a diverse place. The densities of some American states resemble those of some dense nations in Europe. For example, New Jersey has almost exactly the same number of persons per square mile as the Netherlands (and, incidentally, about the same gross domestic product). But the Dutch pay the equivalent of more than $3.00 a gallon in gasoline taxes (compared with $0.25 in New Jersey) and consume about 80 gallons a year per capita, compared with about 450 a year by each resident of the Garden State.[30]

Motorization

The extent of automobile ownership in the United States complicates the politics of gasoline taxation. By 1983 more than 86 percent of all U.S. households owned automotive vehicles. That included 60 percent of the households with incomes below $10,000, 91 percent of those with incomes between $10,000 and $20,000, and 98 percent of those with higher incomes.[31] These motorized multitudes have an intense interest in keeping down the variable costs of their vehicles. And naturally, a society that now averages almost two registered passenger vehicles for every household can generate broader opposition to higher fuel costs than a society with only two-thirds as many vehicles per household (the west European average).[32] The comparatively low voter turnout in this country probably magnifies the political consequences. Voter participation rises with family income, as does the number of cars. In other democracies, where much larger percentages of citizens vote, nonmotorists figure more prominently in the active electorate.

Although the constituency of motorists in the rest of the world remains more modest, it is no longer small. More than three-quarters of all French households, for example, now own a car, and almost a quarter of them own more than one.[33] The figures for western Germany are about the same.[34] At levels like these it is simply no longer credible to argue that most German or French consumers do not feel the bite of motor fuel prices triple those in the United States. In public opinion polls it has not been surprising to find European taxpayers responding much like Americans to the prospect of higher prices. When the French were polled on the subject by the Gallup organization as far back as 1974, a resounding 87 percent disapproved of the government's increasing the cost of gasoline to conserve fuel.[35]

It is true that mass motorization is a relatively recent development outside the United States. Even in Germany the number of automobiles per 1,000 inhabitants was only 81 in 1960. America had reached that level by 1921.[36] Naturally it must have been easy to embed relatively high tax rates in Germany when 90 percent of the population still lacked cars. But that was then. What about now? Today, an overwhelming majority of west German households own at least one automobile. Yet, as recently as 1991, the German government managed to hike its tax on gasoline by 28 percent, sending the price per gallon of regular unleaded fuel from $1.95 to $2.50. (As if that was not enough, another significant increase took effect in 1994.)[37] For politicians to administer gasoline price increases of that magnitude in the United States would have been unthinkable, even several decades ago when fewer Americans possessed cars.

In sum, comparative tax positions have not simply reflected auto ownership. In 1988 western Europe as a whole averaged 400 cars per 1,000 people, or approximately the U.S. ratio in 1970. But Americans were not more tolerant of European-type gasoline taxation back in 1970, and European drivers were not taxed nearly as lightly in 1988 as American drivers were eighteen years earlier. Clearly, the chasm in national excises involves factors beyond ownership rates.

Interest Groups

Can America's political resistance to energy taxes be blamed simply on powerful rural lobbies, Detroit, and "big oil"? And should other countries' hefty gas taxes be imputed to a supposed scarcity of similar interest groups?

Farmers, automakers, and oil companies have had a stake in minimizing fuel taxes. These groups seemingly enjoy disproportionate influence in American politics. Rural states, by way of the Senate, are overrepresented in Congress. The automobile industry employs hundreds of thousands of workers whose geographic concentration in pivotal midwestern states can be critical in close presidential elections. As for the oil producers, their capacity to manipulate "public government for the private objectives of the industry" is reputedly legendary.[38]

But don't policymakers in other national regimes confront pressure groups like these?

FARMERS AND AUTOMAKERS. Some of these interests seem at least as well-organized in various European countries and in Japan as they are in the United States. Look at the political might of the French or Japanese agrarian lobbies. There are more than twice as many farmers in the work forces of France and Japan as in the United States. Not surprisingly, they manage to prevail upon their governments for agricultural subsidies that are 60 to 120 percent larger (as a share of farm income) than the subsidies obtained by U.S. farmers.[39] The fact that the American farm belt has unique influence in the Senate evidently is not enough to equalize farm policies and, in any event, frequently seems irrelevant to energy tax outcomes. During the past twenty years, most legislative proposals to increase the federal gasoline tax were opposed in the House of Representatives. Many never came to a vote in the Senate.[40]

Compared with the auto industries of Europe and Japan, the U.S. auto manufacturers seem to have lost more, not fewer, key political battles during the past couple of decades. While Congress saddled the Big Three with increasingly expensive regulations governing safety, gas mileage, and emissions, British, French, and Italian producers successfully warded off comparable regulatory costs through the 1970s and 1980s.[41] And while General Motors, Ford, and Chrysler managed to pressure the Reagan administration into negotiating an import quota of about 20 percent on Japanese cars, companies like Fiat, Peugeot, and Renault successfully lobbied their governments to limit Japanese imports to under 3 percent of domestic sales.[42]

Naturally, the European and Japanese manufacturers, geared to making small cars, have long been more comfortable with their nations' fuel-excise schedules than American manufacturers have been with proposals to increase the federal gasoline tax. But even these conventions have been changing. For a number of years, at least one American firm, Chrysler, has favored a gas tax hike to stabilize the market for its line of compact and subcompact cars. Recently, Ford and GM have muted their objections, preferring a higher gas tax to new fuel-economy requirements.[43]

OIL LOBBY. The political clout of the petroleum industry may be greater in a producing nation like the United States than in a nation with no oil production, like Italy. This truism, however, still leaves some puzzles.

Several countries—Britain, Norway, Canada—levy larger taxes on petroleum products even though these countries also have large, private producing sectors. True, their local operations are generally younger than those of the well-established petroleum industry in the United States. But that probably does not solve the whole riddle: if the presence of producers is a constraint on energy taxation, why does British Petroleum or Imperial Oil of Canada or the assortment of private firms drilling off the coast of Norway countenance taxes much higher than in the United States?[44]

If the U.S. oil producers are so much more muscular, why was this industry burdened with extraordinary government controls on prices and profits throughout the 1970s and well into the 1980s? And if its goal is to suppress every energy tax, why does the industry not speak with one voice? Some majors (for example, Conoco and Chevron, the nation's biggest refiner) have openly expressed support for higher taxes on gasoline to cut the federal deficit.[45]

Casual observers jumped to the conclusion that the oil lobby ultimately dominated the great energy tax debate of 1993. When Congress sank President Bill Clinton's initial tax proposal in the summer of 1993, it was the oil industry's advocates aboard the Senate Finance Committee who fired the main torpedo.[46]

This interpretation of the events is insufficient, however. There was more than one cause of the demise of this unusual tax on the use of energy (as measured in the British thermal unit, or Btu). The proposal was badly packaged; instead of complementing deep budgetary reductions, it gave the appearance of funding additional public "investment." This defect became one of the reasons why every Republican member of Congress, not just representatives from oil-producing states, opposed the tax. Further, the proposed levy imposed costs on a wide range of industries on the basis of the heat content (Btu) of the energy they employed in manufacturing. The inevitable result was a backlash, not just from energy producers, but from many other businesses. The American Petroleum Institute worked hard to scuttle the tax, but the objections of the National Association of Manufacturers were devastating.

HIGHWAY CLIENTS. Although special interests are neither unique to American politics nor a sufficient explanation for our fabled reluctance to tax energy consumption, the breadth of the antitax coalitions in the United States is admittedly distinctive. Clinton's Btu tax virtually invited broad rejection. But narrower levies, such as proposals to tax gasoline only, typically face widespread organized opposition, too.

Part of the reason is that the sellers of gasoline are usually joined by associations like the Highway Users Federation, an organization representing thousands of firms, from car rental companies and truckers to tire manufacturers and advertising agencies. Alongside groups like these typically stand state highway departments, legislatures, and governors, who fear a loss of revenue from local tolls and excises whenever the federal government threatens to encroach. Then, of course, every congressional district bulges with local roadside businesses (motels, fast-food franchises, shopping malls, and countless other drive-in services) for whom patronage by motorists—and, at bottom, inexpensive gasoline—is the lifeblood.

The potential for this configuration of interests exists in other parts of the industrialized world. But certain political traditions have long ensured its pervasive presence in the United States. As we discuss later in this chapter and the next, the ubiquitous "strip" remains largely an American phenomenon, thanks in no small part to a system of singularly emancipated local governments.

Petrol Taxation in Britain and France

In almost all industrial nations, energy security and environmental concerns have furnished, at best, ancillary excuses for taxing automotive fuels. The primary impetus for these tax policies has been fiscal: the need for revenue to finance expensive public enterprises. This was typically the case earlier in the century and is largely true today. Reliance on the income of fuel taxes has increased the most in countries such as Italy, with an outsized government sector and an undependable system of direct taxation. But costly government projects have also provided the chief motive for taxing gasoline in the United States. The main rationale for U.S. state and federal excises has been to fund highway construction.

Beyond the almost universal use of fuel taxes for public purposes other than energy policy, however, accidents of history and the differing constraints and incentives associated with national political institutions have generated sharply diverse outcomes. Among the most important institutional legacies are those pertaining to budgetary procedures, party systems, and the powers of local government.

Consider Great Britain and France, which highlight key contrasts with the United States.

Roots

It might be thought that Britain's and France's taxes on gasoline and other refined products stem historically from centuries of monarchical excise fees on luxuries, starting with items like salt and tobacco. There is an element of truth to this belief, but it should be noted that at least in

Britain there has also been a long tradition of income taxation. A national tax on income was first levied in England in 1799 to pay for the Napoleonic wars—more than a century before ratification of the Thirteenth Amendment in the United States. The income tax was substantially expanded in 1842 and has since yielded more revenue than any other single component of the British tax system.[47] Britain could have, but did not, follow the American model of minimizing national taxes on consumption and relying overwhelmingly on personal and corporate income taxation.

The link between Britain's petrol taxes and antecedent excises is indirect: the treasury began taxing motorcars at the turn of the century.[48] The car duty, based on horsepower, soon became a convenient trade restriction; it acted as a barrier to imports of American Fords, securing market share for British manufacturers producing cars with smaller engine displacements.[49] By helping to create a domestic fleet of small, thrifty vehicles, the tax coincidentally made it possible to levy increasingly stiff duties on fuel with fewer complaints from the auto industry or from motorists. The duties on petroleum products, in turn, served to protect the coal industry.

Trade protection had other effects. The sheltered British automobile companies continued to make their own parts and components and to assemble vehicles in the fashion of a craft industry, long after U.S. competitors had streamlined production. This practice added to their costs. As early as 1913, when Henry Ford had introduced the moving assembly line, 485,000 cars were produced and sold in the United States, compared with only 34,000 in England, where prices remained substantially higher.[50]

The early fuel taxes and tariffs in France appear to have been part of a broader plan for commercial autarky.[51] As in England, but more deliberately, the system of excises and customs duties ensured an infant-industry niche for, among other groups, native automobile companies producing small cars with lesser (or different) fuel requirements. Vestiges of the pattern persist to the present day. Preferential tax treatment of diesel fuel, for example, is partly designed to enhance the competitive position of Peugeot, a leading producer of small diesel-powered cars.[52]

Budgetary Practices

The two nations' imposts could not have risen from their original rates of only a few pence or centimes per liter to their current levels if, as in the United States, all revenues had been reserved for particular public works.

Short of paving over the realm from Southampton to Aberdeen, the United Kingdom cannot possibly spend on highways all of the £15 billion it collects each year from its levies on motor "spirits." A jealously guarded principle of tax policy in both Britain and France is that the proceeds of any tax are commingled as general revenue.[53] To be sure, there have been attempts to "hypothecate" petrol and motorcar taxes. Lloyd George, chancellor of the Exchequer in 1909, created a special "road fund." However, subsequent treasury ministers repeatedly raided the fund, dismissing as "preposterous" any notion that highway users "are entitled to make binding terms with Parliament as to the application of the taxes levied from them."[54]

Similarly, in France, a separate highway fund was ultimately established: *le Fonds spécial d'investissement routier*, enacted into law in 1952, shortly before the U.S. Federal-Aid Highway Act. Although a portion of the *Taxe intérieure sur les produits pétroliers* (TIPP) was to be allocated annually to the fund, the Ministry of Finance soon began diverting the earmarked TIPP receipts to other priorities.[55]

Thus the yield from these taxes came to be widely distributed, creating new clienteles. Among the natural beneficiaries of high motor-fuel taxation were first the railroads and later the airline industry. Especially in France, but also in Britain, these major public employers would be cross-subsidized in part by gas-tax revenues.[56]

Compare this setting with American fiscal arrangements. In Britain, the process of budget-making is centralized in the treasury, which has great discretion in deciding how to tax and spend. The "budget"—each year's program of taxes and expenditures—is prepared in secret by the Exchequer with minimal give-and-take in the cabinet, to say nothing of legislative participation. It is eventually presented to the House of Commons but only as an indivisible package to be briefly debated and then approved. Parliamentary rejection of any aspect (an extreme rarity) is tantamount to a vote of no confidence and grounds for a full-blown government crisis.

The procedures in France have varied over time, but there, too, (under the Fifth Republic) Parliament does not initiate tax or spending bills, and the autonomous fiscal powers of the Finance Ministry are notorious.[57]

In the American system fiscal policy is fragmented at every stage and level. In the postwar period, divided government has been the rule as much as the exception. With or without unified party control, the executive proposes an assortment of revenue measures and expenditures, but the power of the purse rests squarely with Congress, where it is divided eight ways—among the two chambers' tax-writing, authorizing, appropriations, and budget committees, each of which can defend, modify, or reject what the executive proposes. A budget director or treasury secretary cannot simply decide, as Winston Churchill did about the British road fund, that a legislatively mandated highway trust fund was "absurd" and then promptly sequester or redirect its contents.[58] When the Nixon administration sought to impound some highway funds in 1972, state governments filed a successful lawsuit, and two years later Congress enacted legislation prohibiting impoundments.[59]

Not only is poaching on earmarked trusts against the law; surely an American administration cannot decree, as France's Finance Ministry does on a regular basis, a percentage ad valorem change in various national excise taxes. At a minimum, Congress would reserve the right to punish such "imperialism," and the president would face a constitutional challenge.

The capacity of the executive in Britain and France to set tax rates virtually at will, and to dispose of receipts with little interference from Parliament, is extreme even by the standards of some other European governments.[60] But nowhere is the situation more different than in the United States, where legislators are full participants and the processes of taxing and spending are political minefields. Disputes between and within the governmental branches can rage not only over how high the rates should go, but also how the money might be disbursed. Hence, methods have been sought to depoliticize these questions, often by putting the government on automatic pilot.[61] In the case of the federal gasoline tax, the favored technique has taken the form of limiting the tax effort to a highway user fee, no larger than what is needed to sustain an earmarked trust.

An important result of this accommodation is the absence of significant constituencies pressing for high rates of taxation. Certain lobbies— road contractors, manufacturers of cement and macadam, state highway commissioners, truckers, the American Automobile Association—ensure that the highway trust is adequately maintained, but a tax in excess of that minimal level lacks clients. The lopsided clientelism of the highway fund only began to change, ever so gradually, in recent years. The Surface Transportation Assistance Act of 1982 began diverting a small share of new gas-tax receipts to mass transit improvements, and the 1991 reauthorization now gives states discretion to apportion more than 50 percent of trust fund disbursements to transit.[62]

Party Positions

Republicans in the United States have been reluctant to decouple the national gasoline tax from its dedicated trust accounts for fear of stirring congressional appetites for tax dollars and of abetting more government spending. In Britain, however, where outlays are under tighter executive control reinforced by disciplined party majorities in the legislature, a fiscally conservative government (like that of Margaret Thatcher) can have greater latitude. In fact, higher yields from consumption taxes during the Thatcher years did not portend "bigger government." Petrol fees rose repeatedly under Thatcher amid extensive budgetary retrenchment, privatization, and reductions in other types of taxation.

Thatcherism, of course, is a relatively recent development in the Conservative party. The Tories for most of their history supported a robust central government—less so than in the *étatist* vein of French conservatism, but certainly more strongly than does the modern Republican party in the United States.[63] The continual tax revolt of the more libertarian American right does not come naturally to European conservatives.

Energy taxes tend to be regressive. For this reason, politicians on the left are troubled by them—but evidently much more so in the United States than in Europe. When the socialist government of François Mitterand came to power in 1981, the tax on regular gasoline stood at 54 percent of the retail price. By the spring of 1991, the tax rate had reached 77 percent.[64] In Britain, the Labour party was in the minority throughout this period, but Labour governments in their heyday repeatedly raised the petrol excise.[65] In the British elections of 1992, it was the two parties of the left, Labour and the Liberal Democrats, that fielded in their respective "programmes" the most explicit proposals for higher road and fuel taxes.[66] This position contrasts sharply with that of the U.S. Democratic party. In the budget wrangle of 1990, for example, the Democratic leaders in Congress sought to eliminate a gasoline tax increase of nine and one-half cents proposed in the Bush administration's deficit-reduction package. And in 1992, the winning Democratic candidate for president consistently disparaged the idea of a tax on gasoline as "backbreaking" for the poor and middle class.[67]

Opposition on both ends of the partisan spectrum in the United States dogs most proposals to raise the national gasoline tax. Clearly, no such strange bedfellows bedevil Great Britain or France.

Why the liberals in Great Britain and France react differently from those in the United States is a difficult question. Perhaps they are more confident that the safety nets of their welfare states can lessen the inequity of heavy excise taxation. This form of taxation is also generally less visible than it is in the United States, where almost all local and federal sales taxes are clearly posted. In France, for instance, the gasoline levy at the pump is actually an unmarked mélange of the TIPP, the national value-added tax (VAT), and several other fees, including some minor special collections for a petroleum technology development program, for an independent *Caisse nationale de l'énergie*, and for *l'Institut français du pétrole*. Relatively few French motorists realize how much of the price at the pump represents the government's overall take. In a 1992 survey, only 28 percent of the respondents even came close to estimating the magnitude correctly.[68]

America, too, is not without inequitable tolls (arguably the social security payroll tax, for example) and regressive pricing schemes (costly quotas on imported clothing, for instance). Maybe such policies drew few objections from Democratic congressional majorities, however, for the simple reason that these "taxes," like *les taxes sur l'éssence*, are relatively hidden.

Local Government

In Britain and France local communities have not acquired the political independence found in U.S. metropolitan areas. A suburb of London or Paris does not enjoy wholly autonomous control over the form of its residential development, the location and design of work centers, or the siting of transportation facilities.[69] These critical land-use determinations are subject to regional oversight, or even direct "*aménagement*" by the central government. As a result, growth on the outskirts of these large cities has more often been forced into higher densities, sometimes closely coordinated with plans for public transit investments.[70]

A more compact pattern of urban settlement in Europe has permitted less intensive use of the automobile. In Los Angeles, more than 70 percent of even the poorest households use cars, trucks, or vans, according to the 1990 census.[71] In Greater London, the share of *all* households using cars is less than 60 percent.[72] And because England's lower-income households are much less likely to be among the car owners, high petrol taxes have a less regressive incidence than they would in the United States.[73]

Besides these effects, intergovernmental lobbies, which have traditionally capped the U.S. gasoline tax by dedicating revenues to one or two special-purpose accounts, are far weaker in Britain and France. British local governments repeatedly tried, but failed, to defend a "road fund" throughout the century.[74] (A British road fund lingered on as a legal fiction until 1955, when it was formally abolished.)[75] The bureaucracy in Paris has consistently thwarted locally backed proposals for earmarked infrastructural funds, even after 1982 when a decentralization program strengthened the hand of local authorities.[76]

Variations Elsewhere

Outside the United States, various aspects of the British and French stories can be generalized. For example, lack of transparency is not just a peculiarity of France's fuel taxation. Throughout Europe and in Japan, the sales tax component of the retail price is seldom delineated. Almost everywhere except the United States, VATs and other "indirect" levies (as the Europeans call their consumption taxes and import fees) are simply rolled into final prices, much as production costs are incorporated. The practitioners of these opaque methods of taxing consumers may be enjoying more political cover because buyers are less aware of, hence probably less sensitive to, the composite tax rates.

The stances of political parties toward gasoline taxation in France and Britain seem typical of partisan attitudes in other major European countries—Germany, for instance. Just as Labour governments in London or socialist governments in Paris favored higher rates, the Social Democrats in Bonn promptly doubled the tax on gasoline when they were in power. In the opposition since 1982, the SPD has continued to support steeper rates. Governments of the center right have acted no differently. Chancellor Helmut Kohl's Christian Democratic administrations have been responsible for the massive increases of recent years. In Kohl's conservative coalition, even the most vocal opponents of high marginal taxation in general—for example, the current minister of economic affairs, a member of the laissez-faire "liberals"—recently favored raising the gas tax yet again.[77]

Economic nationalism seems to have been a common initial motive for various energy taxes. Much of Canada's federal fuel taxation originated with a plan to nationalize the country's oil industry by using funds from a so-called Canadian ownership charge.[78] Germany's oil tax, or *Mineralölsteuer*, was originally intended to prop up the German bituminous coal mining industry.[79] Japanese industrial planners in the 1950s used earnings from excise duties on refined petroleum products to subsidize domestic petrochemical producers.[80] As in Britain and France, gainers from the protective effects of the duties developed a vested interest in them.

In some places, the institutional parallels are striking. Canada's parliamentary system, for instance, takes after Great Britain's. The government of Brian Mulroney raised federal taxes on gasoline six times between 1985 and 1990—a cumulative increase of nearly 600 percent. In each instance the process of deliberation in Ottawa closely resembled the Westminster model. The Finance Ministry would decide the rate of taxation largely in secret; the tax provisions were always part and parcel of a budget package; following the formality of a short debate, Parliament would have to cast an up-or-down vote on the entire bundle. Members of Parliament could "take it or leave it," but "leaving it" would have forced the government to resign and to call for new elections. An essentially Britannic form of government, in other words, may have helped Canada adopt a series of fiscal measures that would be hard to imagine in the United States, despite the geographic similarities.

Obviously, however, the United States is not the only major democracy that differs from the English or French paradigms in at least some prominent respects. The interesting question is what, if any, fiscal biases these other systemic nuances create.

Budget-Making in Japan

Nowhere are public choices on taxation and expenditures more decentralized than in the United States, but many other national polities do not consolidate fiscal policymaking as much as the governments of France and Britain do. Tax policies in Japan, for example, have never followed the top-down pattern of British budgetary politics, where the tightly held plans of the treasury may not even be fully vetted with the rest of the cabinet and are sprung on Parliament with practically no consultation.[81]

Important tax decisions in Japan have generally required an extensive interministerial colloquy and an elaborate process of consensus building between the bureaucracy and the majority party in the legislature. Typically, the Ministry of Finance has had to engage in intricate negotiations with the various spending ministries each of which is usually the object of intense lobbying from corresponding parliamentary caucuses (*zoku* representatives) and functional "committees" (*bukai*) of the formerly dominant Liberal Democratic party (LDP) or majority coalition in the

Diet. Through such channels, local governments and other constituent groups have often seen their preferences incorporated in budget drafts.

As a consequence of this porousness to pressures from the bottom, local interests have successfully staked claims on the proceeds of various national taxes. Local governments dispense almost 80 percent of Japan's public expenditures (a higher ratio than in Germany and the United States), with significant funding designated for special local purposes. Revenues from a "gasoline tax," for instance, are supposed to be transferred to a "Road Construction and Improvement Special Account" largely for the benefit of localities.[82] With contractors financing the campaigns of Diet members, the Ministry of Construction assiduously protecting the road construction account, and U.S. trade negotiators frequently pressuring Japan to raise its level of government investment, more than four-fifths of all energy-tax revenues continue to flow into highway repairs or expansions.

Another result is that tax increases, when unpopular with powerful constituencies (including the Petroleum Association of Japan), may encounter rough legislative sledding. Tax measures in Japan are not always indivisible from omnibus budget legislation; they can be, and occasionally are, amended in the lower house of Parliament and may be voted on separately. Government proposals to impose the functional equivalent of a value-added tax perished in 1979 and again in 1987.[83] In general, a fiscal policymaking process that has been considerably less mechanical in Japan than in many European countries has helped keep Japan's overall rate of taxation as a share of gross domestic product (GDP) at the low end of the countries in the OECD.

That said, the capacity of Tokyo to ratchet upward the general level of taxation, and to tax energy consumption in particular, has exceeded the capability in Washington. At the end of the 1980s, Japanese consumers faced the OECD's highest market price for fuel. Yet the government was still able to double that price at the pump by adding various taxes.

Some of this occurs because in Japan, as in France and most other industrial countries, the taxation of gasoline is really an accretion of multiple levies—a separate "petroleum tax," a customs duty on oil, a national consumption tax, and so on—all buried in the price.[84]

And, although the main fuel levy in Japan is traditionally dedicated to road investment, the pressure to spend on construction projects has steadily forced up the earmarked excise on gasoline, from 41 yen in 1955 to 184 yen (or, at the current exchange rate, $1.84) per gallon today.[85] By 1992 the Japanese government was budgeting a larger share of its GNP for roads than was the United States, and indeed was spending almost as much money on these facilities as on its share of compulsory education expenses.[86]

A final factor facilitating Japan's fiscal initiatives, especially during the past decade, was a deepening commitment to budgetary balance.[87] The Japanese consensual style of politics can falter when consensus is lacking. When it is reached, however, fewer veto points remain available than in the American political process. Thus when the LDP finally came to agreement on the urgency of lower deficits, the majoritarian parliamentary machinery overcame earlier obstacles; a VAT-like levy was introduced in 1988, adding another layer of taxation on energy consumption.

Federalism in Germany and Canada

Germany and Canada are not unitary states. This situation sets these regimes apart from those of Britain or France and presumably subjects them to some of the political constraints associated with American federalism. Central and subnational authorities may quarrel over access to excise tax bases, for instance, and the state or provincial governments may vie with one another for economic advantage by lowering tax rates (a phenomenon known as tax competition). Also, the national government is formally twice removed from the activities of local communities.

GERMANY. The superficial similarities among federations often mask quite different ground rules, however. The German states (*Länder*) do not game with one another, or with the central authorities, over the power to tax fuel for a simple reason: the German constitution (or "Basic Law") explicitly assigns the *Mineralölsteuer* to the federal government. The assignment seems arbitrary. Much of the spirit of this article in the Basic Law harks back to 1871 when the taxing powers of the Reich consisted only of a list of specific excises and duties. It was not until the Weimar constitution of 1919 that the national government acquired the authority to tax personal and corporate incomes. To this day, the Federal Republic has exclusive rights to special fees on everything from lamps to sparkling wine (though, for no apparent reason, the *Länder* control the taxation of beer and gambling casinos).[88] When Parliament votes to alter fuel-tax rates, the second chamber (*Bundesrat*) representing the states is not involved.[89]

Arbitrary or not, the constitution settles the question of who taxes what. And the arrangement may even encourage the *Länder* to lobby in Bonn for certain national tax increases. Since 1969 German law has required the central government to share the proceeds of its most productive levies with the states and municipalities.[90] This "pooling" of resources, in the context of constitutionally differentiated tax functions for each level of government, gives state and local politicians extra revenue without the political discomfort of collecting it.

The position of the American states is not the same. Fuel taxation has traditionally been the prerogative of the federal government in Germany, but in the United States it began informally as the domain of the states. The first gasoline excises originated in Oregon in 1919, a dozen years before the first federal gas tax. With no clear demarcation of intergovernmental fiscal responsibilities, the states have been fighting the possibility of federal usurpation ever since. Their guardians, particularly in the Senate, invoke arguments reminiscent of dual federalist theory: a higher national gasoline tax "takes away from the States their right to have control over their own excise taxes."[91]

As gas-tax collectors, the U.S. states face a second challenge: one another. If a higher federal tax may cut into state tax receipts, lower taxes in neighboring states pose the risk of large-scale out-of-state buying.[92] In this competitive environment, few can risk letting their rates rise too far above regional norms.

To be sure, variation exists and gas-tax levels in many states have not been static. In 1991 the rates ranged from a low of 8 cents a gallon in Alaska to a high of 26 cents in Rhode Island. The average state rate (in nominal dollars) doubled after 1980. These developments had their limits, however. State gasoline taxes still averaged 18 cents a gallon in 1991 (less than half the average of the Canadian provinces), and variance from that mean tended to be widest between distant jurisdictions that are thousands of miles apart, such as Alaska and Rhode Island.

CANADA. Canadian federalism is less orderly than the German system; the national and provincial governments levy various overlapping taxes on energy sources. Interestingly, the provincial tax writers have been especially active in recent years. As figure 4-2 demonstrates, provincial fuel taxes began escalating sharply in 1987. The provincial averages have not only risen above the Canadian federal rate but showed a widening gap with their U.S. counterparts. Quebec's tax in 1992, for instance, reached the equivalent of 58.4 U.S. cents a gallon—almost four times the level of Vermont, just across the province's southern border. What explains this activity?

The answer comes down to three basic considerations. Compared with the public sector in the United States, Canada's is large and costly at both

Figure 4-2. Comparison of U.S. and Canadian Gasoline Tax Rates

Nominal U.S. cents a gallon

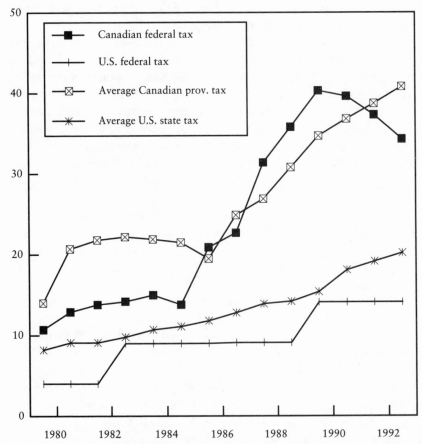

Sources: For the United States: Louis Alan Talley, "Federal Excise Taxes on Gasoline and the Highway Trust Fund: A Short History" (Washington: Congressional Research Service, 1991), p. 8; Federal Highway Administration, *Highway Statistics, Summary to 1985* (Department of Transportation, 1987), p. 134, table MF-205 and *Highway Statistics, 1986–93* (Department of Transportation, 1987–94), annual editions, tables FE-101, MF-1, MF-121T, each year.

For Canada: Data from Statistics Canada, Consumer Price Division, Federal and Provincial Taxes, Ottawa; exchange rates based on International Monetary Fund, *International Financial Statistics, June 1993* (Washington, 1993), p. 141, and *International Financial Statistics Yearbook, 1989* (Washington, 1990), p. 271.

the central and local levels. In 1989 Canadian public expenditures as a percent of GDP were close to 50 percent, compared with 40 percent in the United States.[93] Some of the provinces have built welfare states that bear more resemblance to the social democracies of Europe than to any of the American states.[94] With bigger revenue requirements, no strict tradition of earmarking, and a national constitution that circumscribes local revenue sources to some degree, the provinces have exploited sales taxes on motor fuel more aggressively than have other governments in North America.[95]

Like the states, the Canadian provinces face some interjurisdictional tax competition, including considerable cross-border shopping that siphons sales tax revenue into the United States. But the sheer size of most of the provinces, and the fact that their population centers tend to be some distance from provincial borders, helps insulate them somewhat from these tax-constraining pressures. Tiny Delaware cannot afford to let its gasoline tax jump very far ahead of nearby Maryland's, but Saskatchewan has more options. (A motorist in the middle of Saskatchewan is unlikely to drive east to Manitoba, west to Alberta, or south to Montana in search of lower fuel prices.)[96]

Finally, all ten provinces of Canada are miniparliamentary regimes with party discipline and centralized fiscal decisionmaking uncharacteristic of the U.S. state governments. The Canadians seem capable of lurching more radically in one direction or another, depending on the administration in power. The morning after a new government was elected in Alberta in March 1978, the province abolished its existing gasoline tax. A few years later, the government of the day reinstated a 20-cents-a-gallon tax in a single stroke.

Limits to Localism

Public pressure to minimize gasoline prices in the United States has to do with the extreme dispersion of commercial and residential development in urban areas. Among the many factors that have shaped this cityscape are rapid population growth, abundant land, and low-cost energy. But not all of the sprawl can be imputed to Mother Nature. Much of it is rooted in the deliberate regulatory activities of suburban communities. In the United States these local governments have retained an unmatched discretion over the consignment of land for construction. Suburban land-use policies are commonly designed to maintain a relatively low population per acre. The reason is not just aesthetic. U.S. localities depend heavily on local property taxes to support basic functions of government, including one of the costliest: education. Lower densities provide a means of handling community growth, defending property values, and controlling the costs of public services.

In France and Britain both the spatial planning powers and the fiscal burdens of local authorities are less independent of higher orders of government. A French municipality is not as free to decide on its own to "zone out" a high-density housing project or to "zone in" a shopping strip; its finances are also less likely to turn on these decisions. In a system where *l'état* pays directly for public schools and various other basic services, expenditures by local entities from their own revenue sources represent only about 18 percent of all government spending (compared with at least 26 percent in the United States).[97]

The subordinate position of French local governments is not unique in Europe. If anything, the role of central agencies in monitoring the disposition of local real estate in France seems permissive compared with what goes on, for example, in the Netherlands.[98]

LAND MANAGEMENT IN HOLLAND. Suppose a developer dreams of converting a given parcel of farmland near Amsterdam into the equivalent of an American mall. Like the visionaries of U.S. suburban shopping centers, the Dutch entrepreneur would first need to see whether the town or county zoning map allows the conversion. If so, he would then need to obtain the necessary subdivision and building permits from the local planning commission. Unlike the clearance for a U.S. developer, however, the Dutch builder's compliance with the extant local regulations might not suffice. The regional authorities encompassing Greater Amsterdam (the respective Provincial Executive) must approve the local jurisdiction's land-use plan and can require changes.[99] Even approval by the provincial overseers may not be the last word; technically, the national Ministry of Housing, Physical Planning, and Environment can override their decisions and order the locality to make revisions directly.[100] If this happens, the local parties to the project have little recourse: "As long as the [local] land-use plan has not been revised, no (building or construction) permit can be granted for the works and projects in question."[101]

Rarely does the national planning ministry have to go to such lengths. Local officials function largely as agents of the central government, simply administering its centrally funded services, and following its general directives. The ministry's current program for managing urban growth includes a "location policy" the audacious purpose of which is to put "the right business in the right place."[102] Only a limited class of commercial activities is permitted to locate in suburban fringes accessible primarily by automobile. The rest is confined to contiguous urban zones served almost exclusively by public transport or by bicycles. How is this "site allocation" scheme enforced? When a local government does not cooperate, "pressure is brought to bear," down to the minutest details of its development plan. The number of parking spaces available for a proposed office complex or industrial park, for example, must conform to a set of restrictive "norms" specified by the Ministry of Transportation.[103]

GERMANY'S APPROACH. It is not surprising to find this much national supervision of local planning decisions in a small unitary state whose land is a scarce resource, painstakingly reclaimed from the sea. But even in Germany, with a territory ten times larger than Holland's and with a political system that devolves much more authority to lower tiers of government, the process of urban planning has been organized more hierarchically than in the United States.

German constitutional law empowers the federal government to enact guidelines for local zoning ordinances.[104] The exercise of this regulatory function (or *Raumordnungsklauseln*) has largely been indirect: the *Bundesministerium für Raumordnung* obliges each of the German states to devise a "comprehensive" framework into which communities must fit their building programs.[105] There is considerable variability among the *Länder* in the implementation of Bonn's urban development policy aimed at sustaining "central places." But while the *Land* of Hesse or of Nordrhein-Westfalen has a reputation for stronger supralocal intervention than, say, Lower Saxony or Baden-Württemberg, state and local governments in Germany by and large decide land-use questions less autonomously than in the United States. The incentives of German fiscal federalism are fundamentally different; municipalities and states are far less reliant on local tax bases for revenue, and more mandates are funded because they are attached to a larger quotient of federal grants.[106]

A consequence of these arrangements has been a slower rate of suburbanization in Germany (table 4-1). Despite the pressure of strong population growth earlier in the postwar period, and the fact that entire cities had to be rebuilt after the war, no German metropolis in the automobile age looks like Houston.[107]

Summary

The Europeans and Japanese, as well as the Canadians, do not mandate complex energy regulations for motor vehicles. They simply tax automotive fuel instead. Although this approach may seem relatively elegant and uncomplicated, its historical and political underpinnings are not.

Table 4-1. *Distribution of Population in Metropolitan Areas in West Germany and the United States, 1950–90*

Year	Nation's population distribution (percent)	
	In central cities	
	West Germany	United States
1950	51	56.9
1960	53	50.1
1970	50	45.8
1980	46	39.1
1990	45	40.4
	Outside central cities	
1950	49	43.1
1960	47	49.9
1970	50	54.2
1980	54	60.9
1990	55	59.6

Sources: German data from Bundesforschungsansalt fur Landeskunde und Raumordnung. U.S. data from Bureau of the Census, *Statistical Abstract of the United States, 1971* (Department of Commerce, 1971), p. 16, table 14; *1980 Census of Population, Number of Inhabitants, United States Summary* (Department of Commerce, 1980), p. 1–39, table 6; and *1990 Census of Population, General Population Characteristics, United States Summary* (Department of Commerce, 1990), p. 1-1, table 1.

Statist agendas have favored higher fuel taxes in many countries. Governmental activism directed at air pollution and at energy waste has not been a leading determinant, however. Nor have other societies just shouldered heavier energy-tax burdens because of favorable geography, smaller automotive populations, or docile interest groups.

Particular policymaking institutions in these societies have facilitated the different outcomes. National budgetary procedures, for instance, play an important part. The more executive centered the fiscal policy process, the fewer the opportunities for obstruction by legislators representing tax-sensitive constituencies. Higher rates, in other words, are associated with regimes in which the role of legislative bodies is basically to ratify an executive budget, rather than to formulate individual tax and spending bills. (Interludes of frail minority rule in parliamentary systems may be an exception to this generalization. In 1979 the minority government of Prime Minister Joe Clark was toppled by a legislative insurgency against a proposed 18-cent increase in the Canadian gasoline tax.)[108]

Besides these significant procedural effects, less doctrinal resistance by political parties has enabled foreign governments to take action. America's bipolar opposition to gasoline taxation seems to be one of a kind. With much of the Democratic party insisting that such excises are "unfair" while the GOP ritually regards them only as grist for a profligate federal government, motor-fuel taxation mostly takes the form of a small, explicit "user fee" whose receipts are narrowly earmarked. Except for Japan (where the reverence for earmarking, as for baseball, mirrors that in the United States), other industrial countries do not adhere as religiously to such transparent and limiting contracts with taxpayers. Abetting this tendency has been the fact that their parties of the left and the right are more eager to collect and distribute gas-tax revenues for more purposes and claimants.

Finally, intergovernmental relations in most other countries simply do not foster the same degree of developmental self-government prevalent in American metropolitan areas. Tax penalties on the use of automobiles are almost as unpopular in America's "edge cities" as in its rural hinterlands. The comparatively low density of these communities is not merely a consequence of market forces; it also reflects conscious land-use programs aimed at bracing local finances. The fiscal incentives for this form of development often seem less intense abroad. Moreover, even in foreign federations, such as Germany or Canada, local home rule tends to operate within a more restrictive framework of national or regional planning guidelines.[109]

CHAPTER FIVE

The American Experience

D ISTINCTIVE POLICY INHERITANCES and political dynamics charted a different course for public decisions on fuel consumption in the United States. Here, national taxation of gasoline developed relatively late and has been complicated by a particular institutional environment. Party philosophies, the budgetary gauntlet in Washington, and extreme local control have frustrated serious tax proposals.

But while U.S. energy policymakers have been largely loath to tax, they have been exceptionally ready to regulate. Thus the U.S. effort to spare oil in automotive transportation consists of forcing technological changes on automobile manufacturers rather than altering price signals for consumers. Understanding the American method requires, first, some historical background.

History

Gasoline taxation in the United States began at the state level. Following Oregon's example in 1919, every state adopted gas taxes during the ensuing decade. The consequences of these local initiatives were two-sided. On one hand, the experiments in the states may have created the necessary precedent for federal involvement. Woodrow Wilson had proposed a 2-cent federal tax on gasoline in 1915.[1] Too ahead of its time, the novel idea was perfunctorily dismissed by Congress. But when the federal lawmakers revisited the question a decade later, fuel taxes averaging 4 cents a gallon were already accepted nationwide.

On the other hand, the early action in the states also delayed and constrained the federal role. Washington eventually tapped into the new source of revenue, but not before the state governments had staked a prior claim on it.

Early Initiatives

The dissent of state governors and legislators to proposed federal fuel taxes was to become an important obstacle almost every time Congress debated these bills. The first federal tax, masterminded by President Herbert Hoover, was not adopted until 1932, decades after the first national petrol excises in Britain, and was limited to 1 cent a gallon.

Federal fuel taxation made its debut under inauspicious circumstances; the Great Depression was a poor time to be imposing new taxes of any kind. The federal tax survived the New Deal largely because the Roosevelt administration was not an early convert to countercyclical fiscal policy. A stimulative tax cut was not contemplated; instead, revenues from the gasoline fee were deemed useful to fund programs under the National Industrial Recovery Act.[2] Nevertheless, the tax rate remained essentially flat until 1940, when military preparations finally prompted a slight increase to 1.5 cents.[3] Strict administrative rationing of gasoline during the war temporarily postponed further adjustments.

Throughout the 1930s, the financially strapped states, now dependent on income from various motor-vehicle-related charges and fearing erosion of their base, fought against further federal incursions.[4] Business and farm lobbies (the automobile industry, the American Petroleum Institute, the American Farm Bureau Federation) were able to argue effectively that the combination of higher national and local gasoline taxes was damaging the buying power of common consumers. The argument was persuasive in the American context because ownership of motor vehicles had already become a mass phenomenon. On the eve of the Depression, the average American was eight times more likely to own an automobile than, say, the average Englishman, and more than 60 percent of all new cars were being purchased by persons with incomes under $3,000.[5]

Penny Ante in the Postwar Period

The years immediately following the Second World War briefly offered an opportunity for higher rates, but the window soon began to close as the postwar period's explosive suburban growth (partly powered by federal housing programs) got under way. The national gas levy inched up to

2 cents a gallon after the outbreak of the Korean War in 1950, but by the mid-1950s an additional set of constraints had emerged: the commitment of all revenues to building highways, aimed in part at enhancing the auto-mobility of a burgeoning population in low-density suburbs.[6] The 1956 Highway Act added a cent to the existing tax and authorized collections over a sixteen-year period. What made this prolongation possible was the legislation's principle of strict earmarking, a fiscal device already used in a number of states.[7] Creation of the federal highway trust fund mobilized a particular band of beneficiaries and advocates. Private builders and us-ers of roads, congressional public works committees, and federal and state highway agencies formed a classic three-cornered alliance whose common interest was clear: to expand the road system, collecting just enough automatic receipts from a user fee to replenish the funding source. Although, as noted in chapter 4, the highway trust's "iron triangle" be-came more flexible in the early 1980s, by that time the nation's dominant modal infrastructure and urban form had become irreversible. Imposition of a European fuel tax (two or more dollars a gallon) on a system so thoroughly dependent on automotive transport was utopian.

The Eisenhower administration had underestimated the cost of the prospective interstate highway system in 1956, so three years later the president was forced to request a slight increase in the gasoline tax. It rose to 4 cents a gallon in 1959. This increment was to be the last for nearly the next quarter century.[8]

Neither the oil crises of 1974 and 1979 nor the worsening budget deficits of the 1980s seemed to end the inertia. In the course of its long deliberations on energy policy, Congress turned down proposed tax hikes, ranging from 50 cents to as little as 3 cents a gallon, on at least six sepa-rate occasions in the 1970s. Eventually, a 5-cents-a-gallon surtax (the equivalent of a penny in 1959, in inflation-adjusted dollars) was narrowly approved at the end of 1982, but again, only for purposes of refurbishing the transport infrastructure. With much huffing and puffing a second in-crease of 5 cents was finally included as part of the 1990 budget reconcili-ation, but after Congress first rejected the "temerity" of a 9.5-cent in-crease proposed by the Bush administration.[9] The following year, congressional efforts to ante up another nickel (with what its sponsors called one more "nickel for America") fizzled during the run-up to the 1991 Surface Transportation Reauthorization.[10] And two years after that, an energy tax proposed by President Clinton to help meet budgetary goals fared dismally as well. Clinton's "Btu tax" would have raised the price of gasoline by 7.5 cents over four years. When the dust settled, an increase of only 4.3 cents was adopted.

As of 1994 the average tax on gasoline in the United States (combining the national and state levies) stood at 37.9 cents a gallon, half of the average in the OECD nation with next lowest rate, Canada.[11] In real terms, the U.S. impost today is a fifth less than it was in the early 1960s. Out of the current federal share of gas-tax revenues, two-thirds—$11.5 billion a year—remain dedicated to infrastructural projects, while only $6.8 billion a year are supposed to go toward reducing the deficit. The 1993 gasoline excise was the first in more than sixty years intended exclusively for the latter purpose. As late as 1990, Congress had proved unable to redirect most of its gas-tax dollars; reverting to form, the lawmakers required that at least half of that year's increase still be deposited in the highway fund.

CAFE Society

Having made an earlier and stronger start taxing fuel usage, national governments in western Europe and Japan had unwittingly exerted a powerful formative influence on their domestic automobile industries: small, economical cars predominated in Europe and Japan well before the Arab oil embargo in 1973.[12] Meanwhile, government at all levels in the United States facilitated the development of autocentric urban habitats. And by ensuring low energy prices, it also fostered a different vehicular fleet.

On the eve of the first oil shock, U.S. auto manufacturers were plying the domestic market with products whose size, weight, horsepower, and gadgetry bore little resemblance to those of the rapidly expanding automotive sectors abroad.[13] By the time the day of reckoning was at hand, the automobiles rolling off U.S. assembly lines were actually averaging fewer miles per gallon (13.1 mpg) than the vehicles built in 1960 (14.3 mpg).[14] Uncertain whether market conditions after 1974 would force an end to this anomaly, Congress stepped in to engineer the desired change. As part of a massive piece of legislation adopted in 1975—the so-called Energy Policy and Conservation Act—automakers were ordered to improve the average fuel use of each fleet of new cars, following specified targets and timetables, beginning in 1978. The legislators thus embarked upon an elaborate regulatory operation imitated by no other industrial country.

Table 5-1. House Votes on Gasoline Tax Legislation, 1975–80

Legislation	For	Against
Amendment to H.R. 6860, to increase the federal tax by 2 cents a gallon on a standby basis (June 11, 1975)	72	345
Amendment to H.R. 6860, to increase the federal tax by 3 cents a gallon (June 11, 1975)	187	209
Amendment to H.R. 8444, to increase the federal tax by 5 cents a gallon (August 4, 1977)	82	339
Amendment to H.R. 8444, to increase the federal tax by 4 cents a gallon (August 4, 1977)	52	370
H.R. 7428, to add a 10-cents-a-gallon fee through an oil tariff tilted onto gasoline (June 5, 1980)	34	335

Sources: *Congressional Quarterly Almanac, 1975* (Washington, Congressional Quarterly, Inc., 1976), pp. 66H–67H; *Congressional Quarterly Almanac, 1977* (Washington, 1978), pp. 136H–137H; and *Congressional Quarterly Almanac, 1980* (Washington, 1981), pp. 82H–83H.

Alternatives to CAFE standards were fleetingly discussed at the time. Some congressional leaders and the Carter administration's energy strategists floated plans to promote conservation by taxing fuel. But when put to a vote, this tack was repeatedly rejected (see table 5-1). Throughout the decade, large majorities in the House of Representatives could not bring themselves to solve energy problems with price instruments. Indeed, so intense was this congressional fear of the social dislocations imputed to energy price increases that the 1975 legislation not only avoided new consumption taxes, it professed to protect consumers through price controls. The CAFE scheme comported with this propensity to manipulate energy markets, shifting (or concealing) the burden of conservation from users by regulating producers.

Party Politics

"If this tax is enacted, we will be requiring the people of the heartland of America to carry this burden on both shoulders. It is unfair; it is inequitable; it is grossly discriminatory against the . . . people of this country who do not have access to public transportation."[15] The voice ringing through the House chamber was that of Democrat Bill Alexander of Arkansas, urging his fellow representatives to reject a gasoline tax bill that was being considered in the summer of 1975. Similar perorations could be heard every other time that Congress took up gas tax legislation. And most of the time, scores of legislators from the heartland of America would chime

Figure 5-1. *Pooled House Votes on Gasoline Taxation, 1975, 1977, 1980, 1982, 1990*

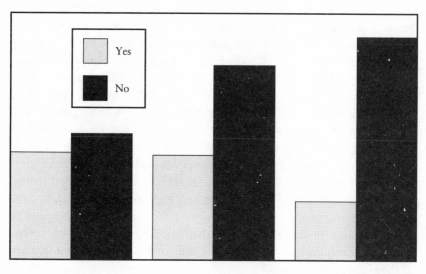

Sources: *Congressional Quarterly Almanac, 1975* (Washington: Congressional Quarterly, Inc., 1976), pp. 66H–67H, votes 207, 208; *Congressional Quarterly Almanac, 1977* (Washington, 1978), pp. 136H–137H, votes 472, 473; *Congressional Quarterly Almanac, 1980* (Washington, 1981), pp. 82H–83H, vote 273; *Congressional Quarterly Almanac, 1982* (Washington, 1983), pp. 116H–119H, votes 389, 395; *Congressional Quarterly Almanac, 1990* (Washington, 1991), pp. 150H–151H, vote 474; and David C. Huckabee, "Congressional Districts of the 99th Congress Classified on an Urban to Rural Continuum" (Washington: Congressional Research Service, September 1985), pp. 13, 19.

in with a chorus of negative votes. That representatives from the country-side would react this way was understandable. As Congressman Alexander asked, "Did you ever hear of anybody catching a subway in Osceola, Arkansas, or a bus in Bugtussle, Oklahoma?"[16]

Ubiquitous Opposition

But members from places like Boston (where it is still possible to catch a bus or even a subway) also behaved as if their constituents were living in Bugtussle. Although rural politicians have traditionally led the attack on gasoline taxation, representatives from metropolitan areas have frequently been their allies. Pooling all of the House votes on gasoline taxes from 1975 through 1990 reveals that members from urban and suburban districts were more likely to oppose tax increases than to accept them (figure 5-1). Congressional displeasure with taxing gasoline, in other words, has not been consistently confined to the hinterlands; it is a nationwide phenomenon.

What makes the legislative resistance so broad-based? Most of the breadth ultimately derives from the fact that "city" folk in America are often no less dependent on, and partial to, affordable automotive transportation than are country folk. Indeed, inside the metropolitan areas where commuters crawl to work in stop-and-start traffic, urbanites driving over shorter distances can spend as much of their income on gasoline as do residents of many rural counties traveling greater distances.[17] By 1990 the voters in no fewer than 170 congressional districts were primarily persons living in suburbs. Spokesmen for these automobile-intensive communities share an interest with the eighty-eight members from rural districts in avoiding higher costs of motor fuel. Of the remaining districts, seventy-nine are "mixed" and only ninety-eight represent central cities. Even if all the central-city representatives in Congress were reconciled to taxing gasoline (presumably because their home towns were viably served by public transportation), they would still constitute less than a quarter of the House membership.

As it happens, even delegations from large, old central cities in the Northeast cannot be counted upon to support a higher gasoline tax. In a 1977 House roll call, for example, the representatives from Boston, Chicago, New York, and Philadelphia voted 17 to 10 against a mere 4-cents-a-gallon boost. In the decision whether to add a levy of 10 cents in 1980, more than two-thirds of the representatives from these cities joined the naysayers. The politics in some cases grew complex. Several of the tax proposals causing consternation in Congress had been bungled by their sponsors; others became, so to speak, collateral casualties of an increasingly gridlocked budgetary process.[18] But besides these considerations, the partisan biases of the legislators mattered. Many liberals seem to disapprove of gasoline taxation on principle. So do many conservatives, although on altogether different ideological grounds.

Democratic Populism

An equitable distribution of income, with a schedule of taxation based on ability to pay, is a maxim of political parties on the left in virtually every democracy. In the U. S. Congress, however, much of the Democratic party has sought progressivity, not just in the aggregate (for the national tax system as a whole), but often in the system's marginal elements.[19] Thus although federal excise taxes now signify a minuscule and declining fraction (less than 4 percent) of the government's income, they continue to come under close critical inspection.[20] Higher gasoline taxes, in particular, are considered inordinately regressive.

The regressiveness of these measures seems to offend their liberal critics regardless of developments in the nation's overall structure of taxes and transfer payments. In the early 1980s gas-tax opponents could make a credible case that systemic inequities had worsened, and that under the circumstances, higher fuel taxes could add insult to injury. As one Democratic senator put it during debate on the Reagan administration's request for a 5-cent hike in 1982, the proposal was doubly "unfair and unwise" in the wake of the 1981 income tax reduction, since "the Government will be extracting the gas tax with one hand from low- and middle-income people, senior citizens, and others of modest circumstances, while, in mid-1983, the Government will be distributing a large tax cut to individuals of high income levels who neither deserve nor need this larger personal tax cut."[21]

But Democratic discomfort with further gasoline levies did not seem to abate after the national tax code was substantially overhauled. The reform of 1986 eliminated several important preferences for the wealthy, including the favorable treatment of income from capital gains. Yet liberals continued to flog the "fairness" issue well into the next decade. At one point during the budget showdown of 1990, the Democratic majority in the House tried to adopt a budget resolution conspicuously deleting any increase in the gasoline tax.[22] Congress had to "show progressivity," explained a chairman of the House Democratic caucus.[23]

Similarly, in the late stages of the budget battle of 1993, Wisconsin Democrat Herbert H. Kohl wielded a crucial swing vote in the Senate. Declaring "I don't think we should tax the middle class" with a 6.5-cent boost on gasoline, his stance threatened to derail the entire budget agreement.[24] Meanwhile, fresh research at the University of Wisconsin estimated that a tax of 7.5 cents a gallon would cost the average family less than two-tenths of 1 percent of its annual income. Of the lowest 30 percent of families (those with incomes under $24,000), according to the Wisconsin study, at most half would bear an increased burden. Many would be compensated by an expanded earned income tax credit, others by food stamps and social security benefits indexed to the cost of living.[25]

Liberal dissidents such as Senator Kohl gave President Clinton headaches as he struggled to cut a budget deal with the 103d Congress. But Clinton had not helped his own cause by voicing populist appeals before coming to Washington. At the end of 1992, for example, the president-elect was still insisting that "the gas tax"—indeed, "consumption taxes generally"—could "aggravate the inequalities of the last decade."[26]

The Liberal Predicament

Tax relief for the poor and "the middle class" may be an alluring issue in electoral campaigns, but it also presents a difficulty: if rationing by price is off limits, but public officials are still convinced that oil dependency is hazardous, how (if at all) can the overconsumption be moderated?

Here, much of the policy discourse is evasive. Take the testimony of Ralph Nader before the House Rules Committee at a critical juncture in the great energy debate of 1975. The theme of Nader's remarks was conservation. "Without a doubt," he insisted, "the top priority of Congress today should be saving energy." This was "the quickest new energy source we have," since "40 percent" was being wasted. According to Nader, however, steeper energy prices would do little to reclaim the waste; this inefficacy was "well known."[27] How, then, was energy to be conserved? There would have to be, somehow, a gradual transition away from the wasteful technology into which the country was locked. None of the committee members asked Nader to back up his assertion that inelasticities for existing energy use were "well known." Nor was he asked to elaborate on how wasteful technology could be improved if not by creating the economic incentives for technological change.

Amid the vagueness, however, emerged one prescription that resonated among the lawmakers: a plea to regulate the fuel mileage of automobiles. This idea had begun to catch the fancy of Congress in 1973, when it became apparent that another regulatory venture, the Clean Air Act of 1970, was worsening the miles per gallon of American automobiles.[28] By 1975 fuel-efficiency regulation had come to seem like an ingenious and relatively painless antidote. Soon the debate turned not on whether to legislate standards but how harshly to enforce them, through a system of tax penalties or of civil fines on manufacturers who failed to comply.[29]

Faith

In truth, the automotive fuel economy program enacted in 1975 proved less painless and ingenious than its proponents had assumed. The law gave the Department of Transportation (DOT) discretion in setting and adjusting the requisite average mpg levels for various fleets of vehicles. A decade later, with world petroleum prices plunging and demand for heavier, fuel-devouring vehicles on the rise, the automobile industry was able to persuade DOT's National Highway Traffic Safety Administration (NHTSA) to scale back its requirements, first for light trucks and a year later for automobiles.[30]

NHTSA's decisions distressed advocates of stringent enforcement at a series of House and Senate oversight hearings in 1985. Rolling back CAFE, however marginally, was regarded as another example of reckless deregulation at the hands of a Republican administration that lacked an energy policy. What few seemed to recall was that the Carter administration had felt similarly compelled to ease the regulatory burden on the ailing U.S. automakers in 1980.[31] At that time, the industry had estimated, plausibly, that it would need to spend some $80 billion through 1985 to comply with the government's timetables for improving fuel economy, along with safety and emission levels.[32] Almost from its inception, the costs of CAFE clashed with other public policy objectives dear to the Democrats—saving jobs in the automobile industry, for instance, and providing protection from Japanese import competition. Those charged with actually implementing the program, not just giving speeches about it, seemed more cognizant of the quandary. As Neil E. Goldschmidt, Carter's transportation secretary, cautioned in 1979, "Energy-efficient automobiles are important, but we don't want to end up with . . . less employment as the end product."[33]

Despite these realities, every few years progressive politicians on the stump, or on Capitol Hill, would wage a campaign to extend or intensify the regulatory effort. In the fall of 1985, the Senate sought to pass a bill designed to overturn the recent NHTSA rulings. In 1989 three sets of Senate committees held hearings on proposals to stiffen CAFE. Among the bills considered was one by Senator Albert Gore (the so-called World Environmental Policy Act of 1989) that would have forced a 65 percent improvement in the fuel efficiency of automobiles by the year 2000.[34] A year later, with a new oil crisis brewing in the Persian Gulf, there were renewed calls in both houses for further CAFE requirements. In 1990 and again the following year, a bill introduced by Senator Richard Bryan, Democrat of Nevada, that would have mandated a 40 percent increase in mpgs within twelve years, was stopped only by the threat of a presidential veto.

During the presidential race in 1992, the CAFE question resurfaced, even making its way into the nationally televised debates. Why? In their manifesto, *Putting People First*, candidates Clinton and Gore had been outspoken; they claimed that "the Republicans in Washington have undermined our national security and cut short our economic growth because they haven't had a national energy policy."[35] "We've fallen behind our competitors in energy efficiency," the Clinton-Gore ticket asserted, "and are in danger of leaving our future generations of Americans in a precarious position of overwhelming debt and dependence." "It's time to make the right energy choices," the pamphlet proclaimed. How? At the very top of its long list of recommendations was: "*Increase corporate average fuel economy standards* from the current 27.5 miles per gallon to 40 miles per gallon by the year 2000." Elsewhere in the platform was a vow to "*oppose federal excise gas tax increases*." On what grounds? Because, the authors reckoned, a federal gas tax would be "backbreaking," and instead of it Americans should try, among other things, "conservation."[36]

Political opponents and editorial writers would infer from such reasoning by "the regulatory left" that it amounted to little more than blame avoidance.[37] American members of Congress are perhaps more likely than European, Canadian, or Japanese parliamentarians to be held individually accountable for their actions. House members, after all, are exposed to an unusually short electoral cycle, and on controversial votes, cannot as credibly invoke the excuse that their hand was forced by legislative leaders.[38] Thus avoiding blame is an important reason (some would say the primary reason) why Congress often shuns blunt policy solutions that, however effective, demand explicit sacrifices from voters.[39] Circuitous regulatory measures are alluring because they deflect responsibility from elected officials to administrators and also help shift or obscure costs.[40] This cover undoubtedly accounts for some of the political charm of CAFE regulation, in contrast to a direct energy tax. The *Washington Post* made the point acerbically: "The consumer will pay in either case, whether for a more efficient car or for more expensive gasoline. But Congress has learned that while people blame the auto companies for higher prices of new cars, they blame Congress for a higher price of gasoline. That's why Congress likes the fuel efficiency law."[41]

Politicians may be blame avoiders, but they can also believe what they say. Among the Democrats, a party preference, not mere opportunism, underpins their defense of CAFE. Senator Bryan, for example, pressed for higher CAFE standards in 1990 and 1991, evidently convinced that there was no alternative; a gasoline tax would fall too "heavily" on people "pushed further out of the economic mainstream of American life."[42]

The Republican Line

While Democrats agonize over the social injustice of consumption taxes, Republicans wonder whether the federal government needs to raise any additional taxes at all.

Much of what animates the Republican theme of "no new taxes" is

Figure 5-2. *Pooled House Votes on Gasoline Taxation, 1975, 1977, 1980, 1982, 1990*

Percentage

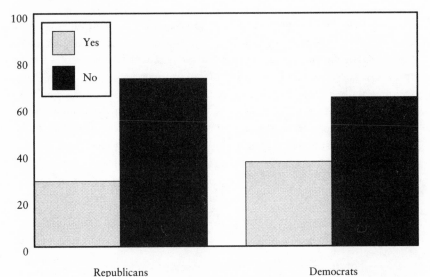

Sources: *Congressional Quarterly Almanac, 1975* (Washington: Congressional Quarterly, Inc., 1976), pp. 66H–67H, votes 207, 208; *Congressional Quarterly Almanac, 1977* (Washington, 1978), pp. 136H–137H, votes 472, 473; *Congressional Quarterly Almanac, 1980* (Washington, 1981), pp. 82H–83H, vote 273; *Congressional Quarterly Almanac, 1982* (Washington, 1983), pp. 116H–119H, votes 389, 395; and *Congressional Quarterly Almanac, 1990* (Washington, 1991), pp. 150H–151H, vote 474.

pure constituency politics. The party's suburban electoral base, predominantly made up of property owners, provides an especially receptive audience.[43] Tax-sensitive suburban voters not only led a series of plebiscitary raids on local property tax rates at the end of the 1970s, they elected Ronald Reagan in 1980 on a pledge to lower the federal income tax. Not surprisingly, the Republican party in Congress has heeded the suburban electorate during most debates on raising the federal gasoline tax.

Besides a core constituency in the suburbs, the Republican base in the West is intensely antagonistic to the federal tax on gasoline, which is said to cost the average household in some western states several times more than the average household in the urban Northeast. The political ecology of the GOP helps explain why, as figure 5-2 demonstrates, Republican lawmakers have opposed gas-tax increases more intensely than have Democrats.[44]

The most notable exception to the pattern came in 1982.[45] On that occasion proponents of a 5-cents-a-gallon increment were able to muster support from a majority of the House Republicans, and then to collect the necessary GOP votes to break a filibuster led by archconservatives in the Senate. The Republican role reversal in 1982 had much to do with the fact that, in this instance, the proposed tax was skillfully sold by a Republican president. Reagan's tax was labeled an essential "user fee" to repair the surface transportation infrastructure. This characterization respected the long-standing norm of federal earmarking. It was also in keeping with a state and local proclivity for special-purpose taxation. Suburban taxpayers were rebellious, but less so when the revenues were raised from specific groups and tied directly to specific functions deemed worthwhile. Framed this way, some of the traditional conservative aversion to a higher federal gas tax was muted. Thus on December 6, 1982, ninety-six Republicans in the House consented to the higher tax, slightly exceeding the eighty-seven Republican members who voted nay.[46]

Politics of Distrust

Not all of the tax rebellion among conservatives is just political expediency. Deeper principles are involved. During the 1970s, for instance, leading Republicans in Congress were no less troubled than their Democratic counterparts by energy shortages. However, their position was less confusing: to eliminate the shortages, controls on oil and natural gas prices had to be removed; no other step ought to take precedence. Democratic energy plans typically worked the other way around: price controls were considered indispensable to protect the consumer, but their wasteful effect was supposed to be offset by fuel-conserving "incentives" and regulations. From time to time, the proposed incentives included higher excises on motor fuels. To skeptics, these contortions were easy to assail. It made no sense for the government to be depressing prices with one hand (through controls) while raising them with the other (through taxes).

Further, most of the tax bills involved rebate schemes or expenditures that aggravated the opposition. A bill crafted by the Democratic majority on the House Ways and Means Committee in 1975, and a similar proposal by the Carter administration two years later, were illustrative. Both called for recycling all tax receipts progressively in the form of income tax credits. The "basic problem," as one Republican congressman noted, was that such legislation turned energy policy into "a form of income redistribution."[47] Rebates also raised doubts about the likely conservation benefits of the taxes. A higher levy on gasoline could discourage people from driving their cars, but the refunded revenue might be spent on heated outdoor jacuzzis.

At the same time, measures that were not revenue neutral worried Republicans the most, for these might feed unwanted government spending. At least until 1991, when a complicated budget agreement finally began capping discretionary spending, the unease of fiscal conservatives was not unfounded. The unrebated portion of proposed energy taxes, especially during the 1970s, was usually accompanied by authorizations to cover dubious additional energy development programs, or "research," or conservation credits, as well as the usual mass transit projects and highways.[48] The single biggest energy excise ever levied by the U. S. government, the 1980 windfall profit tax on deregulated oil producers, authorized a phenomenal $88 billion to fund a Synthetic Fuels Corporation. Even into the 1990s, when reduction of the federal deficit would have first claim on new sources of revenue, activist public interest groups were still recommending that new fuel taxes be levied to serve other ends. One such organization urged policymakers in 1993 to combine the bitter pill of an energy impost with "the sweet syrup" of what it called "energy efficiency."[49] Energy efficiency, it turned out, meant sinking $4.5 billion into low-income housing weatherization, public housing retrofits, tighter federal buildings, new state building codes, state loans for home improvements, research and development for improved equipment, local tax benefits for transit commuters, investment assistance for vehicle manufacturers as well as other industries, and "EPA green programs." Such agendas may have continued to fortify Republican perceptions that energy-tax initiatives would not achieve much budgetary balance.

Some of the complaints from conservatives seemed bogus. For example, it was alleged that "even a modest increase in the federal gasoline excise tax would cost more than two hundred thousand jobs and significant productivity losses throughout the U.S. economy."[50] But such assertions typically dwelt on immediate costs, conveniently ignoring longer-term macroeconomic benefits such as a lower national debt. It was also sometimes implied that a higher federal gasoline tax stole from the states "their right" to control such excise taxes.[51] Gasoline taxation, however, was not an exclusive "right" of local government, and in any case, there was no evidence that increases in the federal tax limited the ability of the states to hike their own rates (figure 5-3), even to the point of swelling state budget surpluses during the 1980s.[52]

Figure 5-3. *Federal and Average State Gas Tax Rate*

Cents a gallon

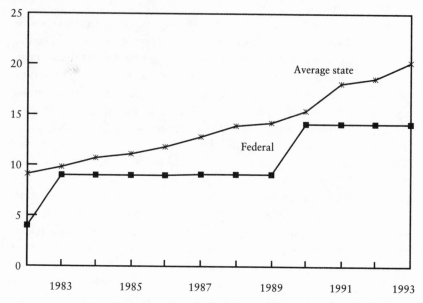

Source: Federal Highway Administration, *Highway Statistics, Summary to 1985* (Department of Transportation, 1987), p. 134, and *Highway Statistics, 1986–93*, annual editions, tables FE-101, MF-1, MF-121T, each year.

CAFE and the GOP

Largely because the Republicans have tended to find so many reasons to scorn fuel taxation, they, too, have been impaled on the horns of the energy-conservation dilemma: how else would the voracious use of oil in transportation be disciplined? During the 1970s, when lifting price controls would have allowed rising market prices to restrain demand, the answer on the Republican side of the aisle was simple in theory: "Deregulate!" But with the Democratic congressional majority refusing to play that card until the end of the decade, price deregulation was a political fantasy. In the 1980s, when decontrol finally arrived but world oil prices collapsed, coming up with other constructive suggestions on energy policy became an even greater challenge. Unwilling to tax, in the end Republicans found themselves with little to fall back on. So the initiative was left to the Democrats, for whom CAFE was the ace in the hole.

To a party that preferred "getting prices right" rather than shackling a major industry with more command-and-control regulations, the fuel-economy scheme was disagreeable, of course. However, without a better idea, it soon became impolitic to dismiss CAFE out of hand. Sharply divided, the Republicans took to fighting a series of rear-guard skirmishes but avoided a frontal assault. In House floor action on CAFE in 1975, they (and a lobbying blitz by the United Auto Workers) helped defeat the sternest enforcement procedures in favor of a less onerous system of fines.[53] Later on, Reagan appointees in the Department of Transportation responded sympathetically to Detroit's pleas for partial regulatory relief, and Senate Republicans repeatedly blocked bills that would have toughened the existing standards, but neither the administration nor its allies in Congress made a concerted effort to dismantle the regulatory program entirely.[54] Moreover, the Republican misgivings on these (and subsequent) occasions seldom seemed to go to the heart of the matter: namely, that CAFE was economically inefficient. Instead, objections were raised on other grounds—for example, that higher standards would cause highway deaths.[55]

In sum, just as the convictions and calculations of the left largely excluded serious fuel-consumption taxes but favored an administrative fuel-use program, party positioning and maneuvering on the right qualified the program but did not advance a viable substitute. This type of partisan interplay had few, if any, parallels in the governments of other advanced industrial countries.

The Budget System

Governments mostly tax motor fuel to raise revenue, not to avoid a need for bureaucratic regulation. This primary quest for revenue inevitably embroils the taxes in national budgetary politics. Nowhere are budgets formulated the way they are in the United States, however.[56] This aspect of American exceptionalism, as well, frustrates efforts to make big changes in the federal excise on gasoline.

In democratic regimes, legislatures grant or deny permission to collect and disburse public funds. But no constitutional democracy vests as much control in the legislature as does the Constitution of the United States. Here, a large and complex bicameral body not only approves each year the government's overall compilation of revenues and expenditures, it also decides what to compile, for it alone has the authority to "lay" the requisite taxes and to distribute their proceeds (which cannot be spent "but in consequence of appropriations" through acts of Congress).[57] In this system, in other words, choices about specific items and amounts, not just about a budget's overall balance sheet, remain very much in the congressional purview.

The reach of this legislative prerogative has remained unique despite various modifications in the mechanics of U.S. fiscal policy. Before 1921 there were no presidential budget submissions; the "budget" (such as it was) consisted of an assemblage of congressional spending and tax bills. Even after the president began submitting a unified budget, congressional committees acted on it separately, tinkering freely with any or all of its parts. The Congressional Budget Act of 1974 constrained this tendency but did not end it. Henceforth each house would adopt resolutions intended to guide individual appropriations and tax measures toward a reconciliation with broad budgetary ceilings. The resolutions were not binding, however. Congress could (and, until very recently, did) continue to assemble an assortment of spending priorities far in excess of estimated revenues.[58]

Nor did the seemingly draconian Balanced Budget Act of 1985 make an immediate difference. This reform (named Gramm-Rudman, after its principal Senate authors) was supposed to force Congress to eliminate the federal deficit within five years. If the intent of the law had been observed, the legislators would promptly have had to contemplate additional taxes (possibly including sizable energy excises) alongside deep cuts in programs reaching well beyond defense. They did neither.[59] Not until the fall of 1990, with the prospect of Gramm-Rudman's automatic axe about to fall, were limits placed on future discretionary spending. At that belated stage, the budgeteers also sought new revenues, including minor adjustments in the gasoline tax.

Perhaps Congress's fiscal decisions through most of the 1980s were more independent and desultory than they might have been with an executive determined to achieve greater budgetary equilibrium. Gratuitous promises of "no new taxes," for example, did little to enhance the president's credibility in budget negotiations or to help him exert discipline over the process. Yet even after a Republican president conceded the need for "increased tax revenues" (as George Bush eventually did in 1990), or when a Democratic president initiated a similar legislative effort to dent the deficit (as Bill Clinton did in 1993), Congress still altered the proposed budgets at will. Controversial elements—notably the energy taxes recommended in both cases—were reworked, almost beyond recognition.

The Power of the Purse

Several specific features distinguish the legislature's fiscal power in the United States. Not only does Congress jealously guard its right to micromanage the details of budgets, it does so with or without divided party control of the legislative and executive branches. Regardless of whether a Democrat or Republican sits in the White House, there is no such thing as an up-or-down verdict on a presidential budget draft; typically, it is susceptible to extensive changes at almost any point.

This is partly because of the strength of the congressional committee structure and partly because the separation of powers in the American system lowers legislative party cohesion. Separately elected, individual members of Congress can defect with impunity from their party leadership's preferred package. The Senate also has unusual influence over the course of the legislation; budgets must pass both houses, but the upper body's procedures afford extraordinary opportunities for amendments and obstructionism.

In a comparative context, the implications of these rules of the game are striking. Difficult fiscal choices may be debated, and sometimes revised, acrimoniously in the parliaments of Germany or Japan, but the debates and the revisions are confined. In the parliamentary politics of these countries, challenging key provisions of an executive budget may ultimately risk bringing down "the government"—something the ruling coalitions normally prefer to avoid. In 1993, by comparison, lawmakers of the governing party in the United States first rewrote their administration's top legislative priority (the budget), then came within a one-vote margin of wrecking it and their presidency.

The congressional minefield is also different in another respect. Unpleasant components of a budget blueprint (energy taxes, for instance) that manage to remain intact in the House of Representatives must still survive the Senate. There, as in 1993, if the majority party's margin is not overwhelming, small factions, even a single member, may yield virtual veto power. The procedural rigors in Germany and Japan are not comparable. Germany's oil taxes, for example, have only had to clear a single hurdle (the Bundestag) instead of two (the Bundesrat, as well). Adoption of Japan's austere budgets in the late 1980s might have been harder if the upper house of the Diet (the House of Councillors) had been in a position to play a coequal role with the lower chamber.[60]

The difficulty of implanting more than token fuel taxes, and of making them stick, was painfully evident in the U.S. budget cycles of 1990 and 1993. The chaotic events bear retelling.

The Ordeal of 1990

The ink was scarcely dry on the Bush administration's fiscal 1991 budget, submitted to Congress at the end of January 1990, when two vulnerabilities became evident. The draft grossly underestimated the likely size of the deficit that year, and it called for less reduction in military spending than the Democratic Congress wanted. Faced with rising deficit projections and much bigger cuts in defense proposed by the congressional budget committees, the president opened bipartisan negotiations (a "summit") in May to seek an accommodation. By the end of June, Bush had acknowledged a need for additional revenue, in return for which the Democratic summiteers would initiate a search for savings in entitlements.

The bridging of differences between the administration and Congress was short lived, however. The GOP rank-and-file in the House promptly went into open revolt, resolving to oppose any new net burden on taxpayers as a means of taming the deficit—and signaling to the Democrats that the president would now be largely at their mercy in devising specific tax provisions. Sensing the opportunity for political hay, leading Democrats moved the "tax equity" issue to the fore. Senate Majority Leader George Mitchell, for instance, said he could not support a prime request of the administration—a lower tax rate on capital gains—without a sharp upward revision in the marginal rate on the wealthy.[61]

The question of "progressivity" deadlocked the summit into the August recess, Republicans insisting on capital gains preferences and Democrats demanding rate increases in the top income tax bracket, along with fewer changes in entitlement programs. (Echoing the general sentiment of his party, California Democrat Henry Waxman dismissed the idea of higher premiums for medicare recipients as "absolutely outrageous.")[62] But when Congress reconvened in September, pressures to end the stalemate had mounted. The end of the fiscal year was imminent. In the absence of a budget that would meet the year's Gramm-Rudman targets, an across-the-board sequester exceeding $100 billion would presumably go into effect. The Iraqi invasion of Kuwait in August and the ensuing deployment of U.S. troops to the Gulf rendered the impending sequester all the more unthinkable. Hence, on the last day of September, a core group of negotiators struck a deal.

Although the tentative settlement of September 30 made a dubious claim of reducing the deficit by half a trillion dollars over five years, it was not a fatuous plan. Discretionary outlays were slated to shrink by some $180 billion. Sacred cows, such as farm subsidies, were not spared; together, various entitlements would lose more than $100 billion. On the revenue side, limits on deductible mortgage interest, and increases in the amounts of income taxed for the medicare trust fund, among other items, would bring in $30 billion annually. Not least, a 10-cents-a-gallon increase in the excise tax on gasoline and diesel fuel, plus a new 2-cents-a-gallon tax on all refined petroleum products, were expected to raise about $57 billion.[63]

But in Washington's fiscal free-for-all, agreements between presidents and party leaders do not necessarily carry weight with backbenchers. Six days later, the summit accord collapsed on the floor of the House. Liberal members concluded that the proposed budget "stunk" because it slashed into some social programs, particularly medicare, and added excises that would touch low- and middle-income taxpayers.[64] Even at the risk of Gramm-Rudman sequestration, conservative representatives seemed to prefer no budget at all to one that raised taxes, especially without firmer guarantees that the projected spending cuts would materialize. More than half of the House Democrats voted against the agreement. More important, fully 60 percent of the Republicans joined them, deserting the president and betting long odds that further budget haggling might somehow produce a better alternative.

After three more weeks of mayhem replete with all-night sessions and a series of eleventh-hour continuing resolutions to keep the government from shutting down, an alternative finally emerged. It was not better. The original summit package had at least required the welfare state to bear more of the brunt of deficit reduction, and it relied principally on consumption taxes rather than higher income tax rates for an infusion of revenue. Under the final reconciliation bill, on the other hand, up went the income tax, from a top rate of 28 percent to 31 percent, and down went the gasoline tax, from 10 cents a gallon to a nickel. Gone, too, was the 2-cent oil tax. Medicare beneficiaries would incur some increased costs, but considerably less than envisioned at the summit. Concurrently, a number of big revenue losers were introduced, including a new entitlement—subsidized child care—estimated to cost more than $22 billion through 1995.[65] Now, however, with time on the budgetary clock having long since expired, this compromise became the only endgame. On November 5, "serious regrets" notwithstanding, the White House signed off on it.[66]

That the final legislation contained any energy tax to combat the deficit was miraculous. The House's version of the budget passed in mid-October omitted such a tax entirely. Simultaneously, on the other side of the Capitol, various liberal and conservative senators were introducing half a dozen amendments to cripple or strike what was left of the administration's proposed gasoline tax.[67] Although the Senate leadership managed to repel these efforts, the vote margins were generally tight and forced important compromises. In one instance, it took twelve hours to kill a measure that would have required every penny of gas-tax revenues to be dedicated to the highway trust fund.[68] To win this bout, the victors ultimately had to give up at least half of the tax proceeds to the fund. Only twice in the preceding ten years, in 1984 and 1989, had the highway trust spent less than 100 percent of its annual intake.[69] Earmarking half the 1990 gasoline tax seemed likely to neutralize the tax's already insignificant contribution to deficit reduction.

More Trouble in 1993

The 1990 budget pact limited some categories of expenditures in the out-years, but not soon enough to prevent the government's fiscal imbalance from deteriorating to $320 billion by the beginning of 1993.[70] So the executive and legislature resumed wrestling with the deficit. This time, however, the contest was supposed to be less excruciating. An energetic, newly elected president would rise to the challenge. For the first time in a dozen years, the chief executive would be backed by friendly majorities in both legislative chambers.

Briefly it did appear that the new circumstances might help. A burst of enthusiasm accompanied Clinton's budget message to a joint session of Congress in mid-February. Within weeks, the House and then the Senate adopted initial resolutions approving the broad outlines of the president's economic plan, which purported to save the same amount, $500 billion, over four years that the 1990 summit agreement was to save over five.[71] But later on, when the legislators began the more difficult process of reconciling specifics with generalities, momentum was lost.

In April the Senate handed the administration its first defeat. While billing his proposal as a bold assault on the deficit to be achieved through an even combination of tax increases and spending restraint, Clinton had also chosen to frontload some $20 billion in additional outlays on the theory that the economy needed stimulation. The proposed pump-priming was ill timed. In the 1992 election, many office seekers had come under public pressure to start by curbing spending, rather than by spilling more red ink. Capitalizing on this mood, the Republican minority in the Senate successfully filibustered Clinton's "jobs bill."

The clash over the stimulus scheme was a public relations victory for the Republicans. It encouraged them to close ranks in an extended crusade to wring additional pork from the prospective budget, and to hold the line on taxes. GOP unity in the Senate, in turn, emboldened a handful of uneasy Democratic senators. Two such senators, David L. Boren of Oklahoma and John B. Breaux of Louisiana, acquired bargaining power in the Senate Finance Committee, where the Democrats held a slim 11–9 majority. Both of these oil-state politicians were especially uncomfortable with a centerpiece of the Clinton plan—the proposed $72 billion dollar energy (Btu) tax—and either of them was now positioned to cast a deciding vote. By May, Boren, who had hailed Clinton's budget initiative when it was unveiled, had all but hitched himself to the Republican bandwagon. Refusing to endorse the Btu tax, he called for an additional $50 billion to $60 billion in entitlement cuts instead.[72]

As the Btu tax (the financial glue for much of the budget package) came unstuck in the Senate, Democrats in the House grew restive. With no assurance the Senate would go along, why follow the president, lemming-like, into the political abyss of steeper taxation? In the days preceding House passage of its version of the budget at the end of May, recalcitrant Democrats extracted promises from the White House that it would accept a milder energy levy at the conference stage. The administration seemed resigned to let the tax, already riddled with loopholes and exemptions, yield perhaps as little as $37 billion.[73] Despite these (and other) concessions, the vote was a cliff-hanger, 219 to 213, with the outcome in doubt until the final minutes.

Back in the Senate, Boren, Breaux, and an armada of business lobbyists blocked the finance committee from pursuing a Btu tax.[74] But unable to make up all of the resulting revenue loss through further cuts in mandatory spending programs (many of which were fiercely protected by liberal members), the committee was obliged to consider at least some nominal energy tax. At this point, however, other obstacles popped up. While Breaux and perhaps Boren could live with a proposed substitute—a 7.3-cents-a-gallon excise limited to transportation fuels—two other Democrats, Max Baucus of Montana and Kent Conrad of North Dakota, announced they could not. Complicating matters, the administration itself did not rally behind the 7.3-cent option. Transportation Secretary Federico Peña, for example, criticized it for including jet fuel.[75] The committee finally settled on 4.3 cents.

Even that paltry effort almost failed on the Senate floor. With the Republicans maintaining their unanimous opposition to virtually all tax increases (and preferring instead to hold out for unspecified "cuts" in appropriations), half-a-dozen defections among Democrats could spell trouble. The 4.3-cent initiative squeaked through the Senate 50–48.[76] A handful of conservative Democrats and at least one liberal, Herbert Kohl of Wisconsin (who intoned that "people cannot afford a gas tax and should not be asked to pay it"), nearly doomed this negligible fee.[77]

If so small a tax could cause such anguish in the Senate, the House's larger rendition (the Btu scheme) would obviously go no further. Only its most quixotic enthusiasts expected it to remain on the table when conferees from the two chambers convened in July. The question now was what, if any, remnant might be salvaged. Having watched the Senate labor for weeks to bring forth a mouse, a bloc of House Democrats began recommending that the conference committee abandon any pretense whatsoever of taxing energy. From moderates came the argument that the meager gain from the Senate's best offer was not worth the political pain.[78] From liberals came renewed pleas to substitute higher corporate and income taxation.[79] Chairman Dan Rostenkowski, the chief tax negotiator for the House Ways and Means Committee, attempted repeatedly to improve the yield of the Senate's tax, suggesting it be raised to 9 cents, or just 7 cents, or at least 6.5 cents, or at a minimum 6 cents.[80] The senators refused to budge, however, and at the end of the day the exasperated Rostenkowski had to settle for their lower figure.[81]

The compromise ultimately helped secure passage of "Clinton's" fiscal 1994 budget—but barely. The final roll call in the House on August 5 was 218 to 216. Forty-one Democrats abandoned the president. The tally in the Senate the next day was even closer—a tie, broken by the vice president. The fiftieth vote was begrudgingly cast by Bob Kerrey of Nebraska, who expressed dismay at the outcome of the budget wrangle. Instead of facing up to the deficit by "collecting $70 billion from consumption," he told the Senate, "we find ourselves with a bill that asks Americans to pay 4.3 cents a gallon more." So trivial was this shared sacrifice, Kerrey concluded, that he would be surprised if people even noticed it and "ashamed" if they complained about it.[82]

The ordeal of 1993, like the one in 1990, left little reason to suppose that even America's mountainous national debt would finally give impetus to bolder federal energy taxation. A few years earlier, lobbyists for organizations like the American Automobile Association had grown fearful that a "'balance the budget at the gas pump' mentality" might begin to grip Washington.[83] Their worries proved unfounded. The epic fiscal confrontations of 1990 and 1993 managed to generate less than $7 billion a year in savings from motor-fuel revenues. Ironically, Herbert Hoover had been more successful in raising $125 million in fuel excises for what he had deemed an urgent matter in 1932—to reduce a $900 million federal deficit by 14 percent—than Bush and Clinton were with their respective fuel levies, which ended up tweaking the deficit by less than 2 percent.[84] The main parallel between then and now was that, for only the second time in the century, budget-makers refrained from making any of their added gas-tax funds available to pave more roads. Even this small concession to the cause of budgetary austerity, however, was startlingly hard to obtain.[85]

Community Control

When former Speaker of the House of Representatives Thomas P. O'Neill quipped that "all politics is local," he must have been thinking only of the United States. Practically no other advanced democracy assigns as much fiscal responsibility to local jurisdictions in urbanized areas, and no other enables these communities to shape development in quite the same way. The American brand of localism has important implications for the nation's urban transportation pattern, and thus ultimately for public choices regarding energy policies in this sector.

Fiscal Self-Defense

The typical structure of government in U.S. metropolitan areas consists of a welter of local authorities responsible for delivering costly services, most of which are paid for through local property tax collections. Localities may not like the spiraling expense of the public goods they are asked to provide, but many avail themselves of development strategies that can help them control the costs while also satisfying other community preferences (regarding the aesthetic or social character of the neighborhood, for example). The pressure to invoke these local growth-managing strategies is especially intense where, as in most American suburbs, 70 percent or more of households are home owners sensitive to property tax rates and anxious to defend the market values of their homes.[86]

The most common local strategy is to use restrictive zoning ordinances, subdivision and building permits, and tax incentives to influence the spatial distribution of residences, shops, and work places. Suburban communities frequently compete to attract commercial real estate that can enhance a town's tax base while they restrain population growth by excluding high-density residential construction. The overall result is a proliferation of work centers and a highly dispersed configuration of dwellings. By often promoting more local jobs than housing units and spreading those units over broad expanses of land, moreover, the local planning policies may contribute to a jobs-housing "imbalance"[87]—or, more precisely, to a wide jobs-housing gulf that commuters can bridge only by traveling considerable distances.

The combination of scattered housing and scattered job sites not only reduces the feasibility or convenience of commuting by transportation modes other than private cars, it reduces vehicular load factors. For a typical household, with two or more wage earners fanning out to separate work locations, the practical solution is to own multiple vehicles and to drive them solo. In metropolitan areas by 1980, persons commuting from one low-density suburb to another outnumbered persons journeying from suburbs to central cities by more than two to one.[88] Fully 77 percent of the commuters drove alone.[89]

Automotive trips configured this way largely explain why traffic in the average American metropolis consumes much more gasoline per capita than in the average European metropolis.[90] Of course, the extreme reliance on personal vehicles inhibits policymakers from sharply increasing prices at the fuel pump.

Comparative Perspective

As noted in chapter 4, other industrial countries organize their urban governments differently. Even in decentralized polities such as the Federal Republic of Germany, municipalities are not left mostly to fend for themselves for resources in the fashion of American cities and towns. Levels of intergovernmental aid and revenue sharing tend to be higher, and expensive functions (such as public education and health care) tend to be centrally funded. Although localities in Europe frequently hold historic rights of home rule, they are seldom as free to devise their own defensive or promotional land-use policies. Physical planning is usually subject to national enabling legislation. Sometimes it is a shared function, with higher orders of government exerting direct influence over local decisions. Not uncommonly, the dominance of historic city centers over peripheral areas has been deliberately preserved, as a matter of national policy, by clustering new housing and commercial establishments in proximity to the centers or to rapid transit lines serving the centers.[91]

Urban government is also far more fragmented in the United States. Whereas regional authorities with general-purpose taxing and land-use powers are common in western Europe, only a handful of metropolitanwide governments have been chartered in this country. One consequence of dividing land-use regulation among scores or even hundreds of jurisdictions, each with a parochial perspective, has been haphazard expansion outside the boundaries of U.S. central cities. With their independent control over the disposition of land, localities in outlying areas have permitted private developers to bypass sites adjoining existing settlements and to construct whole subdivisions in remote locations. This "leap-frogging" style of growth adds to travel distances. West European metropolitan areas have largely avoided it. There, writes Anthony Downs,

> such a "leap-frog" pattern was prevented by deliberate regional or national policies to preserve agricultural uses for as long as possible in the territory immediately outside the densely settled portion of each urbanized area. This policy was enforced by regional authorities who controlled land-use decisions over wide areas. . . . The result is a striking visual difference between the edges of metropolitan areas in Western Europe and in the U.S. In Western Europe, travellers . . . pass from densely-settled urbanized neighborhoods to uninterrupted open farmland. In the U.S., there is a gradual transition from the former to the latter through a broad region of scattered patchwork subdivisions and small outlying residential and commercial areas.[92]

These contrasting urban forms, determined in no small part by differences in local regulatory interventions, help account for the divergent levels of automobile usage—hence, fuel consumption—between the United States and other parts of the industrial world. The fraction of all urban passenger trips made by automobile in modern Germany, for instance, has been almost half the percentage in urban America.[93] Not surprisingly Germany offers the more fertile turf for gasoline taxes, while the United States minimizes them and resorts to CAFE.

Summary

The distinctive cast of American energy policy for automotive transportation has much to do with the formative history of motor-fuel taxes in this country and with the politics of the nation's political parties, budgetary deliberations, and system of local self-rule.

Tax collectors in Washington began drawing revenue from the sale of motor fuels later than did the central treasuries of western Europe and Japan. The late start placed Congress in the awkward position of seeming to intrude on an established source of income for state governments, and of trying to embed the new national excise after the era of mass motorization was well under way. What flexibility the federal government had to bolster its gasoline tax before the Second World War was narrowed in the immediate postwar period. Once the tax was fused to the building of interstate highways, its scope was circumscribed. Increases to meet other needs came to be regarded, at least until recently, as breaching a "trust." Further, Americans increasingly lived in suburbs and, thanks to cheap fuel, drove around in big cars. CAFE standards could eventually find their way into this setting; their timetables for compliance were negotiable in later stages of implementation, and in any case, their costs to the public would be veiled. A policy that would ratchet up, significantly and explicitly, the operating expense of vehicles, however, would prove much harder to square with the American context.

Distaste for the tax option has been pervasive in Congress, not only because most members of Congress represent constituents from metropolitan as well as rural districts, which increasingly share a need for automotive travel at minimum cost, but also because politicians in both parties claim principled objections. The terms of their debate have been unusual from the vantage point of other democratic nations. European conservatives rarely resist the bountiful yield of national fuel taxes. But Republicans in the United States remain wary, preferring to keep a lid on the taxes (or the proceeds) by earmarking them narrowly.[94] At the same time, many Democrats appear to subject gasoline taxation to a more exacting test of fairness than do the socialists of Europe. The upshot of this two-sided critique has been CAFE. Relieved of requiring conservation-by-price, Democrats have generally embraced the regulatory approach exuberantly, while Republicans have acquiesced for lack of a politically palatable alternative.

The energy shortages of the 1970s failed to arouse any congressional enthusiasm for taxing gasoline. And the towering federal deficits of more recent years did not have much effect, either. A basic reason is that the budgetary process in the United States is not governed by an executive presiding over dependable legislative majorities, but by fissile congressional factions, even by the whims of individual members. Every discretionary component of a president's plan for revenues and expenditures is negotiable. With Congress exercising the functional equivalent of a line-item veto, proposed energy taxes can seldom be securely encased in omnibus budget legislation.

Less dispersion of fiscal power at the national level might have helped U.S. policy shift toward a sizable fuel tax, perhaps doing away with CAFE. But how much is hard to say. Americans are extraordinarily sensitive to gasoline prices because, compared with the Japanese or Europeans, Americans not only own more cars but spend more of their lives in them. To a large extent, the layout of most U.S. metropolitan areas does not leave much choice. Alternate transport modes—including one of the most common in Europe, walking—are infeasible where land uses are so spread out. In part, this sprawl is an outcome of public policy, ensured by independent local regulators coping with the fiscal exigencies of their communities.

CHAPTER SIX

New Directions

THE PRIMARY AIM of American energy policy during the past two decades has been to reduce the nation's reliance on oil, especially imported oil. The merits of this priority aside, it is more efficiently promoted by raising the price of motor fuel than by administering mileage mandates for motor vehicles. Although the mandates can slowly improve the energy performance of new vehicle fleets, they do nothing to influence other causes of resurgent oil consumption—most notably, the sheer amount of driving.

Thus we estimate that if a gasoline tax of 25 cents a gallon had been introduced in 1986 to brace the falling price of oil, the United States would have conserved as much petroleum as was saved throughout the life of the cumbersome Corporate Average Fuel Economy (CAFE) program. Five years later such a tax would still have left the average price of gasoline in the United States 125 percent below the average for the rest of the OECD countries and, in real terms, less than 1 percent above the U.S. price prevailing forty-five years ago.[1]

Recapping the Complications

Why has a decision to replace the CAFE program, even with so modest a tax, been elusive?

Politicians, here or elsewhere, have not been in the habit of raising taxes on transport fuels primarily to meet energy goals or environmental plans. Instead, the levies have evolved with other, mostly unrelated, purposes in mind. In many countries, for instance, trade protection for particular domestic industries (automobile manufacturers, coal producers, and so on) was an early determinant of national energy tax systems. All governments raise revenue from fuel users to pay the bills for public works and services. Most have done so on a much grander scale than does the United States, not only because they have proportionately larger government sectors requiring higher overall tax rates, but because many got an earlier start and had in place the necessary institutional and developmental preconditions.

One such prerequisite, for better or worse, has been the ability of the national executive to affix fuel excises to budgetary enactments. Legislative dominance of these determinations, a constitutional certainty in the United States, complicates matters. Each of the past four presidents (Clinton, Bush, Reagan, Carter) was willing to take the political heat of proposing new energy taxes, only to see them filibustered, removed, or pared down by dissenting legislators. The contrarians in Congress regularly included numerous members of a president's own party—eccentric behavior in comparison with the norms of parliamentary regimes in Japan, Canada, or most of western Europe.

In addition, these regimes (with the notable exception of Japan) have avoided the institutionalization of "road funds." Until the 1990s, the propensity of Congress was to funnel all fuel-tax receipts into transportation projects. This requirement had the effect of limiting the taxes and narrowing their clientele, principally to the highway lobby. Less formulaic disbursement of motor-fuel revenues in Europe and Canada generally reached a more diversified set of claimants. These included some powerful interest groups (national railroads, for example) with substantial stakes in raising rates.

Two other interrelated factors are especially important in comprehending America's reluctance to tax fuel consumption. Opposition spans the political spectrum. Liberals and conservatives may concur on little else, but they frequently agree that gasoline taxes are either unjust or unnecessary. This meeting of the minds is more than expediential; it partly expresses authentic partisan attitudes about the proper design and degree of national taxation, attitudes that parties of neither the left nor the right in other democracies affirm with such constancy.

The antitax alliance also has extensive grass roots. Hostility to gasoline taxation runs deep in the United States because, as the architects of the interstate system stressed triumphantly almost forty years ago, "America lives on wheels."[2] Much (not all) of this life-style reflects the extreme decentralization of American metropolitan areas. Their centrifugal growth has not been spun, entirely, by unfettered market forces. Atomistic local governments have had a visible hand. Few other industrial nations have yet acquired an urban geography like that of the United States, partly because few have passed to local jurisdictions as many fiscal responsibilities or as much discretion over the density of development. Representing an overwhelmingly automobile-dependent urban population, Congress cannot comfortably vote to impose highly visible costs on motorists. Hence, it finesses its commitment to conserving motor fuel by resorting to indirect techniques, such as CAFE standards, with delegated enforcement functions and concealed costs.

New Politics?

It is hard to envisage what, if any, national or international events in the foreseeable future could easily dislodge U.S. policy from its attachment to fuel-economy regulations and to low taxes on gasoline.

"Crises"

Depending on its severity, another oil shock might at least reopen the question. Judging from past experience, however, jolts in world oil markets do not necessarily lead to thorough reassessments of energy policy. The Gulf crisis in 1990 was the latest case in point. It stirred in Congress the usual anxiety about growing dependence on imported petroleum, accusations of price-gouging by oil companies, and renewed calls for tougher CAFE controls, but at no point did the emergency create tolerance for energy tax increases.[3]

In recent times, heightened concern about government deficits prompted new consumption taxes in Japan, Germany, Canada, Holland, and various other industrial countries, including the United States. But in the U.S. case, the measures have been very limited excises. Compare U.S. fiscal action with Japan's in the 1989–90 period. The 1990 budget compromise added 5 cents a gallon to the federal tax on gasoline, along with increased charges on such items as tobacco, alcoholic beverages, airplane tickets, yachts, and jewelry, in order to generate an estimated grand total of $66 billion in additional revenues over five years.[4] Japan's value-added tax alone, adopted in 1989, raised nearly $40 billion in its first year.[5] For all the public deficit-bashing in the United States in the early 1990s, the issue never fundamentally transformed the terms of the national tax debate.

The same goes for environmental issues. During the Rio Earth Summit in 1992, environmental groups chastised the U.S. government for declining to curtail greenhouse gases according to specific targets and timetables. Global climate change may or may not be a real danger, but if it is, the efficient solution for every country is an energy tax (in this case, aimed at carbon emissions). At Rio, however, some factions entertained instead the notion that members of the OECD, led by the United States, ought to spend billions buying reductions of carbon dioxide from developing countries.[6] Although the environmental movement is hardly monolithic, much of it has seemed too disposed to favor lavish subsidies or laborious regulatory remedies for the problems it sees. Nowhere has this tendency been more evident than in debates about energy conservation. For the most part, environmentalists remain unwavering advocates of CAFE regulation.

New Transportation Policies

Federal transportation funding formulas have been changing of late. The sanctity of the highway trust fund was challenged in the 1990 and 1993 budget agreements, and also by the Intermodal Surface Transportation Efficiency Act of 1991 (ISTEA), which allows states to reallocate more federal funds from road construction to public transit. Could these departures from past practice begin to create a constituency for higher gasoline taxes?

The trouble is that the changes are tardy. Most U.S. cities, particularly in the West, now lack the critical mass needed to support larger public transportation networks cost effectively. To be sure, state governments will be increasingly unhappy with the mounting traffic congestion and air pollution. State transportation planners will also welcome their newly granted discretion to consider a wider range of federally supported investments. But proponents of conventional transit systems will be hard pressed to justify costly expansions (and the additional state taxes needed to secure the federal matching grants) on the basis of potential ridership where the vast majority of commuters journey from one low-density suburb to another, not to and from central cities.

The new flexibility in funding bears resemblance to foreign models, but only up to a point. Once there was only one way (laying asphalt) to use the proceeds of gas taxes in the United States. Now there are more possibilities. The available options, however, are far from open-ended; plenty of strings are still attached. The surface transportation funds commonly subsidize fixed-rail projects that are hopelessly ill-suited to most U.S. metropolitan regions, and only a fraction of federal income from fuel taxes is no longer earmarked.[7] The fungibility of revenues in British, French, or German budgets remains greater. With a multiplicity of claims on the money, the taxes in these countries stay much higher.

Defenders of the new U.S. urban transportation policy can rejoin that it is better to start late than never. At least some future growth in and around cities might be concentrated by more diversified transportation plans than those traditionally envisioned by state highway engineers. Scattered evidence around the country provides some reasonable basis for this expectation. The rapid transit system serving metropolitan Washington, D.C., has magnetized considerable new development in the downtown area and at nodes along the system's lines in the suburbs. The less ambitious transit improvements in Honolulu, Portland, San Diego, Dallas, Minneapolis, Chicago, and a few other sizable cities may induce some similar results. If enough inhabitants in these places eventually acquire viable substitutes for automotive travel, local resistance to steeper gasoline taxation may abate somewhat.

Free Wheeling?

Even for residents with access to alternatives, private motor vehicles will remain the heavily favored mode of transportation and cheap gasoline the favored policy—all the more so because a number of government programs and procedures, apart from transport financing, have solidified this public preference.

The federal government bears some direct responsibility. Federal Housing Administration and Veterans Administration mortgage insurance helped finance a substantial part of the postwar period's suburban sprawl.[8] Petroleum price controls throughout the 1970s held gasoline prices below market levels, thereby indulging wasteful cars and drivers. The federal tax code encourages the provision of free parking at work places and commercial locations, a potent inducement to the use of automobiles.[9] The Internal Revenue Code permits employers to claim this fringe benefit as a business expense, and the benefit is tax-free to employees.[10] Meanwhile, transit riders do not receive an equally generous tax break for their commuting expenses.

Rethinking one-sided incentives like these can be helpful.[11] During the 1980s the removal of price regulations, not only on petroleum products but also on natural gas, corrected the most irrational elements of federal energy policy. Partial redress of federal tax biases by way of the National Energy Policy Act of 1992 has finally begun to level the playing field for transit users.[12]

But even if officials in Washington right more of the distortions that contribute to the transportation system's fuel intensity, they would still be left with a sobering reality: in the United States the important decisions are also made at the local level. Local zoning ordinances play a larger role than FHA mortgage subsidies in the dispersal of jobs and housing in metropolitan areas. Caprice by the IRS does not explain the prevalence of subsidized parking; much more telling are the local subdivision statutes that typically require developers of residential and commercial real estate to provide ample on-site spaces, gratis.[13]

In unitary political systems, like those of France or Britain, central authorities can delimit such powers of cities and towns directly. In the American system, as in Germany or Canada, the constitutional authority to do so rests largely with subnational entities. Yet the provincial or state governments of Canada and Germany generally permit less local rugged individualism in deciding the uses of urban land. Although our state legislatures engage in much guidance of localities on other matters, involvement with local zoning and subdivision practices to reshape metropolitan densities and transportation requirements is relatively rare. At the same time, municipalities eager to create the conditions for sustainable investment in public transportation sometimes find that state law hampers their efforts. Thirty-one states, for instance, continue to set aside all their revenues from road-related user fees for highway extensions and repairs.[14]

Some Suggestions

A meaningful "vision of change" has not come into focus in U.S. energy policy for automotive transportation, and one purpose of this book has been to explain why.[15] Another, though, has been to consider the costs of the status quo and to explore new directions.

Adjustments from the Bottom Up

A suitable place to start is in the states. Pricing policies that substantially raise the real cost of transportation fuels will remain a hard sell, but their prospects may get even dimmer unless more state governments begin to exert a different influence on patterns of urban growth and physical mobility.

To be sure, most of the forces configuring urban America lie well beyond the reach of officials in state capitals or anywhere else. America's contemporary cityscape reflects, in large part, a rapidly growing population through most of the postwar period.[16] An expanding urban population must either be crowded into dense dwellings and high-rises or dispersed into suburbs. Of the two possible outlets, the second makes sense for a country still blessed with plentiful, relatively inexpensive land along its metropolitan fringes. Concentrating development in cities is not a goal to maximize. The cheek-by-jowl density of people and functions in the Tokyo area, to take an extreme example, is no boon to the Japanese economy. So congested is the Japanese capital that government planners have been trying hard to encourage decentralization.[17]

The dispersion of metropolitan economic activity and households in the United States has important benefits. During the 1980s alone, more than six million immigrants entered the United States, an influx that dwarfed the immigration to every other industrial country. One may wonder whether nations that force their inhabitants into much tighter physical proximity could absorb as much demographic pressure and ethnic diversity. Liberal use of space over which to distribute a bulging, extraordinarily diverse society may provide an essential social buffer in America. In any event, ownership of detached single-family homes, with substantial private space separating each housing unit, satisfies a traditional preference of most American households.

Yet the rapid pace of American suburbanization over the past thirty years has also left in its wake some less desirable consequences.[18] It has severed inner-city minorities from job sites, generated regional traffic jams, and frustrated efforts to better the air quality of a number of cities. Not least, the accelerating sprawl conflicts with national energy conservation objectives. Inasmuch as some of these effects are induced by the interventions of governments, not just the free operation of real estate markets, corrective steps might be contemplated.

STATE LAND USE POLICIES. The states may need to oversee more closely the exercise of local regulatory powers that warp urban housing and land markets.[19] Experiments with statewide or regional land-use policies have been under way for a number of years in Oregon, New Jersey, Georgia, Florida, Hawaii, Rhode Island, Maine, and Vermont.[20] In a few locations (most notably Portland, Oregon) significant progress has been made in controlling haphazard growth.[21] But with the exception of Florida, big states experiencing the most explosive growth in recent decades generally have not been in the forefront. Just three of them—California, Texas, and Florida—captured more than half of the nation's total population growth from 1980 to 1987, and nearly 42 percent of it during the preceding decade. A substantial share of development in the past twenty years could have been organized differently in the megalopoli of southeast Texas and southern California, if authorities in these states had interceded as Oregon did, beginning in 1973.[22] The activities of states such as California have been curiously unbalanced. On one hand, California (along with New York and Massachusetts) scarcely hesitated to mandate truly radical measures against automobile emissions; by the year 2003 a minimum of one out of ten new cars sold in California must be a zero-emission vehicle.[23] On the other hand, the mode of urban land development—a root cause of urban smog—has received far less attention from the activists in Sacramento.

FISCAL BURDEN SHARING. Well short of commandeering community land-use controls, state governments could do more to alter the underlying structure of local finance, which indirectly gives impetus to the American suburban diaspora. States have been assuming a larger share of the costs of key services (public schools, for instance).[24] If this trend toward intergovernmental cost-shifting continues, it eventually could diminish the fiscal incentive of local jurisdictions to maintain low densities through exclusionary zoning. Regional revenue-sharing arrangements could enable communities to cluster their commercial activity and housing and to be less preoccupied with the implications for their immediate tax bases.

State initiatives along these lines admittedly lack political support; they presuppose that suburban towns and counties can be persuaded or compelled to redistribute substantial resources, if not relinquish substantial regulatory sovereignty, to regional agencies. The counties and towns almost always command enough representation in state legislatures to prevent this expropriation.[25] Occasional surprises are possible, however, and they merit attention. For many years, Minnesota has showcased a successful tax-base sharing system in the Minneapolis-St. Paul area.[26]

Federal Efforts

The federal government can facilitate financial and developmental policy innovation in the states. For states to relieve more of the fiscal burdens on local governments, Washington needs to desist from imposing unfunded mandates on the states. The rising cost of medicaid, for instance, accounted for a large part of the deterioration of state finances after 1985.[27] Judicious health care reform, if it can rein in the costs of medical insurance programs, could eventually ease a major source of strain on state budgets.[28] States fashioning new regional land management systems to influence the course of local growth may get a lift from recent federal legislation.[29]

PRICING POLICIES. But before revamping American fiscal federalism or endorsing an expansion of federally sponsored regional planning authorities, policymakers would do well to take the recent reforms in federal transportation programs a step farther. Transportation bills since 1982 have been releasing a greater share of dedicated tax revenues for multiple applications. The applications, however, still do not reach much beyond capital improvements for roads or, to a lesser extent, municipal transit systems. National transportation policy should promote, instead, the sophisticated use of pricing methods to ration the existing infrastructure.

The 1992 presidential campaign abounded with vows to revitalize the nation's decaying transport facilities. Candidates alleged a grave lag in public investment, and came to the (debatable) conclusion that more government spending on everything from expressways to high-speed rail lines would boost the productivity of the economy.[30] Budgetary constraints have since trimmed the investment plans of the Clinton administration, but existing commitments still favor capacity renovation and expansion rather than cost-effective utilization of the ample capacity that already exists in most localities. "Efficiency" is in the very title of the ISTEA; nonetheless, the act authorized $155 billion in conventional highway and transit spending for fiscal years 1992–97. Other types of projects—for example, the Department of Transportation's Intelligent Vehicle-Highway Systems (or smart cars/smart highways) initiative and experimentation with congestion pricing—remain eligible for only a small fraction of this largesse.[31] The priorities ought to be inverted, advancing the relatively low-budget road-pricing and traffic-demand management experiments *before* allocating the additional billions to construction projects.[32] This would send a clear message that efficiency is truly an aim of national policy in the transportation sector. Indeed, such a message might also reach the debate on automotive fuel-economy standards—and perhaps help legitimize changes that are long overdue.

NEW TECHNOLOGIES. The age of gasoline- and diesel-powered vehicles will not last forever. One day the commercialization of new propulsion technologies and alternative fuels could revolutionize vehicular transport throughout the industrial world. Until that day arrives, however, energy policymakers may misallocate resources if they keep trying to force-feed new technologies on producers and consumers amid unreceptive market conditions.

The policies of Republican and Democratic administrations have been remarkably similar in this respect. President Bush's *National Energy Strategy* duly noted that the low cost of gasoline had "dampened consumer interest in more fuel-efficient vehicles," and that "in the absence of predictable consumer demand, the development of new transportation technologies can be costly and risky, especially to U.S. industry."[33] Nevertheless, in the next breath, the *Strategy* recommended "enhanced" efforts to develop a wide assortment of such technologies, from automotive gas turbines and advanced diesels, to high-temperature ceramic materials, high-performance batteries, electric vehicles, and alternative-fuel vehicles. After President Clinton had campaigned vigorously against raising the price of gasoline, his administration launched an ambitious venture in research and development to produce, inside a decade, "a new generation of vehicles up to three times more fuel-efficient than today's."[34]

The desired technological breakthroughs may or may not prove feasible within the foreseeable future, but to accelerate a conversion to them by pushing an industrial policy in the face of relatively low oil prices will be, at best, frustrating. If energy strategists deem it necessary to move more quickly than markets to introduce better vehicles or fuels, the government should at least start by setting consistent price signals. The Department of Energy may be eager to promote a supercar by emulating a Japanese-style public-private partnership. But no one should be surprised if, in the end, the Japanese sell one first.[35] Surely, the incentive to do so remains more intense in a market where the cost of fuel at the pump nears $4 a gallon (Japan), compared with a market where a gallon of fuel is now cheaper than bottled water (the United States).

Toward Policy Coordination

Flawed schemes such as the CAFE legislation examined in this book raise larger questions about the composition of the public agenda in the United States. The nation is nearing the end of the century facing intense international pressures. As a signatory to the Rio agreement on climate change, for instance, the U.S. government will be expected to show more progress in curbing carbon emissions. As the mainstay of a wider General Agreement on Tariffs and Trade (GATT), this country, too, will have to harmonize more of its domestic regulatory practices with those of others. A tumultuous, much more competitive world will demand of us supple, complementary policy responses at home and abroad. Now more than ever, Americans can ill afford to carry an ever-expanding load of government programs operating with dubious efficacy and at cross-purposes.

When lawmakers and regulators began devoting attention to the conservation of energy two decades ago, the issue was framed more or less discretely: amid the physical shortages of those years, petroleum was regarded as a scarce resource to be husbanded. Few paused to ask how various plans to conserve fuel might touch other important public concerns. The CAFE initiative was typical. Its purpose was viewed narrowly, as a device intended to "save" oil. Whether the device would also prove helpful in addressing the country's fiscal exigencies, international trade disputes, or even transportation and environmental woes was not carefully considered. The myopic approach may be understood as a rudimentary, reactive policy conceived during the emergency conditions of the 1970s. But perpetuating it today, while continuing to pass up a far more versatile alternative, seems increasingly incongruous.

Intersecting Foreign Trade

Consider the awkward interface of the CAFE law with the trade issue. Not only was CAFE recently the subject of a European protest before the GATT on the grounds that the unique U.S. law might constitute a discriminatory nontariff barrier against European exports of luxury cars, parts of the law aggravate our own trade grievances as well.[36] The regulations distinguish between fleets of imported and domestically produced vehicles, even though most automobile manufacturers are multinational corporations that make various combinations of both. An "import" is arbitrarily defined as a vehicle with less than 75 percent domestic value added. Imports and domestics must each meet CAFE's mpg standards separately; a firm cannot simply average the sale of its domestically made cars with those produced abroad, even if they are assembled by a wholly owned subsidiary. Ironically, since import fleets consistently score higher mpg ratings than domestic fleets, the effect of these provisions on U.S. manufacturers can be to drive more of their production or sourcing offshore.[37] At one point Ford Motor Company, for example, turned to importing at least 26 percent of the parts for its Crown Victoria and Grand Marquis models. This strategy enabled Ford to roll in these large, energy-intensive cars with its thriftier line of imports, thereby prettying the fuel-economy rating of its domestic fleet.

Further, the fuel-economy regulations insouciantly hand foreign rivals an artificial advantage over U.S. firms. During the past three years, Japanese manufacturers accumulated large reserves of CAFE "credits" by exceeding the law's mpg requirements. U.S. companies, by contrast, remained near or even below the requirements. Thus, although the regulatory gate is wide open for Japanese companies to shift upscale into larger, more profitable exports, regulation continues to constrain American companies. Induced to raise prices on their large cars and engines in order to meet CAFE standards, the Americans have inevitably attracted a new wave of competition—now from the likes of Lexus, Infiniti, Diamante, and Acura.

Not all of us suffer sleepless nights over the vicissitudes of automobile commerce. The trend in oil imports, however, is of potentially greater importance.[38] Imported autos and auto parts may represent a big part of the U.S. multilateral trade deficit, but at least the nation has never experienced an embargo on cars. Imported petroleum accounts for an even bigger part of the deficit—and a large volume is purchased from a region that has repeatedly disrupted supplies. As has been stressed throughout this book, the CAFE program has fallen well short of providing an optimal hedge against this uneasy oil dependency for the simple reasons that consumption is a function of vehicle miles traveled, not just vehicular miles per gallon.

Getting More Mileage from Energy Policy

In recent years, Congress has added to its extensive list of aspirations a desire to raise the national rates of saving and investment through budgeting and tax revisions. However genuine this desire, so far it has been satisfied primarily by spending less on discretionary activities (principally national defense) and levying more taxes on income. Not only do the budget's "nondiscretionary" big-ticket items remain largely off limits, so do new instruments in the fiscal tool-kit. Nudging more federal tax policy toward the taxation of consumption, and away from the double taxation of savings (first on earnings, then on interest from those earnings), might seem warranted for a society that is said to save too little. No amount of automotive fuel-economy rules will further this objective. But replacing those rules with a higher gasoline tax obviously could.

Similarly, it seems increasingly odd to bewail snarled traffic, polluted city air, and supposedly inadequate investment in transport infrastructure while stubbornly enforcing energy regulations that do not relieve such problems. America became an energy-conscious nation in the course of the 1970s. Still the average number of miles driven annually per motor vehicle continued to rise. Whatever else contributed to this oil-consuming increase, the CAFE regime has probably played a part. By raising the mileage per gallon of new motor vehicles, but not the real price of motor fuels, CAFE lowers the marginal cost of driving. And by adding to the expense of purchasing new vehicles, but not the cost of running older ones, CAFE renders the vehicular fleet as a whole less efficient, and less environmentally benign, than it would be under a simpler policy of taxing fuel.

In any case, policymakers cannot continue to have it both ways: wringing their hands about the national debt, gridlocked freeways, global warming, unbalanced trade, unfair foreign competitors, and reliance on insecure oil, while clinging to unsatisfactory policies such as the 1975 automotive fuel-use statute. Either the government will have to worry less, or, if worry it must, discontinue pet programs that often add to the difficulties it perceives.

Econometric Analysis of the CAFE Program

T HE ANALYSIS of the effects of the Corporate Average Fuel Economy (CAFE) program or fuel prices on vehicle miles traveled (VMT), new-car weight and new-car performance, and the domestic companies' pricing strategies discussed in chapter 2 reflects a series of econometric analyses described in detail in this appendix.

Vehicle Miles

David Greene has argued that the feedback effect of CAFE on vehicle miles, induced by lowering the cost of driving in newer cars, is quite small. His conclusion is based on some straightforward estimates of the determinants of VMT for light-duty vehicles.[1] His regression equation is simply:

(A-1) $VMT = a + b\,CPM + c\,GDP + d\,DRIVERS,$

where VMT is vehicle-miles traveled in light-duty vehicles, CPM is the *average* real cost of fuel per mile driven, GDP is real GDP, and $DRIVERS$ is the number of licensed drivers. Equation A-1 is estimated in linear and logarithmic form. Because the estimates of b are generally small, with implied elasticities in the range of -0.05 to -0.15, Greene concludes that the "snapback" effect of CAFE through greater VMT is relatively small.

Greene's analysis utilizes Federal Highway Administration (FHWA) data on fuel consumption and miles traveled by passenger cars and light trucks to calculate vehicle miles per gallon (MPG) for light-duty vehicles. He then divides this measure into the real price of fuel to obtain the cost per mile traveled, CPM. Unfortunately, this approach does not capture the effect of higher CAFE standards on the *marginal* cost of travel in newer vehicles. Indeed, because of measurement errors in the components of mpg,[2] even the *average* cost per mile may be measured badly.

CPM can be divided into its MPG and fuel-price (p_f) components to see how well each performs in an equation such as A-1. Using all available data from 1966 through 1992, we obtain the following estimates for a logarithmic version:[3]

$$LVMT = -1.06 + 0.043\ LMPG - 0.10\ Lp_f + 0.52\ LGDP$$
$$(t = 0.35) \quad (t = -3.33) \quad (t = 4.79)$$

(A-2)
$$+ 0.91\ LDRIVERS - 0.019\ D74 - 0.016\ D79,$$
$$(t = 5.89) \quad (t = -2.54) \quad (t = -2.08)$$

$$R^2 = 0.998$$
$$DW = 1.962$$

where the L prefix indicates the natural logarithm of the variable and $D74$ and $D79$ are dummy variables for the gas-rationing years of 1974 and 1979.[4] The low value of the t-statistic for the estimated coefficient of LMPG suggests that the FHWA's estimate of mpg is not a good proxy for the incremental mpg of the light-duty fleet. The estimated elasticity for fuel prices is only -0.10, but this estimate may be biased toward zero by the absence of a well-measured mpg variable.

We delve further into the empirical estimation of vehicle miles traveled in chapter 3, emphasizing the difference between short-term and long-term elasticities. For the present, note that most estimates of the effects of real gasoline prices on VMT, holding MPG constant, cluster around -0.5. We would expect the effects of CAFE to be similar for new cars because an increase in MPG, other things being equal, is analogous to a reduction in fuel prices to the individual consumer.

Vehicle Weight

To test for the effects of CAFE as distinct from factor prices, we estimated a regression equation in which the fleet-average weight of all new passenger cars, W, is the dependent variable.[5] We expect fuel and steel prices, p_f and p_s, respectively, to influence design decisions with a four-year lead time to the introduction of the vehicle model and current fuel prices to influence current-year choices by consumers.[6] Since CAFE targets are generally known in advance, we include $CAFER$, the ratio of the CAFE standard to the pre-CAFE fleet-average fuel economy (15.79), without a lag. In addition, because Japanese voluntary export restraints constrained consumer choices in 1983-86, a dummy variable is included, *VER*, equal to one in 1983-86 and zero otherwise.

The period of estimation is 1968-92, all years for which data are available. The results explain 94 percent of the variance and show that factor prices and CAFE drive the final fleet-average weight:

(A-3)

$$W = 66650 - 1234 \quad CAFER - 586 \, p_{f,-4} - 282 \, p_f$$
$$(t = 15.92) \qquad (t = 2.97) \, (t = 1.69)$$

$$- 480 \, p_{s,-4} \quad + 390 \, VER,$$
$$(t = 2.28) \qquad (t = 4.79)$$

$$R^2 = 0.942$$
$$DW = 2.116$$

The t-statistics in parentheses show that all coefficients except that for the current price of fuel are statistically significant at the 99 percent confidence level.[7] Thus CAFE surely affects the weight of cars offered by manufacturers, but higher fuel prices and steel prices also reduce weight. The VERs on Japanese exports increased average weight by 390 pounds as consumers were denied the opportunity to purchase additional smaller, fuel-efficient Japanese models.

Performance

The best single indication of vehicle performance is acceleration, which is generally measured by the time required to accelerate from 0 to 60 miles per hour. Between 1978 and 1986, average new-car acceleration changed very little despite substantial reductions in average engine size (table 2-2).[8] Part of the reason was the substantial reduction in vehicle weight. Since 1985, however, with fuel prices falling, acceleration has improved substantially despite relatively constant engine size and rising vehicle weight.

There is little evidence, however, that engine displacement has responded to anything except the declining weight of the car. Data on the average displacement of passenger cars (*DISP*) are available from 1970 through Murrell, Hellman, and Heavenrich.[9] Using these data, we estimate a model of displacement whose determinants are average weight, time (to reflect technical progress), *CAFER*, and the real price of motor fuel. Weight is endogenous, depending on past and present fuel prices, *CAFER*, and the lagged real price of steel. The results of a loglinear regression show that only weight (*LW*) and *TIME* (technical progress) affect displacement, not real fuel prices or *CAFER:*

(A-4) $LDISP = -6.45 + 1.49\ LW - 0.017\ TIME +$
$(t = 9.17) \quad (t = 4.74)$
$0.09\ CAFER + 0.0044\ p_f.$
$(t = 0.76) \quad\quad (t = 0.10)$
$R^2 = 0.993$
$DW = 1.584$

Thus CAFE or real fuel prices affect the size of the vehicle, but not its engine displacement for given average vehicle weight.

Technical Improvements in Fuel Efficiency

To estimate the effect of CAFE and real fuel prices on technical fuel efficiency on individual models, we employ a cross-sectional database composed of all of the domestic passenger cars tested by *Consumer Reports* from the 1970 model year through the 1993 model year. The fuel efficiency of the ith model may be modeled as:

(A-5) $LMPG_i = a + b\ LW_i + c\ LDISP_i + dT_i + u_i,$

where mpg is miles per gallon, *W* is vehicle weight, DISP is engine displacement, *T* is technology, *u* is a random error term, and the *L* prefixes once again indicate natural logarithms.[10] If technology improves at an exponential rate, calendar time (*TIME*) may be substituted for *T*. To estimate equation A-5, we use data for all domestic passenger cars, excluding station wagons and sporty cars, tested by Consumers Union for the model years 1970 through 1993 for U.S. producers. In all, 268 observations are available over twenty-four years, or about eleven a year.

The results of estimating equation A-5 appear in table A-1. Weight is highly significant, with a coefficient of about 0.8, and the exponential rate of improvement in technical fuel efficiency is about 1.6 percent a year (column 1). In column 2 the time trend is broken into five separate periods to examine the temporal pattern of technical improvement. When fuel prices rise in the early and late 1970s, technical fuel efficiency accelerates after a lag of about four years, the design lag. However, when real fuel prices begin to decline in the early 1980s, technical progress also decelerates, suggesting that producers respond to energy price signals in designing individual models.

To estimate the effects of CAFE and gasoline prices, we test to see if

Table A-1. *Estimates of the Determinants of Average Fuel Economy Using a 268-Passenger-Car Cross Section, 1970–93 Model Years*

Variable	(1)	(2)	(3)
Constant	9.73	9.40	9.30
LW	−0.79	−0.77	−0.76
	(t=11.10)	(t=11.56)	(t=10.90)
LDISP	−0.13	−0.11	−0.13
	(t=3.35)	(t=3.02)	(t=3.46)
TIME	0.016		0.015
	(t=18.26)	. . .	(t=5.28)
TIME 70-75		0.004	
	. . .	(t=0.80)	. . .
TIME 76-80		0.017	
	. . .	(t=6.87)	. . .
TIME 81-85		0.019	
	. . .	(t=11.67)	. . .
TIME 86-90		0.017	
	. . .	(t=12.81)	. . .
TIME 91-93		0.013	
	. . .	(t=11.80)	. . .
CAFER			0.0026
	. . .	. . .	(t=0.04)
$P_{f, -4}$			0.15
	. . .	. . .	(t=3.52)
$\bar{R}^2$	0.913	0.931	0.921

Source: See text.

technical change responds to either *CAFER* or the real price of motor fuel lagged four years, the typical design lag. In column 3 of table A-1 the coefficient of the lagged price of gasoline is highly significant, but *CAFER,* the ratio of the CAFE standard to the preexisting level of mpg, is not significant. This confirms that higher gasoline prices are associated with a greater rate of adoption of new fuel-saving technologies, but that CAFE apparently is not.

A different approach to estimating equation A-5 is simply to include a separate dummy variable for each model year, other than 1970, as regressors instead of TIME. The coefficients of each of these variables provide an estimate of the proportionate improvement in fuel economy in the relevant model year over the average 1970 level. The results of this exercise appear in table A-2. The results are shown for 1970–93 as well

Table A-2. *The Determinants of Technical Fuel Efficiency Using a 268-Passenger-Car Cross Section, 1970–93 Model Years, with Individual Time Dummies*

Variable	1970–93	1970–83	1984–93
Constant	9.28	9.11	9.37
LW	−0.73	−0.68	−0.75
	(t=−11.21)	(t=−8.72)	(t=−5.58)
LDISP	−0.13	−0.18	−0.08
	(t=−3.77)	(t=−3.97)	(t=1.34)
D1976	0.13	0.12	
	(t=6.15)	(t=5.78)	. . .
D1977	0.13	0.12	
	(t=5.33)	(t=4.82)	. . .
D1978	0.13	0.12	
	(t=5.54)	(t=5.12)	. . .
D1979	0.15	0.15	
	(t=7.15)	(t=6.61)	. . .
D1980	0.14	0.12	
	(t=4.33)	(t=3.76)	. . .
D1981	0.20	0.19	
	(t=7.12)	(t=6.51)	. . .
D1982	0.21	0.20	
	(t=8.66)	(t=7.67)	. . .
D1983	0.29	0.28	
	(t=13.38)	(t=12.29)	. . .
D1984	0.23		
	(t=9.12)	. . .	. . .
D1985	0.30		0.06
	(t=11.40)	. . .	(t=1.92)
D1986	0.27		0.03
	(t=1.42)	. . .	(t=0.86)
D1987	0.26		0.02
	(t=7.92)	. . .	(t=0.58)
D1988	0.32		0.08
	(t=12.56)	. . .	(t=2.52)
D1989	0.35		0.10
	(t=13.78)	. . .	(t=3.21)
D1990	0.25		0.01
	(t=7.95)	. . .	(t=0.15)
D1991	0.29		0.04
	(t=11.17)	. . .	(t=1.31)
D1992	0.28		0.03
	(t=11.99)	. . .	(t=1.09)
D1993	0.27		0.02
	(t=9.53)	. . .	(t=0.58)
R^2	0.933	0.930	0.796

as for two subperiods—the 1970–83 period, during which fuel prices were generally rising, and 1984–93, when it had become clear that fuel prices would no longer be rising.[11] The results in table A-2 clearly show that technical progress accelerated after 1975, reaching an apparent peak in the 1988–89 model years. There was no perceptible progress in 1971–75; that is, the coefficients of the time dummies for these years were not statistically significant and therefore the results for an equation including them are not reported. After 1983, there was little apparent technical progress in fuel efficiency. The coefficients of the 1988 and 1989 dummy variables are equal to 0.08 and 0.10 (column 3) respectively, but by the 1990s the coefficients are again statistically insignificant even though CAFE is clearly binding in 1990–93 at 27.5 mpg.

These results decidedly cast doubt on the proposition that government administrators must instruct producers to recognize the need for conservation. Price signals are much more likely to affect the rate of technical improvement in energy conservation than is a change in the CAFE standard.

The Effects of CAFE on Relative Vehicle Prices

To test for the CAFE-induced effect on relative car prices, we use the 268-car database for 1970–93 models to estimate a semilogarithmic hedonic model of the real price, P_i, of the ith passenger car:

(A-6) $LP_i = f(W_i, A_i, R_i, PS_i, PB_i, AT_i, AB_i, ANB_i, S_i, D_i, T_i)$,

where W is weight; A is acceleration (seconds required to go from 0 to 60 mph); R is an index of the quality of ride from *Consumer Reports; PS, PB, AT, AB, ANB* are dummy variables indicating that the car has power steering, power brakes, automatic transmission, air bags, and antilock brakes, respectively; S is a set of three dummy variables reflecting three of the five size classes (intermediate, full size, and luxury); D_i is a set of three dummy variables for the 1973–75 model years, reflecting a period of government price controls; and the Ts are three time trend variables for the 1970s, 1980s, and 1990s, respectively.[12] The real price variable is the manufacturers' suggested retail price of the car deflated by the consumer price index.

Equation A-6 is estimated with two additional variables to capture the effect of CAFE. Given that the vehicle producers should be attempting to shift consumers away from large, powerful cars after 1983 to meet CAFE, the coefficients of W (weight) and A (acceleration) should change after

Table A-3. *The Determinants of Real Vehicle Prices, 1970–93 Model Years*

Variable	Coefficient	t statistic
Constant	7.27	90.42
W	0.00015	7.54
A	−0.011	−3.37
R	0.017	1.25
PB	0.076	3.59
PS	0.077	3.73
AT	0.085	3.99
AB	0.016	0.43
AnB	0.14	3.51
D73	−0.062	2.45
D74	−0.19	5.44
D75	−0.12	4.19
Intermediate	0.036	1.87
Full size	0.078	3.09
Luxury	0.40	9.79
T70s	0.0082	2.77
T80s	0.015	5.88
T90s	0.0085	3.63
W*D84ff	0.00017	7.58
A*D84ff	−0.025	6.11
$\bar{R}^2 = 0.912$	. . .	. . .

Source: See text.

1984. Thus, each variable is entered separately and with a multiplicative post-1983 dummy variable. In table A-3 these variables are shown as W*D84ff and A*D84ff. Each takes the value of zero before 1984 and the value of W or A from 1984 through 1993. We expect W*D84ff to have a significantly positive coefficient, reflecting producer decisions to place a price premium on heavy cars, and A*D84ff to have a negative coefficient, reflecting producer decisions to raise the price of acceleration from 1984 through 1993.

The estimates of equation A-6 shown in table A-3 confirm our expectations in almost every respect. The only coefficients that are not statistically significant are those for air bags and intermediate-size class. The coefficient for car weight more than doubles after 1983, and the coefficient for acceleration more than triples. It is thus clear that beginning in 1984, the vehicle producers used their pricing discretion with a vengeance to attempt to move customers to smaller, less powerful vehicles. CAFE has induced downsizing and a substantial mix shift from vehicle producers to achieve a 27.5 mpg.

The Effects of a Fuel Tax:
Empirical Methodology and Results

T HIS APPENDIX provides a detailed description of the methodology and the results of the empirical estimates summarized in chapter 3. We focus on the determinants of vehicle-miles traveled (*VMT*) and vehicle fuel efficiency (*MPG*).

Vehicle-Miles Traveled

Our analysis of *VMT* is based on time-series data for the 1960–91 period.[1] Vehicle-miles of travel and *MPG* are derived from Federal Highway Administration estimates; the real price of fuel is the consumer price index for motor fuel divided by the overall CPI; real GDP is from the Commerce Department's Bureau of Economic Analysis; and the number of licensed drivers (*DRIVERS*) is based on Federal Highway Administration estimates. The equation estimated from time-series data is logarithmic:

$$\text{(B-1) Log } VMT_t = a_0 + a_1 \text{ Log } p_{f,t} + a_2 \text{ Log } MPG_t + a_3 \text{ Log } GDP_t \\ + a_4 \text{ Log } DRIVERS_t + a_5 D74_t + a_6 D79_t + u_t.$$

D74 and *D79* are dummy variables for the years of significant gasoline rationing, 1974 and 1979, and u_t is a random error term.

Equation B-1 is estimated with no lags and with Almon distributed lags for the real price variable. The results for both passenger cars and all light vehicles are shown in table B-1. The results provide no support for the model that includes average mpg. The real price of gasoline provides significantly negative coefficients, as expected, and a distributed-lag formulation of these prices (using the current price and four years of lags) seems to work best.[2] The long-run price elasticity of *VMT*, using the

Table B-1. *Estimates of the Determinants of Vehicle-Miles of Travel,*
1966–92

Variable	Passenger cars		Light-duty vehicles	
Constant	1.50	1.99	−1.06	−0.91
Log p_f	−0.10	...	−0.10	...
	(t=2.83)		(t=3.33)	
Log p_f (sum of five-year Almon lags)	...	−0.30	...	−0.23
		(t=5.34)		(t=5.96)
Log GDP_t	0.42	0.44	0.52	0.55
	(t=3.44)	(t=3.47)	(t=4.79)	(t=5.54)
Log $DRIVERS_t$	0.75	0.70	0.91	0.89
	(t=3.79)	(t=4.46)	(t=5.89)	(t=7.26)
D74	−0.019	−0.027	−0.019	−0.027
	(t=2.30)	(t=3.32	(t=2.54)	(t=3.90)
D79	−0.020	−0.025	−0.016	−0.021
	(t=2.49)	(t=3.08)	(t=2.08)	(t=3.10)
Log MPG_t	0.012	...	0.043	...
	(t=0.08)		(t=0.35)	
$\bar{R}^2$	0.995	0.995	0.998	0.998
DW	1.937	1.665	1.962	1.896
ρ_1	1.44	1.20	1.27	1.14
ρ_2	−0.55	−0.70	−0.42	−0.78

Source: See text.

Almon lag structure, is between −0.20 and −0.30 for both categories
of vehicles. If we eliminate the years in which CAFE is binding, 1984
to 1991, the estimated elasticity rises to −0.31, substantially below
(in absolute value) the −0.55 average that Carol Dahl reports in her
1986 survey.[3]

Miles per Gallon

The equation estimated over the 1966–92 time period[4] for mpg is of
the following form:

(B-2) $$MPG_t = f(p_{f,t} \cdot \cdot p_{f,t-4}, p_{s,t-4}, TIME_t).$$

In addition, the CAFE standard is introduced into equation B-2 in two
ways. First, as in chapter 2, it is equal to one before 1978 and the ratio
of each year's CAFE standard to the average fuel economy in 1974 (the

Table B-2. *Estimates of the Determinants of Fuel-Economy for Passenger Cars, Using-Time Series Data, 1966–92*

Variable time period	New cars			All cars on the road		
	1968–92	1968–92	1968–83	1966–92	1966–92	1966–83
Constant	1.86	1.93	1.49	2.36	2.52	2.79
Time	0.026	0.032	0.024	0.012	0.017	−0.0003
	(t=5.18)	(t=10.36)	(t=10.88)	(t=2.76)	(t=3.41)	(t=0.26)
Log $p_{s,t-4}$	0.27	0.29	0.73	...	...	...
	(t=1.91)	(t=1.82)	(t=5.81)			
Log p_f	0.39	0.42	0.43	0.004	0.087	0.63
(Sum of four-year Almon lags)	(t=2.64)	(t=2.62)	(t=3.51)	(t=0.33)	(t=0.57)	(t=10.87)
CAFER (lagged two years)	0.25 (t=2.15)	...	...	0.15 (t=1.67)	...	...
CAFE84ff	...	0.082 (t=1.34)	...	...	−0.38 (t=1.77)	...
$\bar{R}^2$	0.986	0.984	0.987	0.989	0.990	0.974
DW	2.254	1.942	2.163	2.060	2.362	2.259
ρ_1	1.03	0.96	0.08	1.51	1.64	0.86
ρ_2	−0.50	−0.37	−0.64	−0.60	−0.71	−0.58

Source: See text.

year before the legislation was passed) for all subsequent years (*CAFER*). Second, it is equal to one for all years before 1984, the year in which CAFE generally becomes binding, and to *CAFER* thereafter. This variable is denoted *CAFE84ff*. The second approach assumes that CAFE has no role until 1984 in vehicle production or purchase decisions because producers respond only to fuel-price signals in designing and pricing their vehicles. Equation B-2 is estimated in logarithmic form separately for passenger cars and for light trucks.

The estimates of equation B-2 for passenger cars are shown in table B-2. The first three columns exhibit the results for the average new car, 1968–92; the second group of three columns shows the results for all cars on the road.[5] Note the significantly positive effect of fuel prices, estimated with Almon lags, especially for the 1968–83 or 1966–83 periods.[6] Before CAFE became binding, MPG responded to changes in fuel prices with a long-run elasticity of between 0.43 and 0.63. After CAFE was binding, approximately 1984, the fuel-price elasticity falls. In no case is the coefficient of *CAFE84ff* statistically significant, but the coefficient of *CAFER*, lagged two years, is statistically significant for new passenger

Table B-3. *Estimates of the Determinants of Fuel Economy for New Passenger Cars, U.S. Big Three Producers, 1978–92*

Variable	Chrysler	Chrysler	Ford	General Motors
Constant	2.39	2.43	2.49	2.55
TIME	0.037	0.030	0.016	0.011
	(t=6.86)	(t=2.27)	(t=2.02)	(t=1.07)
Log P_f	0.65	0.58	0.30	0.15
(Sum of four-year Almon Lags)	(t=4.14)	(t=3.46)	(t=3.07)	(t=1.17)
CAFER	. . .	0.085	0.24	0.28
(lagged two years)		(t=0.44)	(t=2.21)	(t=2.09)
$\bar{R}^2$	0.880	0.861	0.914	0.905
DW	2.163	1.596	2.072	2.261
ρ_1	0.703	0.466	0.340	0.604
ρ_2	0.418	. . .	−0.492	−0.567

Source: See text.

cars. This suggests that new-car manufacturers adjust to CAFE after a lag, through weight reductions and relative price changes for large and small cars.

Lagged steel prices are significant in the new-car average fuel-economy equations, but not in the estimates for all cars on the road. For this reason, results that include lagged steel prices are not reported on the right-hand side of table B-2.

Note the significant exogenous rate of technical progress in the average mpg of new cars: 2.4 to 3.2 percent a year. The rate of progress for all cars on the road is much lower because only a small share of cars is replaced each year.

The results for individual manufacturers, shown in table B-3, are in stark contrast to those reported by David Greene in an earlier paper.[7] When the mpg ratings for the Big Three manufacturers are used to estimate equation B-2, very different results are obtained for each company (table B-3). The most rapid temporal rate of progress in mpg, as measured by the coefficient of *TIME*, is for Chrysler, but Chrysler's progress is much more highly responsive to fuel prices than is the progress for the other two manufacturers. Ford and GM's mpg ratings respond to CAFE, but only after a two-year lag, while Chrysler's mpg rating is not significantly affected by CAFE.

Table B-4. *Estimates of the Determinants of Fuel Economy for Light Trucks, Using Time-Series Data, 1966–92*

Variable	New trucks		All light trucks on the road		
	1975–92	1975–92	1966–92	1966–92	1966–83
Constant	2.05	2.29	2.23	2.17	2.19
TIME	0.019	0.030	0.017	0.016	0.015
	(t=2.88)	(t=9.30)	(t=17.88)	(t=27.76)	(t=10.93)
Log p_f	0.59	0.53	0.065	0.073	0.12
(Sum of four-	(t=5.95)	(t=4.73)	(t=1.13)	(t=2.16)	(t=2.35)
year					
Almon lags)					
CAFER	0.43	...	−0.082	...	...
(lagged two	(t=1.70)		(t=1.63)		
years)					
$\bar{R}^2$	0.910	0.901	0.991	0.990	0.981
DW	1.817	1.624	2.072	2.086	2.060
ρ_1	0.13	0.29	0.79	0.81	0.64
ρ_2	...	...	−0.49	−0.38	−0.31

Source: See text.

Greene estimated a complex pooled cross-section, time-series model of individual company average mpg ratings based on a theory that the impact of fuel prices and CAFE vary according to the proximity of realized mpg to the CAFE standard. This approach is of rather dubious validity; why should all vehicle producers respond in the same way to changes in prices or CAFE standards? Indeed, our results suggest that they did not. Moreover, assume that one company produces mostly large, powerful cars and another produces very small subcompacts. What if neither changes its vehicle designs very much in response to changes in fuel prices or fuel-economy regulation, but consumers can migrate between them? Then estimating the effect of CAFE or fuel prices on the mpg level of *individual* manufacturers may lead to the erroneous conclusion that CAFE induced a major response from each manufacturer when it simply induced Buick buyers to switch to existing Plymouth Shadows.

The results for light trucks, those with two axles and four wheels, are shown in table B-4. The results for new trucks, on the left-hand side of the table, are estimated only over the 1975–91 period because average mpg data do not exist for earlier years. The results for all light trucks on the road are estimated for years after 1965 because the Federal Highway Administration did not produce comparable data for earlier years. Once again, fuel prices seem much more important than CAFE regulation in driving new-truck mpg, but less effective in influencing on-the-road mpg. The real price of steel does not affect truck mpg and is therefore dropped from the equation in this exercise. The temporal rate of progress, the coefficient of TIME, is similar for trucks and passenger cars even though light-truck CAFE is a much less severe constraint.

Notes

Notes to Chapter 1

1. Former French foreign minister Jean-François Poncet, quoted in the *Washington Post*, March 27, 1992, p. A21.

2. The goal was most recently reaffirmed in the Comprehensive National Energy Policy Act of 1992. The act calls for a further reduction in the nation's oil dependence from the 1990 level of approximately 40 percent of total energy use to 35 percent by the year 2005.

3. See Pietro S. Nivola, "Gridlocked or Gaining Ground? U.S. Regulatory Reform in the Energy Sector," *Brookings Review*, vol. 11 (Summer 1993), pp. 36–41.

4. Joel Darmstadter, Joy Dunkerley, and Jack Alterman, *How Industrial Societies Use Energy: A Comparative Analysis* (Johns Hopkins University Press for Resources for the Future, 1977), pp. 100, 191.

5. Energy Information Administration, *Annual Energy Outlook, 1993* (Department of Energy, 1992), p. 90.

6. General Accounting Office, *Other Nations' Policies to Reduce Oil and Coal Use in Transport and Industry* (May 1993), p. 42.

7. Energy Information Administration, *Monthly Energy Review* (Department of Energy, September 1994), p. 15. Energy Information Administration, *Annual Energy Outlook 1994 with Projections to 2010* (Department of Energy, 1994), p. 68. Since 1985, net imports have risen at an average rate of over 7 percent a year. James Tanner, "U.S. Crude-Oil Output Hits 35-Year Low and Many Say Turnaround Is Unlikely," *Wall Street Journal*, July 15, 1993, p. A2.

8. See Douglas Ostrom, "Oil Prices and the Japanese Economy," *JEI Report*, no. 33A, Washington, Japan Economic Institute, August 24, 1990, p. 5. See also Clay Chandler and Marcus W. Brauchli, "How Japan Became So Energy-Efficient: It Leaned on Industry," *Wall Street Journal*, September 10, 1990, pp. A1, A4.

9. Fried and Trezise conclude, "Another sizable oil disruption has to be rated a possibility, simply because so much of the world's oil needs, a growing propor-

tion in fact, is supplied from an area of chronic volatility—the Middle East." Edward R. Fried and Philip H. Trezise, *Oil Security: Retrospect and Prospect* (Brookings, 1993), p. 87. In 1973 the principal oil exporter to the United States was Canada, which sold America 1.32 million barrels a day, whereas the United States bought only 0.49 million barrels a day from Saudi Arabia. In 1992 Saudi Arabia was by far the largest supplier, selling the United States 1.72 million barrels a day. Energy Information Administration, *Monthly Energy Review* (Department of Energy, July 1993). It should be recalled that even the minishock of 1990 had appreciable economic consequences. Oil prices jumped temporarily to $35 a barrel and helped precipitate a recession in the ensuing months.

10. Alan J. Krupnick, "Vehicle Emissions, Urban Smog, and Clear Air Policy," Discussion Paper QE92-09 (Washington: Resources for the Future, 1992). Light-duty vehicles in urban areas have accounted for approximately 45 percent of hydrocarbon and nitrogen oxide emissions (the principal causes of smog) and about 80 percent of carbon monoxide emissions. Tougher pollution controls have had difficulty bringing these levels down, not only because of the continual increase in VMTs, but because of travel conditions. Vehicles operating on increasingly congested roads emit more noxious effluents per unit of time or distance. Increased trip volumes pose an equally large problem: cold starts account for most of a vehicle's harmful HC and CO emissions.

11. Michael Cameron, *Transportation Efficiency: Tackling Southern California's Air Pollution and Congestion* (Oakland, Calif.: Environmental Defense Fund and Regional Institute of Southern California, 1991), p. 21.

12. As of 1991, ninety-eight metropolitan areas, with a total population of 140 million people, did not meet ozone air quality standards under the Clean Air Act. Forty-two metropolitan areas violated the act's carbon monoxide standards. General Accounting Office, *Energy Policy: Options to Reduce Environmental and Other Costs of Gasoline Consumption* (September 1992), p. 12. The number of metropolitan areas with an alarming annual smog problem is much smaller. The Environmental Protection Agency is required by law to establish, in a very cautious fashion, national ambient air quality standards for each pollutant. The standard for ozone, for example, is set at 0.12 parts per million daily maximum one-hour concentration, not to be exceeded more than once a year on average at any monitoring site in the region. Though entire metropolitan regions are classified as "attainment" or "nonattainment" areas, a reading of 0.12 parts per million at a single recording station may be deemed in "exceedance." In the 1990–92 period, forty-five areas that were "nonattainment" actually exceeded the 0.12 ozone standard for fewer than one and a half days a year. Another twenty-seven experienced fewer than three days annually in which measurements exceeded 0.12. Only nine of the ninety-eight "nonattainment" areas had more than seven days a year of "exceedance" readings. Based on unpublished data, Environmental Protection Agency, Office of Air Quality Planning and Standards, "Ozone and Carbon Monoxide, Air Quality Data Update Fact Sheet," Washington, 1993.

13. Congress finally authorized the use of force in the Gulf crisis on January 12, 1991. The vote in the House was 250 in favor, 183 against. Republican support for the resolution was almost unanimous, whereas the Democratic majority divided two-to-one against the resolution. The vote in the Senate was 52 in favor,

47 against. Again, there was near unanimity on the Republican side. Democratic senators opposed the resolution 45 to 10. *Congressional Quarterly Almanac 1991* (Washington: Congressional Quarterly, Inc., 1992), pp. 2-H, 2-S.

14. Consumption rose an average of 1.3 percent annually between 1973 and 1989, but was 2.6 percent a year after 1983.

15. By 1988 the average U.S. price of gasoline (taxes included) had sagged to $1.06 a gallon. In real terms (1991 dollars), gasoline prices were 40 percent higher in 1947! Increasingly efficient automobiles and lower gasoline prices have combined to create a strong incentive to drive with abandon in recent years. In real terms, the cost of gasoline per mile driven dropped from 13.2 cents in 1980 to 5.4 cents in 1991. See Daniel Yergin, *Gasoline and the American People* (Cambridge, Mass.: Cambridge Energy Research Associates, June 1991), pp. 2, 8.

16. Based on figures from Motor Vehicle Manufacturers Association, *Motor Vehicle Facts and Figures '92* (Detroit: MVMA, 1992), p. 85. The 28 mpg improvement is almost certainly an exaggeration. The Environmental Protection Agency's ratings assume that only 55 percent of all vehicle mileage is on urban roads. This figure is now widely considered low. Moreover, worsening urban traffic congestion and shorter length of trips have increased fuel intensity, perhaps by as much as 15 percent to 25 percent more than official estimates.

17. Estimated from Federal Highway Administration, *Highway Statistics 1991* (Department of Transportation, 1992), p. 193, table VM-1; and Federal Highway Administration, *Highway Statistics, Summary to 1985* (Department of Transportation, 1987), p. 232, table VM-201A.

18. Increasingly stringent regulation (for safety and for emissions, as well as for gas economy) is partly responsible for the slower turnover. Tougher regulatory standards entail higher new-car prices and, therefore, lower new-car sales.

19. Estimated from Oak Ridge National Laboratory, *Transportation Energy Data Book: Edition 13* (Oak Ridge, Tenn.: ORNL, 1993), p. 2-7; and Motor Vehicle Manufacturers Association, *Motor Vehicle Facts and Figures '92*, pp. 13, 82.

20. If the present trend persists, vans, pickups, and jeeps will gain the dominant share of the market by the end of the decade. Mary Beth Vander Schaaf, "Automotive News Staff Looks at 1999," *Automotive News*, November 29, 1989, p. 236. This mix of vehicles is troublesome from an energy and environmental standpoint. Light trucks are generally 25 percent less fuel efficient than automobiles and spew into the air more hydrocarbons, nitrogen oxides, and carbon monoxide per mile of travel.

21. See, for instance, Charles Lave, "The Spread of the Automobile Demon: What Can We Do?" paper prepared for the 1993 annual meeting of the Western Political Science Association.

22. Although population growth in the United States is slowing, the populations of most European countries and of Japan are growing even more slowly. During the 1980s, the U.S. population grew by 16 million, while Europe's increased by only 6 million persons. Several countries, including Austria, Belgium, Denmark, and Sweden, registered no population growth at all. It is hard to see how VMT growth rates can converge internationally without faster population growth abroad. Growing participation of women—from 32 percent of the work

force in 1950 to almost 46 percent in 1992—has also been a major factor in the continuing rise of vehicle miles traveled in the United States. Female labor participation is expected to approach 50 percent of the work force by the year 2005—far higher than projected levels in Germany and Japan. Data from Bureau of Labor Statistics, "People Patterns," *Wall Street Journal*, December 31, 1993, p. A9. At the limit, of course, saturation of vehicles is logically inevitable. The limit, however, is hardly imminent. From 1980 to 1990 the absolute number of registered vehicles rose 34.4 million, or 55.2 percent more than the country's population. Part of the reason was that an increasing percentage of suburban households are advancing beyond two vehicles per household to three or more. In various suburbs of the Washington, D.C., area, for example, the number of households with three or more vehicles increased by as much as 50 percent during the 1980s. See Dan Beyers, "Not the Family Car, but the Family Fleet," *Washington Post*, April 4, 1993, p. A1.

23. Lest it be thought that this sample of countries misrepresents the overall trend, the IEA *World Energy Outlook* (Paris: OECD, June 1991), which reports the average annual mileage for the light-duty vehicle fleets of all members of the OECD, observed a widening gap between North America and the rest of the OECD countries after 1987.

24. See Anthony Downs, *Stuck in Traffic: Coping with Peak-Hour Traffic Congestion* (Brookings, 1992), pp. 20–21. According to the Department of Transportation, average miles driven per vehicle increased 22 percent between 1983 and 1990.

25. The fuel intensity of the American light vehicular fleet was more than 13 liters per 100 kilometers in 1988, compared with a European fleet average of 9 liters per 100 km. Lee Schipper and others, "Mind the Gap: The Vicious Circle of Measuring Automobile Fuel Use," *Energy Policy*, vol. 21 (December 1993), p. 1181. The persisting disparity occurred largely because of the expansion of light trucks in the U.S. passenger fleet. Between 1982 and 1987, the total amount of gasoline used by U.S. automobiles rose very slightly, by only 1 percent. Consumption by light trucks, however, grew by 35 percent. International Energy Agency, *Fuel Efficiency of Passenger Cars* (Paris: OECD/IEA, 1991), pp. 9–11.

26. In 1988 as in 1970, the United States consumed just under twice as much gasoline and diesel/gas per vehicle in overall road transport as the average for the OECD countries of Europe. (The ratio with respect to Japan actually seems to have deteriorated, to more than twice as much fuel consumed.) Organization of Economic Cooperation and Development, *The State of the Environment* (Paris: OECD, 1991), pp. 214, 216. Part of the reason for the relatively high average consumption of U.S. vehicles is that they have been logging more miles. Whereas the annual distance traveled per vehicle remained stable in Germany and Japan, and fell sharply in Italy, during the period 1974 to 1988, it increased in the United States. International Energy Agency, *Fuel Efficiency of Passenger Cars* (Paris: OECD/IEA, 1991), p. 18.

27. GDP data from Central Intelligence Agency, *The World Factbook, 1993–94* (Washington: Brassey's, 1993), pp. 127, 174, 244, 239. For fuel use data, see Schipper and others, "Mind the Gap," pp. 1173–90, and Schipper and others,

"Fuel Prices and Economy: Factors Affecting Land Travel," *Transport Policy*, vol. 1, no. 1 (1993), pp. 6–20.

28. IEA, *Fuel Efficiency*, p. 50.

29. John Pucher, "Urban Travel Behavior as the Outcome of Public Policy," *Journal of the American Planning Association*, vol. 54 (Autumn 1988), pp. 512–13.

30. The tax component of U.S. gasoline retail prices was a mere 15 percent of the average of Germany, Great Britain, France, and Italy. GAO, *Energy Policy*, pp. 9, 21, 22.

31. For example, one thoughtful critic observes that in Western Europe and Japan, where gasoline prices are $2 to $4 a gallon, new car fuel economies are "only" 27 mpg to 36 mpg. Deborah Gordon, *Steering a New Course: Transportation, Energy, and the Environment* (Cambridge, Mass.: Union of Concerned Scientists, 1991), p. 118. Twenty-seven to 36 mpg is a very wide range. It was not surprising that in Germany, Japan, France, Sweden, and England, where real fuel prices after the oil price crash of 1986 fell below their 1973 levels, little improvement occurred in the average fuel economy of their vehicle fleets. But in Denmark and Italy, where major tax increases raised real prices to levels higher than in 1973, fuel economy did continue to improve. Lee Schipper and others, "Fuel Prices, Automobile Fuel Economy, and Fuel Use for Land Travel" (Berkeley, Calif.: Lawrence Berkeley Laboratory, 1992), p. 7. In Italy, by 1987, the light-duty vehicle fleet was almost twice as efficient as that of the United States. James J. MacKenzie, "Toward a Sustainable Energy Future: The Critical Role of Rational Energy Pricing," *WRI Issues and Ideas* (Washington: World Resource Institute, May 1991), p. 7.

32. Schipper and others, "Mind the Gap," p. 1181.

33. Clearly, the physical shortages and administrative rationing accompanying the two oil shocks also contributed substantially to these results.

34. See Joe W. Russell, Jr., *Economic Disincentives for Energy Conservation* (Ballinger, 1979), p. 75; see also *Gallup Opinion Index*, Report 149 (December 1977), p. 22, and Report 164 (March 1979), p. 17.

35. When Gallup queried a sample of motorists in mid-1979 about the feasibility of giving up driving for the equivalent of one day each week, 2 percent said they didn't know, 14 percent claimed it would be fairly difficult, 22 percent said very difficult, and 62 percent said not very difficult. *Gallup Opinion Index*, Report 170 (September 1979), p. 22.

36. Imports of crude oil from these three shaky sources in 1991 reached almost 30 million barrels. National Energy Information Center, *Petroleum Supply Annual 1991*, vol. 1 (Department of Energy, 1992), p. 54, table 21. The long-run price elasticity of gasoline used for work trips has been calculated as approximately –0.35. See Charles River Associates, *Price Elasticities of Demand for Transportation Fuels* (Cambridge, Mass., 1976), p. 42. We estimate that U.S. commuters used approximately 890 million barrels of crude oil in 1991. Department of Energy, International Energy Agency, *Supplement to the Annual Energy Outlook* (March 1994), pp. 124–25, tables 24 and 25.

37. D'Vera Cohn and Stephen C. Fehr, "Lone Drivers Clogging Area's Subur-

ban Roads," *Washington Post*, April 21, 1992, p. A1. Nationally, according to the 1990 census, almost 75 percent of all workers drove to work alone, creating an average peak-hour load factor of only 1.13 persons per car—seemingly a vast underutilization of the rolling-stock resources.

38. Wharton Econometric Forecasting Associates, *Economic Analysis of Gasoline Tax Increases* (Philadelphia: WEFA, May 1987).

39. A sober study of the externalities associated with driving in the Los Angeles basin estimated that a better accounting of the social costs would add 50 percent to the current private costs of owning, maintaining, and operating an automobile in the region. Cameron, *Transportation Efficiency*, p. 21.

40. See Yergin, *Gasoline and the American People*, pp. 17, 21. Personal consumption expenditures for transportation as a percentage of total personal consumption expenditures were 12.4 percent in 1989, compared with 14 percent in 1972 (in constant 1988 dollars). Oak Ridge National Laboratory, *Transportation Energy Data Book: Edition 14* (Oak Ridge, Tenn.: ORNL, May 1994), p. 2-32.

41. Several studies of the effects of raising the tax on gasoline have estimated that an increase of 10 cents a gallon (excluding diesel fuel) would reduce real output by 0.2 to 0.3 percent, while causing the consumer price index to rise by 0.3 to 0.4 percent. For analyses of the effects of motor fuel tax increases, see Mark W. French, "Economic Analysis of Gasoline Tax Increases," in House Committee on Public Works and Transportation, *Proposals to Increase the Federal Gasoline and Diesel Taxes for Deficit Reduction Purposes*, 100 Cong. 1 sess. (Government Printing Office, 1987); Energy Information Administration, *Cost and Benefit Analysis of a Motor Fuels Tax* (Department of Energy, March 1987); Department of Energy, *Energy Security: A Report to the President of the United States* (March 1987), pp. E1–E7; and Brian W. Cashell and Salvatore Lazzari, "Macroeconomic Effects of Increases in the Gasoline Tax," 93-213 E, Washington, Congressional Research Service, February 10, 1993.

42. See Congressional Budget Office, *Federal Taxation of Tobacco, Alcoholic Beverages, and Motor Fuels* (GPO, June 1990), pp. 88–91.

43. In 1990 the U.S. trade deficit, minus shipments of foreign oil, would have been $39.5 billion instead of $101.7 billion. Pietro S. Nivola, *Regulating Unfair Trade* (Brookings, 1993), p. 181, note 38.

44. See CBO, *Federal Taxation*, p. 90.

45. For an example of an elegant but regrettably unrealistic proposal, see Robert J. Barro, "Deficit Reduction Made Easy," *Wall Street Journal*, May 26, 1993, p. A18.

46. Energy Information Administration, *Residential Transportation Energy Consumption Survey: Consumption Patterns of Household Vehicles, 1985* (Department of Energy, April 1987).

47. See Matthew L. Wald, "50-Cents-a-Gallon Tax Could Buy a Whole Lot," *New York Times*, October 18, 1992, p. E5. Note that other estimates of regional incidence find a narrow disparity. See, for instance, William U. Chandler and Andrew K. Nicholls, "Assessing Carbon Emissions Control Strategies: A Carbon Tax or a Gasoline Tax," ACEEE Policy Paper 3 (Washington: American Council for an Energy-Efficient Economy, February 1990), pp. 24–25.

48. See James M. Poterba, "Is the Gasoline Tax Regressive?" in David Brad-

ford, ed., *Tax Policy and the Economy* (MIT Press, 1991), pp. 145–64. Low-income households receive a substantial share of their incomes in the form of indexed transfer payments that reflect the tax on gasoline. Therefore, the lowest income decile may bear a lower burden from gasoline taxation than any other decile. See chapter 3 in this volume.

49. There has been a robust direct correlation between state levels of population per square mile and the average price of natural gas, as well as residential and industrial electric rates. See Pietro S. Nivola, *The Politics of Energy Conservation* (Brookings, 1986), p. 207.

Notes to Chapter 2

1. There have been three small increases in the federal gasoline tax since 1975, but none was promoted as part of a conservation policy.

2. Joseph P. Kalt, *The Economics and Politics of Oil Price Regulation: Federal Policy in the Post-Embargo Era* (MIT Press, 1981).

3. The EPA's tests of vehicles had been developed for the purpose of certifying compliance with the Clean Air Act. The measurement of mpg during such tests could be achieved at nominal additional cost.

4. The standards for light trucks, as shown in table 2-1, were initially separated into two standards—one for four-wheel drive vehicles and one for two-wheel drive vehicles—for model years 1979–81. These standards were combined in the 1982 model year.

5. The CAFE standards could be binding even when real fuel prices are high if producers decide to ensure against potential future fuel-price declines by exceeding the standard so as to accumulate credits that carry over for three years to meet future CAFE deficiencies.

6. *Economic Report of the President, February 1994*, pp. 335, 357.

7. See the empirical results in appendix A.

8. Even in this period, there were a few foreign suppliers, such as Volkswagen, who competed successfully in the U.S. market, though not at the scale of the Japanese in the late 1970s and 1980s.

9. Light trucks include small pickups, vans, and sport-utility vehicles.

10. Both sought some relief from CAFE in 1986–90 when gasoline prices plummeted, but neither company was a strong opponent of the program. Indeed, the legal proceeding that sought to reverse the Department of Transportation's 1990 CAFE standards was filed by two public interest groups, the Competitive Enterprise Institute and Consumer Alert, not Ford or GM. Surprisingly, Chrysler opposed a reduction in CAFE in 1986–87, perhaps because it believed that a 27.5 mpg CAFE would hurt GM and Ford in the short run or that it would so raise large-car prices as to make Chrysler's reentry into this market attractive.

11. The automobile companies formed the Coalition for Vehicle Choice to lobby against CAFE.

12. Toyota produces more Camrys than Corollas in the United States, importing small cars, such as the Tercel, and its luxury car, the Lexus. Honda pro-

duces more Accords than Civics in the United States but imports the Acura. Nissan has recently moved to produce its midsized sedan, the Altima, in the United States while importing the Maxima and the Infiniti.

13. There has been speculation that Ford might pursue this strategy with its Crown Victoria–Grand Marquis large-car line, but it still reports that 80 percent of the parts are domestic for these models. AAMA, "Key Facts about America's Car Companies" (Washington, 1994).

14. John E. Kwoka, "The Limits of Market-Oriented Regulatory Techniques: The Case of Automotive Fuel Economy," *Quarterly Journal of Economics*, vol. 98 (November 1983), pp. 695–704; and Andrew N. Kleit, "The Effect of Annual Changes in Automobile Fuel Economy Standards," *Journal of Regulatory Economics*, vol. 2 (June 1990), pp. 151–72.

15. Robert W. Crandall and others, *Regulating the Automobile* (Brookings, 1986), chap. 6.

16. Robert A. Leone and Thomas W. Parkinson, *Conserving Energy: Is There a Better Way? A Study of Corporate Average Fuel Economy*, prepared for the Association of International Automobile Manufacturers (May 1990), pp. 31–35.

17. All values expressed by Leone and Parkinson are in 1990 dollars. It should be noted that they do not analyze the full societal welfare gains from reductions in fuel consumption, including reductions in pollution, congestion, or energy dependence. Because they are comparing the effects of a fuel tax with CAFE in achieving a given level of conservation, there is no need to address these external effects.

18. Charles River Associates, "Policy Alternatives for Reducing Petroleum Use and Greenhouse Gas Emissions," prepared for the Motor Vehicle Manufacturers Association, Detroit, September 1991, pp. 64–70.

19. David L. Greene, "CAFE or Price?: An Analysis of the Effects of Fuel Economy Regulation and Gasoline Price on New Car mpg, 1978–89," *Energy Journal*, vol. 11 (July 1990), pp. 37–57; David L. Greene and Jin-Tan Liu, "Automobile Fuel Economy Improvements and Consumer Surplus," *Transportation Research*, vol. 22A (1988), pp. 203–18; and David L. Greene, Nabil Meddeb, and Jin-Tan Liu, "Vehicle Stock Modeling of Highway Energy Use: Tunisian and U.S. Applications," *Energy Policy*, vol. 14 (October 1986), pp. 437–46.

20. Robert W. Crandall, "Policy Watch: Corporate Average Fuel Economy Standards," *Journal of Economic Perspectives*, vol. 6 (Spring 1992), pp. 171–80.

21. See the discussion of this result in appendix A.

22. These results are shown in appendix A.

23. Technically, these are coefficients of dummy variables for each model year, 1970 through 1993, in a pooled time-series, cross-section regression. See appendix A.

24. When CAFE is included without the lagged real fuel price, it is statistically significant. However, CAFE does not significantly add to the explained variance of the equation when lagged real fuel prices are included. See appendix A.

25. See appendix A for these results.

26. We provide empirical evidence on these propositions in appendix A.

27. *Competitive Enterprise Institute and Consumer Alert v. NHTSA*, 956 F.2d 321 (D.C. Cir., 1992). This challenge was based in part on research reported

by Robert W. Crandall and John D. Graham, "The Effect of Fuel-Economy Standards on Automobile Safety," *Journal of Law and Economics*, vol. 32 (April 1989), pp. 94–118.

28. The National Highway Traffic Safety Administration has commissioned several studies on the effects of vehicle size. See, for example, "Effect of Car Size on Fatality and Injury Risk," 1991.

29. Leonard Evans, *Traffic Safety and the Driver* (Van Nostrand Reinholt, 1991), p. 77; and Crandall and Graham, "Effect of Fuel-Economy Standards," p. 115.

Notes to Chapter 3

1. Carol A. Dahl, "Gasoline Demand Survey," *Energy Journal*, vol. 7 (January 1986), pp. 67–82; and Carol Dahl and Thomas Sterner, "Analyzing Gasoline Demand Elasticities: A Survey," *Energy Economics*, vol. 13 (July 1991), pp. 203–10.

2. Margaret A. Walls, Alan J. Krupnick, and H. Carter Hood, "Estimating the Demand for Vehicle-Miles-Traveled Using Household Survey Data: Results from the 1990 Nationwide Personal Transportation Survey," Discussion Paper ENR 93-25 (Washington: Resources for the Future, September 1993), p. 21.

3. Dahl, "Gasoline Demand," p. 73.

4. The law allows manufacturers to carry back or forward any excess CAFE (mpg) ratings for three years. As a result, those companies that exceeded the CAFE standard of 22.0 mpg in the 1981 model year, for example, could carry these excess "credits" forward as far as the 1984 model year to meet the 27.0 mpg standard in that year.

5. National Highway Traffic Safety Administration, "Summary of Fuel Economy Performance" (Department of Transportation, September 1993).

6. David L. Greene, "CAFE or Price?: An Analysis of the Effects of Fuel Economy Regulation and Gasoline Price on New Car mpg, 1978–89," *Energy Journal*, vol. 11 (July 1990), pp. 37–57; David L. Greene and Jin-Tan Liu, "Automobile Fuel Economy Improvements and Consumer Surplus," *Transportation Research*, vol. 22A (1988), pp. 203–18; David L. Greene, Nabil Meddeb, and Jin-Tan Liu, "Vehicle Stock Modeling of Highway Energy Use: Tunisian and U.S. Applications," *Energy Policy*, vol. 14 (October 1986), pp. 437–46; and Dermot Gately, "The U.S. Demand for Highway Travel and Motor Fuel," *Energy Journal*, vol. 11 (July 1990), pp. 59–73.

7. The analysis is limited to 1966–92 because the data compiled by the Federal Highway Administration for the years before 1966 are not consistent with the data for the more recent time period.

8. Specifically, we allow real fuel prices to drive average vehicle weight and vehicle miles of travel in the equations estimated in appendixes A and B. Engine displacement is driven by vehicle weight and exogenous technical change, and technical fuel efficiency occurs at the rate estimated for 1970–83 by the cross-sectional database used in appendix A.

9. James M. Poterba, "Is the Gasoline Tax Regressive?" in David Bradford,

ed., *Tax Policy and the Economy 5* (National Bureau of Economic Research and MIT Press, 1991), pp. 145–64.

10. We report Poterba's truncated distribution, which excludes the bottom 5 percent of the income distribution as unduly affected by random measurement errors ("noise," in Poterba's parlance).

11. Poterba also shows the ratio of expenditures less automobile purchase (an investment) plus imputed owner-occupied housing rent. These adjustments lead to slightly greater regressivity in the eighth to tenth deciles.

12. Howard Chernick and Andrew Reschovsky, "Is the Gasoline Tax Regressive?" Discussion Paper 980-92 (University of Wisconsin-Madison, Institute for Research on Poverty, August 1992).

13. *Economic Report of the President, February 1994*, p. 286.

14. Gasoline taxes obviously account for an even smaller share of consumption because they currently account for only about 30 percent of the retail price of gasoline.

15. Poterba, "Is the Gasoline Tax Regressive?" p. 158.

16. Chernick and Reschovsky, "Is the Gasoline Tax Regressive?" p. 26.

17. It was for this reason that the Bush Council of Economic Advisers did not press for gasoline tax increases. The council was concerned about their effect on transfer payments and, therefore, the feedback effect on future deficits.

18. Howard Chernick and Andrew Reschovsky, "The Gas Tax and the Deficit: Is It Fair to Use One to Cure the Other?" Working Paper 19 (University of Wisconsin-Madison, Robert M. La Follette Institute of Public Affairs, July 1993), pp. 12–14.

19. Authors' calculations updating figures in Robert W. Crandall, "Policy Watch: Corporate Average Fuel Economy Standards," *Journal of Economic Perspectives*, vol. 6 (September 1992), pp. 171–80.

20. Brian W. Cashell and Salvatore Lazzari, "Macroeconomic Effects of Increases in the Gasoline Tax," 93-213E, Washington, Congressional Research Service, February 10, 1993, p. 6.

21. Howard G. Borgstrom, "Strategic Petroleum Reserve: An Analysis of Fill Rate Decisions," Ph.D. dissertation, George Washington University, School of Business and Public Management, 1991, p. 79.

22. The administrative and storage costs are currently about $250 million a year. *Budget of the United States Government, Appendix: Fiscal Year 1995*, pp. A407–08. The implicit annual interest cost of a stock of oil acquired at a total cost of more than $15 billion is another $900 million at an interest rate of 6 percent (unpublished data provided by Howard Borgstrom, Department of Energy, December 1993). If one includes the capital losses from acquiring the inventory at prices that were about $11 a barrel above current (1994) prices, the annual cost of the SPR has been more than $1.5 billion a year.

23. Borgstrom, "Strategic Petroleum Reserve." A regression analysis of the "fill rate" for the SPR over the period 1981 through 1989 shows that these purchases are a direct function of the price of oil but are unrelated to the excess capacity in the SPR. The elasticity of the fill rate with respect to oil prices is about 1.4. Thus a 10 percent rise in crude oil prices induces a 14 percent increase in

acquisitions for the SPR. In addition, if one accounts for the perverse effect of oil prices, the fill rate has been falling at a rate of about 2 million barrels a year.

24. Borgstrom, however, finds only weak empirical support for this provocative hypothesis.

25. These calculations exclude the beneficial effects of reducing smog, congestion, or other externalities through reduced fuel consumption. These offsetting benefits would be greater for the fuel-tax alternative because higher taxes would reduce VMT at a higher rate than would the energy-saving equivalent regulatory standards.

Notes to Chapter 4

1. Environmental Protection Agency, Office of Mobile Sources, *Automobile Emissions: An Overview*, Fact Sheet OMS-5 (Washington, January 1993), p. 3.

2. Department of the Environment, Government Statistical Service, *Digest of Environmental Protection and Water Statistics* (London: Her Majesty's Stationery Office, 1991), p. 15. Recent tax penalties on leaded petrol, in Britain and elsewhere in Europe, have since induced a shift to unleaded fuel.

3. The 1990 Clean Air Act limits benzene content to not more than 1.0 percent by volume. The EC's current standard allows 5 percent. A German proposal to the European Commission, suggesting a tougher standard, was not acted upon. Federal Ministry of Economics, "Energy Policy for the United Germany," Bonn, December 11, 1991, p. 109.

4. Centre for Global Energy Studies, "Carbon Taxes: Levelling the Playing Field," *Global Oil Report*, vol. 3, no. 3 (May–June 1992), p. 28. In 1990 and 1991, two Scandinavian countries, Sweden and Norway, raised their fuel levies to penalize CO_2 emissions. As yet, a much-discussed EC carbon tax has not been promulgated.

5. Since 1987 the Dutch have levied separate air pollution and "noise nuisance" duties on the use of cars. H. L. van der Kolk, *Benefits and Burdens of Car Ownership and Use: The Issues Weighed* (The Hague: Institute for Research on Public Expenditure, 1990), p. 8.

6. Ministry of Transport, *Second Transport Structure Plan* (The Hague: Ministry of Transport, 1990), p. 6.

7. Information from Energy Policy Planning Division, Agency of Natural Resources and Energy, Ministry of International Trade and Industry, Tokyo, March 1, 1993, p. 1.

8. Ibid., pp. 2–3. Only 1.5 percent of gasoline sold in Japan was leaded by 1988.

9. International Energy Agency, *Fuel Efficiency of Passenger Cars* (Paris: OECD/IEA, 1991) p. 45.

10. See, for instance, David Vogel, "Representing Diffuse Interests in Environmental Policymaking," in R. Kent Weaver and Bert A. Rockman, eds., *Do Institutions Matter? Government Capabilities in the United States and Abroad* (Brookings, 1993), pp. 237–71.

11. Conseil économique et social, *Les droits d'accise*, no. 13 (Paris, 1991), p. 108.

12. Harvey Feigenbaum, Richard Samuels, and R. Kent Weaver, "Innovation, Coordination, and Implementation in Energy Policy," in Weaver and Rockman, *Do Institutions Matter?* pp. 78–79.

13. In Japan's fiscal 1992 budget, fully 87 percent of all disbursements from the various petroleum-related taxes went toward infrastructural facilities and "rationalization" of the coal industry. The Ministry of International Trade and Industry's "oil policy" accounted for the remaining 13 percent, but under that budget line, almost 90 percent was spent on strategic stockpiling.

14. International Energy Agency, *Energy Conservation in IEA Countries* (Paris: OECD/IEA, 1987), pp. 115–16.

15. The figures are for 1990. International Energy Agency, *Energy Balances of OECD Countries 1990–1991* (Paris: OECD/IEA, 1993), pp. 188, 195.

16. International Energy Agency, *Energy Prices and Taxes, Fourth Quarter 1988* (Paris: OECD/IEA, 1989), p. xxii.

17. International Energy Agency, *Energy Conservation in IEA Countries*, p. 116.

18. Ministry of Transport, *Second Transport Structure Plan*, pp. 10, 12, 28, 30, 38.

19. Several European countries also allow deductions from income taxes of a fixed amount per kilometer and per working day for taxpayers who use cars to commute to work. On the German provision, see Gerold Krause-Junk, "The Taxation of Gasoline in Germany," Institut für Ausländisches und Internationales Finanz- und Steuerwesen, Universität Hamburg, 1992, p. 3.

20. On the "company car" distortion, see Lee Schipper and others, "Fuel Prices, Automobile Fuel Economy, and Fuel Use for Land Travel: Preliminary Findings from an International Comparison" (Berkeley, Calif.: Lawrence Berkeley Laboratory, 1992), pp. 4, 6, 10; Lee Schipper and others, "Mind the Gap: The Vicious Circle of Measuring Automobile Fuel Use," *Energy Policy*, vol. 21 (December 1993), p. 1180; and Mark Ashworth and Andrew Dilnot, "Company Cars Taxation," *Fiscal Studies*, vol. 8 (November 1987), pp. 24–38.

21. The current share of urban driving is realistically estimated as 63 percent, not the 55 percent assumed in EPA tests, and is projected to exceed 70 percent by the year 2010. Deborah Gordon, *Steering a New Course: Transportation, Energy, and the Environment* (Cambridge, Mass.: Union of Concerned Scientists, 1991), pp. 45–46. Ninety-seven percent of the miles traveled by American motorists each year are in trips of fifteen miles or less. James J. MacKenzie, "Toward a Sustainable Energy Future: The Critical Role of Rational Energy Pricing," *WRI Issues and Ideas* (Washington: World Resources Institute, May 1991), p. 8. The quotation belongs to Energy Secretary James Watkins (Americans "love to drive on the open plains"). Jessica Mathews, "The Myth of the American Car Cult," *Washington Post*, March 31, 1991, p. B7.

22. Motor Vehicle Manufacturers Association, *Motor Vehicle Facts and Figures '90* (Detroit: MVMA, 1990), p. 49. Schipper and others, "Fuel Prices," p. 9. Schipper and his associates report that the average length of trips by car in Germany, for instance, evidently increased between 1976 and 1982, while it de-

creased in the United States. Lee Schipper and Stephen Meyers, *Energy Efficiency and Human Activity: Past Trends, Future Prospects* (Cambridge University Press, 1992).

23. Schipper and others, "Fuel Prices," p. 9.

24. Lee Schipper and others, "Energy Use in Passenger Transport in OECD Countries: Changes since 1970," *Transportation*, vol. 19 (February 1992), pp. 37–39. Schipper and Meyers, *Energy Efficiency and Human Activity.*

25. Air travel, as a share of passenger kilometrage, doubled between 1970 and 1987 to almost 10 percent in the United States. Meanwhile, it remained under 1 percent in Germany, Italy, and Great Britain. See Schipper and others, "Energy Use in Passenger Transport," pp. 37–39.

26. This point seems widely misunderstood. During congressional hearings on fuel economy standards in 1989, for instance, a spokesman for General Motors Corporation stressed that "the Europeans operate under vastly different circumstances," such as "more mass transit systems." "This difference," he added, "explains most of the divergence between America's use of fuel in surface transportation and that of European countries with which it is frequently compared." Hearing before the Subcommittee on Energy Regulation and Conservation of the Senate Committee on Energy and Natural Resources, 101 Cong. 1 sess. (Government Printing Office, 1989), p. 188.

27. Daniel Sperling and others, "Environmentally Benign Automobiles," *Access* (Berkeley: University of California Transportation Center, 1992), p. 1; Schipper and others, "Energy Use," pp. 37–39. The dominance of the automobile in the modal split of European intercity passengers has been evident for years. Private autos accounted for 83 percent of total travel in France as early as 1972. See, for instance, Réné Parès, *Le Chemin de fer en France* (Paris: La documentation française, 1974), p. 43.

28. In the Los Angeles area, an estimated 57 percent of all peak hour trips and 70 percent of all daily trips are *not* work related. Michael Cameron, *Transportation Efficiency: Tackling Southern California's Air Pollution and Congestion* (Oakland, Calif.: Environmental Defense Fund, March 1991), pp. 28–29. In U.S. cities, less than 10 percent of commuter trips are by walking or bicycling, compared with 40 percent in typical European cities. Gordon, *Steering a New Course*, p. 156.

29. Canadians consumed about 26 percent less gasoline per capita than did Americans in 1990. Australians consumed almost 40 percent less per capita. Estimated from Energy Information Administration, *International Energy Annual 1991* (Paris: OECD/IEA, 1992), pp. 48–49; and International Monetary Fund, *International Financial Statistics* (Washington, January 1993).

30. Approximately one-third of motor-fuel consumption in the Netherlands is in the form of diesel oil and liquid petroleum gas. The gap between New Jersey and Holland would look somewhat narrower if the use of these fuels is considered.

31. Motor Vehicle Manufacturers Association, *Motor Vehicle Facts and Figures '89* (Detroit: MVMA, 1989), p. 46.

32. Schipper and others, "Fuel Prices," p. 5.

33. Institut national de recherche sur les transports et leur securité, *Un milli-*

ard de déplacements par semaine: La mobilité des français (Paris: La documentation française, 1989), passim, cited in James A. Dunn, Jr., "Group Politics and Governing the Automobile in France: The Politics of Highway Finance," paper presented at the 1991 annual meeting of the Northeastern Political Science Association, p. 3.

34. As of 1993, approximately 77 percent of all households in the territory of the former West Germany owned a car, and an estimated 19 percent owned more than one. Estimated by Verband der Automobilindustrie, Frankfurt, correspondence, July 23, 1993.

35. George H. Gallup, *The Gallup International Public Opinion Polls, France 1939, 1944–1975*, vol. 2 (Random House, 1976), pp. 1072–73. The same year, a Gallup poll in Great Britain found 68 percent opposed to any increase in the national value-added tax applied to petrol. Gallup, *The Gallup International Public Opinion Polls, Great Britain 1937–1975*, vol. 2 (Random House, 1976), p. 1318.

36. United Nations, *Statistical Yearbook* (New York, 1962); Federal Highway Administration, *Highway Statistics: Summary to 1965* (Department of Transportation, 1967), p. 23.

37. Including the VAT, the tax on a liter of gasoline rose from 92 pfennig to 110 pfennig per liter as of January 1994.

38. For one of the many assessments in this vein, see Robert Engler, *The Politics of Oil: A Study of Private Power and Democratic Directions* (University of Chicago, 1961), p. 8.

39. See Edward Carr, "The New Corn Laws," *Economist*, December 12, 1992, p. 4.

40. Pietro S. Nivola, *The Politics of Energy Conservation* (Brookings, 1986), p. 217.

41. On the U.S. case, see Robert W. Crandall and others, *Regulating the Automobile* (Brookings, 1986); on the European experience, see Sonja A. Boehmer-Christiansen, "Curbing Auto Emissions in Europe," *Environment*, vol. 32 (July–August 1990), pp. 17–39.

42. Bela and Carol Balassa, "Industrial Protection in the Developed Countries," *World Economy*, vol. 7 (June 1984), p. 186.

43. Warren Brown and Frank Swoboda, "GM Joins in Supporting Gas Tax Hike," *Washington Post*, December 18, 1992, pp. A1, A21; Neal Templin and Timothy Noah, "Auto Firms Urge Higher Gasoline Tax to Avert Tougher Fuel-Use Standard," *Wall Street Journal*, January 22, 1993, p. A4.

44. In the United Kingdom, for example, the government extracts from the industry license royalties and a petroleum revenue tax, in addition to corporate taxes and high sales taxes on refined products. Her Majesty's Treasury, Foreign and Commercial Office, *Britain's Tax System* (December 1991), p. 14.

45. Matthew L. Wald, "50-Cents-a-Gallon Tax Could Buy a Whole Lot," *New York Times*, October 18, 1992, p. E5.

46. See, for instance, "Energy Taxes, Please," *New Republic*, June 21, 1993, p. 9.

47. Her Majesty's Treasury, *Britain's Tax System*, p. 7.

48. For tax purposes, the government's Select Committee on Luxury Taxation

in 1918 grouped motorcars together with "fans, boas, billiard tables, cocktails and yachts." William Plowden, *The Motor Car and Politics, 1896–1970* (London: The Bodley Head, 1971), p. 13.

49. Plowden, *Motor Car*, pp. 167–68, 178, 218, 287, 305. The protectionist intent of the vehicle tax was openly acknowledged. A Treasury memorandum to the British Board of Trade in 1929 stated plainly that "low taxation of high-powered cars [such as Ford Model A's] would give the foreigner exporting to this country an advantage that he does not possess" (p. 288).

50. See James A. Dunn, Jr., *Miles to Go: European and American Transportation Policies* (MIT Press, 1981), p. 98.

51. The geopolitical setting was as follows: "The First World War left France with a strategic problem to which there was no good solution. France was the most damaged of the belligerent countries; Germany remained relatively intact territorially, its economic capacity undiminished. France's powerful ally on Germany's eastern flank, Russia, temporarily disappeared from European politics. The security guarantees expected from Britain and the United States were, in the end, disappointing. Strategic considerations therefore dominated French political thinking in the postwar years and led to a notion, never fully elaborated, of an autonomous commercial policy serving national security needs." Jan Tumlir, *Protectionism: Trade Policy in Democratic Societies* (Washington: American Enterprise Institute for Public Policy Research, 1985), pp. 23–24. For a full account of France's autarkic energy plans, see Harvey B. Feigenbaum, *The Politics of Public Enterprise: Oil and the French State* (Princeton University Press, 1985).

52. The lower tax rate on diesel fuel, however, originated as an attempt to compensate the trucking industry for competitive disadvantages created by subsidies to the national railways. See Albert Boyer, *Les Transports Routiers* (Paris: Presses Universitaires de France, 1973), p. 55.

53. Hugh Heclo and Aaron Wildavsky, *The Private Government of Public Money* (Macmillan, 1974), pp. 353–54.

54. Quoted in Plowden, *Motor Car*, pp. 190–91.

55. See James A. Dunn, Jr., "The Politics of Motor Fuel Taxes and Infrastructure Funds in France and the United States," *Policy Studies Journal*, vol. 21 (Summer 1993), pp. 271–84. By 1981, the *Fond*, which had survived in name only, was formally absorbed into the *Budget général de l'état*. Conseil économique et social, *Les droits d'accise* (Paris: 1991), p. 108.

56. In every European country, save Britain, the state is the sole owner of the railways. In general, subsidies pay an average of half the total costs of the systems. The railroads as government agencies are often the largest national employer. Department of Transportation, *National Transportation Strategic Planning Study* (1990), p. 6-12.

57. See, for instance, J. E. S. Hayward, *Governing France: The One and Indivisible Republic*, 2d ed. (London: Weidenfeld and Nicolson, 1983), p. 179.

58. Quoted in Plowden, *Motor Car*, p. 212.

59. *State Highway Commission of Missouri* v. *Volpe* (1973). The Eighth U.S. Circuit Court of Appeals ruled in April 1973 that the administration had withheld funds illegally. Under the 1956 Federal Aid Highway Act, according to the court, funds appropriated by Congress "are not to be withheld from obligation for pur-

poses totally unrelated to the highway program." Quoted in CQ Almanac 1973 (Washington: Congressional Quarterly, Inc., 1974), p. 253. The practice of impoundment was subsequently enjoined by the Budget Reform Act of 1974.

60. Heclo and Wildavsky go so far as to characterize MPs as "distinctly uninterested in the spending process." Heclo and Wildavsky, The Private Government, p. 245.

61. See R. Kent Weaver, Automatic Government: The Politics of Indexation (Brookings, 1988).

62. The 1982 legislation raised the federal gasoline tax by 5 cents a gallon, with 1 cent going to a new Mass Transit Account.

63. See Samuel H. Beer, British Politics in the Collectivist Age (Vintage Books, 1969), chap. 3.

64. Comité professionnel du pétrole, Pétrole 90: Éléments statistiques (Rueil-Malmaison: CMP, 1991), p. D14.

65. Harold Wilson did so on no fewer than six occasions between 1964 and 1969, for instance. See Plowden, Motor Car, p. 360, and pp. 290, 319.

66. Peter Hughes, "Is Transport Policy Going to Head Left, Right or Centre?" Local Transport Today, April 2, 1992, p. 11.

67. Quoted in Steven Pearlstein and Thomas W. Lippman, "Industry Analysts See Broad-Based Energy Tax in Clinton's Future," Washington Post, January 1, 1993, p. A4.

68. "L'image des entreprises pétroliéres en France," Études et documents (Paris: BIP, May 25, 1992), p. 3.

69. For a detailed account of the comparatively centralized process of urban planning in Greater London, see, for instance, Stephen L. Elkin, Politics and Land Use Planning: The London Experience (Cambridge University Press, 1974), especially chaps. 1–2. See also H. V. Savitch, Post-Industrial Cities: Politics and Planning in New York, Paris, and London (Princeton, 1988), pp. 281–83.

70. The higher densities may also be a product of various other government policies—lavish agricultural subsidies, for instance, which keep more land under cultivation, and reduce incentives for farmers to sell acreage to developers. More generally, see Anthony Downs, "Contrasting Strategies for the Economic Development of Metropolitan Areas," Brookings, September 1991.

71. Bureau of the Census, American Housing Survey for the Los Angeles-Long Beach Metropolitan Area in 1989 (Department of Commerce, December 1991), p. 15.

72. Paul Johnson, Steve McKay, Stephen Smith, The Distributional Consequences of Environmental Taxes (London: Institute for Fiscal Studies, July 1990), p. 24.

73. In the United Kingdom, households in the richest decile are, on average, over 11 times more likely to have use of a car than are households in the poorest decile. Johnson, McKay, and Smith, Distributional Consequences, p. 21. In the United States, 62 percent of all households with incomes under $10,000 (1987) own cars. See Energy Information Administration, Household Vehicles Energy Consumption, 1988 (Department of Energy, February 1990), p. 73. Although tax incidence may be less regressive in the United Kingdom, the impact of petrol taxes on the nontrivial number of families with moderate incomes that are dependent

on automotive transport (in less densely populated regions such as East Anglia, South-West England, and Wales) is undoubtedly severe. Moreover, even the incidence may be regarded as regressive, if the high British tax rates ultimately deter low- and moderate-income households from owning automobiles in the first place. Finally, in the United States, where excise taxation has represented a shrinking share of total federal tax revenue, the relative burden of additional excises on lower-income families may be overstated by using "income" instead of expenditures as the point of reference. "A family's expenditures may be a better indicator than its annual income of the family's true economic circumstances. Measured as a percentage of total family expenditures, excise taxes are more nearly the same for low-, middle-, and higher-income families." Congressional Budget Office, *Federal Taxation of Tobacco, Alcoholic Beverages, and Motor Fuels* (Washington, June 1990), p. xvii.

74. Plowden, *Motor Car,* p. 196.

75. The Miscellaneous Financial Provisions Act of 1955 closed the road fund down. Dunn, *Miles to Go,* p. 104.

76. Dunn, "Group Politics," p. 17. On the so-called *loi Deferre,* see Sonia Mazey, "Power Outside Paris," in Peter A. Hall, Jack Hayward, and Howard Machin, eds., *Developments in French Politics* (St. Martin's, 1990), pp. 152–70; and Yves Mény, "The Socialist Decentralization," in George Ross, Stanley Hoffman, and Sylvia Malzbacher, eds., *The Mitterand Experiment: Continuity and Change in Modern France* (Oxford University Press, 1987), pp. 248–62.

77. *Süddeutsche Zeitung,* November 12, 1992.

78. Harvey Feigenbaum and others, "Innovation, Coordination, and Implementation in Energy Policy," in Weaver and Rockman, *Do Institutions Matter?* p. 69.

79. Sprachendienst Bundesministerium der Finanzen, *An ABC of Taxes in the Federal Republic of Germany* (Bonn: Bundesministerium der Finanzen, 1989), p. 119.

80. Chalmers Johnson, *MITI and the Japanese Miracle: The Growth of Industrial Policy, 1925–1975* (Stanford University Press, 1982), p. 236. The Japanese government still spends revenues from its oil import tariffs on subsidies to coal miners. General Accounting Office, *Other Nations' Policies to Reduce Oil and Coal Use in Transport and Industry,* GAO/RCED–93–139 (May 1993), p. 60.

81. The following discussion draws heavily on Eisuke Sakakibara, "The Japanese Politico-Economic System and the Public Sector," in Samuel Kernell, ed., *Parallel Politics: Economic Policymaking in Japan and the United States* (Brookings, 1991), especially pp. 70–78; Yukio Noguchi, "Budget Policymaking in Japan," in Kernell, *Parallel Politics,* especially pp. 125–127; and Ministry of Finance, Budget Bureau, *The Japanese Budget in Brief, 1992* (Tokyo, 1992), pts. I, II.

82. Ministry of Finance, *An Outline of Japanese Taxes, 1990* (Tokyo, 1990), p. 180.

83. See Michio Muramatsu and Masaru Mabuchi, "Introducing a New Tax in Japan," in Kernell, *Parallel Politics,* pp. 184–85.

84. Ministry of Finance, *Outline,* pp. 332–33.

85. PIARC Economic and Finance Committee and Economic and Finance Committee of Japan, "Finance System for Road Investment in Japan," Tokyo, April 27, 1993, p. 17.

86. While Japan was investing 1.87 percent of its GNP on road work as of 1992, the United States was investing 1.12 percent, England 1.01 percent, and Germany 0.73 percent. "Finance System for Road Investment in Japan," p. 2. According to the Ministry of Finance, the FY 1992 budget devoted 2,396.1 billion yen to road improvements. Expenditures for the national government's share of compulsory education expenses came to 2,726.3 billion yen. Ministry of Finance, *The Japanese Budget in Brief, 1992*, pp. 56, 59.

87. See Noguchi, "Budget Policymaking in Japan," p. 121.

88. Sprachendienst Bundesministerium der Finanzen, *An ABC of Taxes*, pp. 2–11, 76–77.

89. Krause-Junk, "The Taxation of Gasoline in Germany," p. 4.

90. Ibid., p. 13.

91. Senator Donald L. Nickles, Republican of Oklahoma, during debate on a proposed increase in the federal gas tax in 1982. *Congressional Record*, daily ed., December 23, 1982, p. S33547.

92. See Anthony Downs, *Stuck in Traffic* (Brookings, 1992), p. 69.

93. Organization for Economic Cooperation and Development, *OECD Economic Surveys: United States* (Paris: OECD, 1992), p. 53.

94. See in general, Keith G. Banting, *The Welfare State and Canadian Federalism*, 2d ed. (McGill-Queen's University Press, 1987), especially pp. 74–76.

95. The Canadian constitution, for instance, denies the provinces jurisdiction over forms of taxation that allow the taxpayer to "recover the amount [of the tax] by means of an advance in price" (as in value-added taxation, for example). See Richard J. Van Loon and Michael S. Whittington, *The Canadian Political System: Environment, Structure and Process*, 4th ed. (McGraw-Hill Ryerson, 1987), pp. 276–77, 666–67. Only about 7 percent of federal and provincial fuel tax revenue is earmarked for roads. Canadian Automobile Association, "Rough Road Ahead?" *News*, November/December, 1992, p. 1.

96. Accordingly, Saskatchewan has been able to boost its gasoline tax to more than 40 cents a gallon (U.S.), considerably higher than its neighbors on all sides. To minimize cross-border buying in Manitoba and Alberta, however, Saskatchewan tapers its rates at the periphery. Clearly, only a vast jurisdiction can successfully implement such an elaborate arrangement.

97. Edmond Preteceille, "From Centralization to Decentralization: Social Restructuring and French Local Government," in Chris Pickvance and Edmond Preteceille, eds., *State Restructuring and Local Power: A Comparative Perspective* (London: Pinter Publishers, 1991), p. 138; and Bureau of the Census, *Government Finances*, series GF, no. 5 (Department of Commerce, 1991, 1992, 1993).

98. There is actually more local self-rule in France than commonly assumed. Mark Kesselman, *The Ambiguous Consensus: A Study of Local Government in France* (Knopf, 1967).

99. Ministry of Housing, Physical Planning, and Environment, *The Rules of Physical Planning, 1986* (The Hague, October 1987), pp. 17–18.

100. Ibid., pp. 14–16. These powers of direct oversight have been in effect since 1985, when the National Physical Planning Act of 1962 was amended.

101. Ibid., p. 15.

102. Ministry of Housing, Physical Planning, and Environment, *Fourth Report (Extra) on Physical Planning in the Netherlands*, Comprehensive Summary (The Hague, n.d.), p. 15; and Ministry of Housing, Physical Planning, and Environment, *The Right Business in the Right Place: Towards a Location Policy for Businesses and Services in the Interest of Accessibility and the Environment* (The Hague, n.d.), pp. i, 18–21.

103. Ministry of Transportation, *Second Transport Structure Plan*, part d, p. 12.

104. A legal opinion handed down by the Federal Constitutional Court in 1954 cleared the constitutional grounds for federal legislation regulating physical planning at the local level. See Manfred Konukiewitz and Hellmut Wollmann, "Physical Planning in a Federal System: The Case of West Germany," in David H. McKay, ed., *Planning and Politics in Western Europe* (St. Martin's Press, 1982), pp. 73, 82.

105. Federal Building Act of 1960 and Federal Spatial Planning Act of 1965. Konukiewitz and Wollmann, "Physical Planning in a Federal System," pp. 82–83.

106. Ibid., p. 75. Less than a third of all local government income derives from local revenues in Germany. Two-thirds of the income of urban governments in the United States comes from local revenue sources. See Dennis R. Judd, *The Politics of American Cities: Private Power and Public Policy*, 3d ed. (Scott, Foresman, 1988), p. 201. On the widening federal role after the Financial Reform of 1969, see Hartmut Häubermann, "The Relationship between Local and Federal Government Policy in the Federal Republic of Germany," in Chris Pickvance and Edmond Preteceille, eds., *State Restructuring and Local Power: A Comparative Perspective* (London: Pinter Publishers, 1991), especially pp. 92, 93, 99. This writer observes: "Regarding the tax system and financing of tasks, the municipalities in the Federal Republic are so closely tied to the higher government levels that their functions and scope for action cannot be designated as autonomous in any way" (p. 99).

107. It should be stressed that a different result was conceivable. The West German population went from 43 million on the eve of the Second World War to 56 million by 1961. With an enormous influx of refugees from the East, large-scale rural-to-urban migration, and the need to reconstruct a decimated housing stock, Germany's modern cities could have assumed much more of the form of the urban agglomerations of the American sunbelt. Instead, West Germany's urbanized population lived at an average density of 6,000 inhabitants per square mile in 1980, compared with an average urban density of only 3,327 per square mile in the United States. Dunn, *Miles to Go*, p. 68.

108. On this episode, see more generally Jeffrey Simpson, *Discipline of Power: The Conservative Interlude and the Liberal Restoration* (Toronto: Personal Library, 1980), chap. 1.

109. Canada adopted a national Land Use Planning and Development Act in 1979 aimed at encouraging regionalization of development controls. See Pierre

Hamel and Lizette Jalbert, "Local Power in Canada: Stakes and Challenges in the Restructuring of the State," in Chris Pickvance and Edmond Preteceille, eds., *State Restructuring and Local Power: A Comparative Perspective* (London: Pinter Publishers, 1991), p. 188.

Notes to Chapter 5

1. John Chynoweth Burnham, "The Gasoline Tax and the Automobile Revolution," *Mississippi Valley Historical Review*, vol. 48 (December 1961), p. 443.

2. Indeed, the tax was briefly increased, by half a cent for the 1933 fiscal year, to finance the National Industrial Recovery Act.

3. The half-cent increase was part of a tax package "designed to meet the present emergency for defense expenditures." *Revenue Act of 1940*, Hearings before the House Ways and Means Committee, 76 Cong. 3 sess. (Government Printing Office, 1940), pt. 1, p. 6.

4. By 1931 the states were collecting, on average, nearly 38 percent of their total revenues from motor-vehicle-related taxes. The taxes accounted for almost half the revenue of some states, North Carolina, for instance. *Revenue Act of 1934*, Hearing before the Senate Finance Committee, 73 Cong. 2 sess. (GPO, 1934), pt. 1, p. 477.

5. See James A. Dunn, Jr., *Miles to Go: European and American Transportation Policies* (MIT Press, 1981), p. 98; *Revenue Revision, 1932*, Hearings before the House Ways and Means Committee, 72 Cong. 1 sess. (GPO, 1932), pt. 1, p. 768. Adjusted for inflation, $3,000 in 1932 was equal to the median income in 1990, $29,800.

6. Section 489 of the Revenue Act of 1951 authorized the 2-cent rate to continue until March 31, 1954. The so-called Excise Tax Reduction Act of 1954 extended the tax for an additional year, whereupon the Tax Rate Extension Act of 1955 renewed it again. FHA and VA mortgage insurance programs helped finance an estimated one-quarter of all new single-family homes built during the immediate postwar period.

7. A favorite tactic of the highway lobby was to insert earmarking provisions directly into state constitutions. Minnesota became the first state to adopt such an amendment in 1920. Kansas followed in 1928. By 1962 fifteen state constitutions earmarked gasoline taxation.

8. Eisenhower requested a 1.5-cent increase in 1959. Although supporters of the interstate system ultimately prevailed, the administration's request was scaled down to 1 cent and took several months to adopt. During the debate on the Federal Aid Highway Act of 1959, a number of state governors reopened "states' rights" objections to further federal increases in gasoline taxes, and even Speaker of the House Sam Rayburn seemed to agree that "the federal government] should have left that field of taxation . . . or what's left of it." *Congressional Quarterly Almanac, 1959* (Washington: Congressional Quarterly, Inc., 1959), p. 286; "29 Governors Fight New U.S. 'Gas' Tax," *New York Times*, January 26, 1959, p.

A12. The tax rate of 4 cents a gallon was extended under the highway acts of 1961 and 1970.

9. *Congressional Record*, daily ed., October 17, 1990, p. S15482. Between 1983 and 1990, a period of sharply declining crude oil prices, there was one other minuscule change in the taxation of gasoline: the Superfund Revenue Act of 1986 authorized a tenth of a cent a gallon to be raised for a "Leaking Underground Storage Tank Trust Fund" from 1987 until September 1990.

10. *Congressional Quarterly Almanac, 1991* (Washington: Congressional Quarterly, Inc., 1992), p. 143.

11. Energy Information Administration, *Petroleum Marketing Monthly* (September 1994), p. 158; International Energy Agency, *Energy Prices and Taxes: Second Quarter 1994* (Paris: IEA/OECD, 1994), p. xxv; and Government of Canada, Department of Natural Resources, *Federal and Provincial Petroleum Product Taxes* (Ottawa, July 1994), p. 10, table 3. In the United States, the structure of taxation of gasoline varies among states. Most state taxes are simply levied on a cents-a-gallon basis. Ten states have some form of variable tax based on a percentage of the wholesale price, and ten states also cover motor fuels under their general sales taxes, besides levying specific excises on the fuels.

12. The average fuel intensity of automobiles and personal light trucks in the United States (measured in liters per 100 kilometers for the full, on-road fleet) was at least twice that of the vehicles in France, Germany, Great Britain, and Japan in the early 1970s. Lee Schipper and others, "Mind the Gap: The Vicious Circle of Measuring Automobile Fuel Use," *Energy Policy*, vol. 21 (December 1993), p. 1181.

13. By 1975, for example, automatic transmissions, estimated to decrease gasoline mileage by at least 10 percent, had become standard equipment in General Motors cars. Denis Hayes, *Energy: The Case for Conservation* (Washington: Worldwatch Institute, 1976), pp. 7, 26.

14. Ann Pelham, *Energy Policy*, 2d ed. (Washington: CQ Press, 1981), p. 9.

15. *Congressional Record*, June 11, 1975, p. 18435.

16. Ibid.

17. Persons commuting in, say, Nassau County, Long Island, adjacent to New York City, spend more than 4.5 times longer on their commutes to work as do residents commuting to work in Mitchell County, Kansas (a rural county with the nation's shortest average commuting time). Dirk Johnson, "Fear of Gas Tax Where Commuting Time Is Most," *New York Times*, July 6, 1993, p. A12.

18. On the consequences of policy mismanagement during the debates of the 1970s and early 1980s, see Pietro S. Nivola, *The Politics of Energy Conservation* (Brookings, 1986), pp. 223–41.

19. In so doing, the critics of gasoline taxation may be committing the classic fallacy noted by Alfred Marshall. Marshall urged tax reformers to judge a tax system by its overall fairness, even when some particulars of a system would inevitably be inequitable. See, for instance, Alfred Marshall, *Official Papers* (London: Macmillan and Company, 1926), p. 339.

20. All federal excise tax revenues in 1989 represented 3.44 percent of total federal revenues, down from 19.14 percent in 1950. Federal motor-fuel tax reve-

nues equaled 1.44 percent of total federal revenues in 1989. They had supplied 2.26 percent of the government's total revenues in 1960. Congressional Budget Office, *Federal Taxation of Tobacco, Alcoholic Beverages, and Motor Fuels* (Washington, June 1990), pp. 102, 105, tables A–1, A–4.

21. Senator Donald W. Riegle, *Congressional Record*, daily ed., December 21, 1982, p. S15896.

22. Vote no. 474 on HR 5835, "Fiscal 1991 Omnibus Reconciliation Act/ Democratic Alternative," *Congressional Quarterly Almanac, 1990* (Washington: Congressional Quarterly, Inc., 1991), p. 150H.

23. Congressman Vic Fazio, Democrat of California, quoted in George Hager and Pamela Fessler, "Negotiators Walk Fine Line to Satisfy Both Chambers," *Congressional Quarterly Weekly Report*, vol. 48 (October 20, 1990), pp. 3476, 3477.

24. Eric Pianin and David S. Hilzenrath, "Hill Agrees to Raise Gas Tax 4.3 Cents," *Washington Post*, July 30, 1993, p. A1.

25. Howard Chernick and Andrew Reschovsky, "The Gas Tax and the Deficit: Is It Fair to Use One to Cure the Other?" Working Paper 19 (University of Wisconsin, Robert M. La Follette Institute of Public Affairs, July 1993), p. 13. The authors came to the conclusion that "the hardship imposed on low-income families by a 7.5 cent increase in the gas tax would be relatively small, and for the vast majority of such families, fully compensated by other changes in the budget or by automatic adjustments in existing government transfer programs." Less than half of all low-income families own cars, and those that do drive them half as much as the national average.

26. David Wessel, "Clinton Faces Decision on Raising Gas Tax," *Wall Street Journal*, December 28, 1992, p. A1.

27. See Nivola, *Politics of Energy Conservation*, p. 55.

28. At the end of 1973, on a vote of 75 to 15, the Senate adopted a bill authored by Henry Jackson, Democrat of Washington, which required auto manufacturers to increase gasoline mileage of cars by an average of 50 percent between 1974 and 1984. However, the House was not prepared to take similar action until two years later.

29. In the end Congress settled on a system of fines. A manufacturer failing to comply with mpg standards would be liable for $5 on each one-tenth of a mile a gallon that a new car fell below the standard, multiplied by the total number of such cars built or imported by the company.

30. Warren Brown, "Ford, GM Ask 1-Year Delay on Truck Fuel Ratings," *Washington Post*, August 1, 1984, p. F4; Warren Brown, "Truck Fuel Standards Reduced," *Washington Post*, October 17, 1984, p. F3. In 1984 the mileage requirements for new light trucks made between 1985 and 1986 were set at 19.5 mpg and 20 mpg, respectively, instead of 21.0 mpg and 21.5 mpg. In 1985 NHTSA lowered the mandatory 27.5 mpg requirement for auto fleets to 26.0 mpg starting in 1986.

31. See *Congressional Quarterly Almanac, 1980* (Washington: Congressional Quarterly, Inc., 1981), p. 487.

32. Reginald Stuart, "U.S. May Ease Auto Regulations in Effort to Save Industry Money," *New York Times*, December 17, 1979, p. B13.

33. Ibid.

34. *Congressional Record*, daily ed., June 22, 1989, p. S7259. See also *Motor Vehicle Fuel Efficiency Act of 1989*, Hearing before the Subcommittee on the Consumer, 101 Cong. 1 sess. (GPO, 1989), p. 5.

35. Governor Bill Clinton and Senator Al Gore, *Putting People First: How We Can All Change America* (Times Books, 1992), pp. 89–92.

36. Ibid., pp. 90–92. Emphasis in the original.

37. See editorial, "Mr. Bush's Energy Policy," *Washington Post*, December 17, 1990, p. A10.

38. See Paul D. Pierson and R. Kent Weaver, "Imposing Losses in Pension Policy," in R. Kent Weaver and Bert A. Rockman, eds., *Do Institutions Matter? Government Capabilities in the United States and Abroad* (Brookings, 1993), p. 111.

39. See, for instance, R. Kent Weaver, "The Politics of Blame Avoidance," *Journal of Public Policy*, vol. 6 (October–December, 1986), pp. 371–98.

40. For a general exposition of the shift-the-responsibility thesis, see Morris P. Fiorina, "Group Concentration and the Delegation of Legislative Authority," in Roger G. Noll, ed., *Regulatory Policy and the Social Sciences* (University of California Press, 1985), especially pp. 188–93.

41. Editorial, "How Not to Save Gas," *Washington Post*, April 22, 1992, p. A20.

42. Margaret E. Kriz, "Energy Crunch: Round 3," *National Journal*, September 15, 1990, p. 2185.

43. See the interesting analysis of suburban "operational conservatism" by William Schneider, "The Suburban Century Begins," *Atlantic*, July 1992, especially pp. 37–39.

44. On the other hand, a few errant Republicans sometimes seemed more adventuresome on the gas-tax issue. Senator Charles H. Percy of Illinois, for instance, proposed a tax of 30 cents a gallon in 1978.

45. Although the Bush administration pushed through a 5-cent increase in the gasoline tax as part of a budget compromise in 1990, it should be recalled that Bush's legislation was passed mostly with Democratic, not GOP, support. In the deciding vote, on October 27, 1990, House Republicans rejected the compromise by 126 to 47. Republicans in the Senate also rejected it, 25 to 19. See, respectively, votes nos. 528 and 326 on HR 5835, the Fiscal 1991 Budget Reconciliation Act/ Conference Report, *Congressional Quarterly Almanac, 1990*, pp. 166H, 63S.

46. See vote no. 395 on HR 6211, the Surface Transportation Assistance Act of 1982, *Congressional Quarterly Almanac, 1982* (Washington: Congressional Quarterly, Inc., 1983), p. 118H. After overcoming a two-week filibuster led by the two Republican senators from North Carolina, Jesse Helms and John P. East, a majority of Republicans in the Senate voted to adopt this legislation, but there, too, the party was split (35 supporting the president's bill, 15 opposing it). See vote no. 463 on HR 6211, December 20, 1982, Ibid., p. 76S.

47. Connecticut Republican Stewart B. McKinney, in *Congressional Record*, daily ed., June 10, 1975, p. 18046.

48. Such was the case with the 3-cent tax rejected by the House on June 11, 1975, the 4-cent tax rejected on August 4, 1977, and Carter's 50-cent tax pro-

posal in 1977. Carter's proposed 10-cent import fee was defeated on June 5, 1980, partly because many members suspected it would be used by the administration to balance an election year income tax cut. See *Congressional Quarterly Weekly Report*, vol. 33 (June 14, 1975), p. 1268, vol. 35 (August 6, 1977), p. 1690, and vol. 38 (June 7, 1980), p. 1606.

49. See Howard Geller, John DeCicco, and Steven Nadel, "Structuring an Energy Tax So That Energy Bills Do Not Increase," Washington: American Council for an Energy-Efficient Economy, March 8, 1993, p. 1. A generally centrist liberal think tank, the Progressive Policy Institute, endorsed the concept of a 50-cent increase in the gasoline tax, but on condition that its revenue be transferred to the social security trust fund. Robert N. Stavins and Bradley W. Whitehead, *The Greening of America's Taxes: Pollution Charges and Environmental Protection*, Policy Report 13 (Washington: Progressive Policy Institute, February 1992), p. 21. Compensatory designs like these invited criticism. In the words of one skeptical lobbyist during the most recent energy-tax debate, "If you want to make everybody whole, don't bother [raising the tax]." Quoted in David Wessel, "Clinton Faces Decision on Raising Gas Tax," *Wall Street Journal*, December 28, 1992, p. A1.

50. Institute for Research on the Economics of Taxation, "Gas Tax Increase Would Cost Jobs, Productivity," press release, July 17, 1992, in *The Impact, Shifting, and Incidence of an Increase in the Gasoline Excise Tax* (Washington: IRET, 1992), p. 30.

51. See, for instance, Senator Donald L. Nickles, Republican of Oklahoma, during debate on the 1982 Surface Transportation Assistance Act. *Congressional Record*, daily ed., December 23, 1982, p. S16045.

52. Between fiscal 1983 and fiscal 1989, budget surpluses in the states widened from 1.5 percent of total expenditures to 4.8 percent. National Governors' Association and National Association of State Budget Officers, *The Fiscal Survey of States* (Washington, April 1993), p. 23. Excise and sales taxes on gasoline still represent a relatively underexploited source of total state revenues, less than 7 percent. Petroleum Industry Research Foundation, Inc., "The Rising Tax Burden on Gasoline," PIRF, December 1991, p. 7.

53. See the successive roll calls on amendments by Congressmen Fisher, Jacobs, Ottinger, and Sharp on HR 6860 on June 12, 1975. Republicans voted to adopt the Sharp amendment, substituting fines for tax penalties, 77–56. *Congressional Quarterly Almanac, 1975* (Washington: Congressional Quarterly, Inc., 1976), p. 68H. The legislation finally adopted had at least two political advantages, which, although not acknowledged openly, were well known in the cloakrooms. The president could lift fines if the automobile manufacturers showed that they were unable to meet the law's efficiency standards. Also, by fining fleet averages rather than targeting taxes on models with low gasoline mileage, penalties would not show up as conspicuously on the sticker prices of big cars. (The UAW was particularly concerned that plants manufacturing large vehicles would be forced to shut down or lay off workers.) David E. Rosenbaum, "House Rejects a Stiff Tax on Low-Gas-Mileage Cars," *New York Times*, June 13, 1977, pp. 1, 44.

54. Republican senators voted 34–16 on July 29, 1985, against a resolution that would have put the "sense of the Senate" on record against the National

Highway Traffic Safety Administration's downward revision of CAFE standards. See *Congressional Quarterly Weekly Report*, vol. 43 (August 3, 1985), p. 1564. Similarly, on September 25, 1990, Senate Republicans voted 29–15 against a cloture motion that would have ended a filibuster on the Bryan bill. *Congressional Quarterly Almanac, 1990*, p. 50S.

55. This, for example, appeared to be a major argument used by the Bush administration's energy and transportation secretaries to stop the Bryan bill in 1990. See Kriz, "Energy Crunch," p. 2186. There is a safety issue associated with rising CAFE standards. See Robert W. Crandall and John D. Graham, "The Effect of Fuel Economy Standards on Automobile Safety," *Journal of Law and Economics*, vol. 32 (April 1989), pp. 97–118. Yet, to make safety the overriding issue in the debate on CAFE seemed distracting. The United States, after all, has long enjoyed the world's lowest highway fatality rate, measured in fatalities per 100 million vehicle miles traveled. Total European road deaths, for example, were more than 45 percent higher in 1986 than in the United States. Department of Transportation, *National Transportation Planning Study* (Washington, 1990), p. 6-4. The goal of encouraging a more energy-efficient automotive fleet competed with the ideal of maximizing auto safety, but auto safety was surely one "crisis" America did not have, at least in comparison with other countries.

56. See, in general, Joseph White and Aaron Wildavsky, *The Deficit and the Public Interest: The Search for Responsible Budgeting in the 1980s* (University of California Press and Russell Sage Foundation, 1989), chap. 1.

57. Article I, sections 8 and 9, respectively, of the Constitution of the United States of America.

58. Allen Schick, *Congress and Money: Budgeting, Spending and Taxing* (Washington: Urban Institute Press, 1980), p. 568, also, White and Wildavsky, *The Deficit and the Public Interest*, chap. 16.

59. Lawrence J. Haas, *Running on Empty: Bush, Congress, and the Politics of a Bankrupt Government* (Homewood, Ill.: Business One Irwin, 1990), pp. 6–9.

60. Under Japan's constitution, both bodies must approve the budget, and, as in the United States, any differences between the two versions have to be reconciled by a conference committee. However, "if the Houses don't come to a consensus in the Conference Committee, or if the House of Councillors doesn't take final action within 30 days after receipt of the Draft passed by [the] House of Representatives, the conclusion of the House of Representatives shall be that of the Diet." Ministry of Finance, Bureau of the Budget, *The Japanese Budget in Brief, 1992* (Tokyo: MOF, 1992), pp. 27–28.

61. *Congressional Quarterly Almanac, 1990*, p. 114.

62. Ibid., p. 132.

63. Ibid., pp. 135–136.

64. Ibid., p. 136.

65. Ibid., pp. 139–40.

66. Bush began expressing "regrets" at a postelection news conference on November 7. Ibid., p. 166.

67. The barrage of amendments on October 17 and 18 came from senators David L. Boren of Oklahoma, Kent Conrad of North Dakota, Albert Gore of Tennessee, Carl Levin of Michigan, and Steve Symms of Idaho. George Hager

and Pamela Fessler, "Negotiators Walk Fine Line to Satisfy Both Chambers," *Congressional Quarterly Weekly Report*, vol. 48 (October 20, 1990), pp. 3479–83.

68. This defense of earmarking by Senator Symms, Republican of Idaho, eventually failed, but on a 48 to 52 vote. Ibid., p. 3483.

69. Mike Mills, "Trust Fund 'Sanctity' Crumbling under Pressure from Budget," *Congressional Quarterly Weekly Report*, vol. 48 (October 20, 1990), p. 3502.

70. A mild recession and the costs of the savings and loan bailout were principally responsible for the growth of the deficit after 1990.

71 George Hager, "President Throws Down Gauntlet," *Congressional Quarterly Weekly Report*, vol. 51 (February 20, 1993), p. 357.

72. David S. Cloud and George Hager, "Clinton's Economic Agenda at Stake in Deficit Bill," *Congressional Quarterly Weekly Report*, vol. 51 (May 1, 1993), p. 1065. Later in the month, Boren made his position rather clear: "I'm not going to vote for a Btu tax in committee or on the floor, ever, anywhere. Period. Exclamation point." Quoted in David S. Hilzenrath and Eric Pianin, "Sen. Boren Targets Clinton Energy Tax," *Washington Post*, May 21, 1993, p. A20.

73. George Hager and David S. Cloud, "Democrats Pull Off Squeaker in Approving Clinton Plan," *Congressional Quarterly Weekly Report*, vol. 51 (May 29, 1993), p. 1340. Also, Eric Pianin and Ruth Marcus, "Final Hours Saw President Signal Energy Tax Compromise," *Washington Post*, May 29, 1993, p. A1. At one point, exemptions were multiplying so quickly, it seemed as if the administration was granting them just for the asking. Timothy Noah, "BTU Tax Is Dying Death of a Thousand Cuts as Lobbyists Seem Able to Write Own Exemptions," *Wall Street Journal*, June 8, 1993, p. A18.

74. Michael Weisskopf, "Fanning a Prairie Fire," *Washington Post*, May 21, 1993, p. A1.

75. Eric Pianin and Richard M. Weintraub, "Peña Criticizes Tax on Transport Fuels," *Washington Post*, June 11, 1993, p. A1.

76. The key vote came on June 24 on a motion to kill an amendment by Senator Don Nickles, Republican of Oklahoma, that would have eliminated all of the 4.3-cent tax. *Congressional Quarterly Weekly Report*, vol. 51 (June 26, 1993), p. 1689.

77. *Congressional Record*, June 23, 1993, p. S7729.

78. Eric Pianin, "House Democrats Seek to Kill Energy Tax, Use Income as Offset," *Washington Post*, June 30, 1993, p. A5.

79. These, for example, were the expressed positions of Representatives Charles W. Stenholm of Texas and of David R. Obey of Wisconsin, respectively. George Hager and David S. Cloud, "Democrats Seek Wiggle Room as Conference Begins," *Congressional Quarterly Weekly Report*, vol. 51 (July 17, 1993), p. 1855.

80. David S. Cloud, "It's Democrats v. Democrats as Conference Nears," *Congressional Quarterly Weekly Report*, vol. 51 (July 10, 1993), p. 1800.

81. "They can't pass anything," groaned Rostenkowski. David S. Cloud and George Hager, "With New Budget Deal in Hand, Clinton Faces Longest Yard," *Congressional Quarterly Weekly Report*, vol. 51 (July 31, 1993), p. 2026.

82. *Congressional Record*, August 6, 1993, p. S10707.

83. Quoted in James A. Dunn, Jr., "The Politics of Federal Gasoline Taxes: Iron Triangles Issue Networks and Policy Change," paper delivered at the 1990 annual meeting of the American Political Science Association, p. 22.

84. Hoover's tax was proposed for purposes of deficit reduction, not highway construction. The tax's yield during its first year was equivalent to $1.15 billion in current dollars. The amount finally devoted to deficit reduction under the 1990 tax increase was $2.5 billion. Congressional Research Service, "Federal Excise Taxes on Gasoline and the Highway Trust Fund: A Short History," *CRS Report for Congress* (Washington, March 14, 1989), pp. 1–2.

85. At a critical juncture, Senator Hank Brown, Republican of Colorado, had offered an amendment requiring that all revenues from the forthcoming 4.3-cent gas tax be deposited for use in the transportation trust funds. The amendment passed easily, 66 to 32, but was eventually stricken in the House-Senate conference.

86. Inside metropolitan areas, but exclusive of central cities, the level of home-ownership was 71 percent in 1990. Bureau of the Census, *1990 Census of Housing: General Housing Characteristics*, (Department of Commerce, 1991), p. 1, table 1.

87. Anthony Downs, *Stuck in Traffic: Coping with Peak-Hour Traffic Congestion* (Brookings, 1992), pp. 19, 94, 102.

88. ENO Foundation for Transportation, *Commuting in America: A National Report on Commuting Patterns and Trends* (Westport, Conn., 1987), p. 38.

89. Federal Highway Administration, *New Perspectives in Commuting* (Department of Transportation, July 1992), p. 12.

90. For a very rough attempt to estimate the average differences, see Peter W. G. Newman and Jeffrey R. Kenworthy, *Cities and Automobile Dependence* (Hants, UK: Gower Publishing Co., 1989), p. 35.

91. Anthony Downs, "Contrasting Strategies for the Economic Development of Metropolitan Areas," unpublished paper, Brookings, September 1991, pp. 4–5.

92. Ibid., pp. 5–6.

93. In western Europe, the share of all urban passenger trips made by automobile has ranged from a low of 30.6 percent in Italy to a high of 47.6 percent in Germany. The U.S. figure is more than 82 percent. John Pucher, "Urban Travel Behavior as the Outcome of Public Policy," *American Planning Association Journal*, vol. 54 (Autumn, 1998), p. 510.

94. This is not to say that Republicans have never been willing to depart from a commitment to earmarking. The Bush administration did so in the fiscal 1991 budget. In 1975 President Gerald Ford had proposed legislation that would have left the highway trust fund with only one-quarter of the income from the government's gasoline tax of 4 cents a gallon. Half would have gone to the Treasury's general purpose fund, and the remaining quarter to the states for their unrestricted use. Ford believed that the highway trust was "a classic example" of a federal aid program "distorting the priorities of [state and local] governments." (Congress disagreed and extended the life of the fund.) *Congressional Quarterly Almanac, 1975*, p. 735.

Notes to Chapter 6

1. International Energy Agency, *Energy Prices and Taxes, First Quarter 1993* (Paris: IEA/OECD), p. 293, table 2; and Energy Information Administration, *Annual Energy Review, 1992* (GPO, 1992), p. 167, table 5.22.

2. Treasury Secretary George M. Humphrey, quoted in Richard O. Davies, *The Age of Asphalt: The Automobile, the Freeway, and the Condition of Metropolitan America* (Phila.: Lippincott, 1975), p. 4.

3. On the contrary, the minimal levy of 10 cents a gallon suggested by the Bush administration during the fall's budget proceedings was slashed in half. For congressional allegations of the oil industry "gouging American consumers" see *Congressional Record*, Senate, September 17, 1990, pp. S13225–28, and *Congressional Record*, House, September 28, 1990, pp. H8316–17. See also David Shribman and Michel McQueen, "Office-Seekers Revive 1970s Campaign Strategy of Bashing Oil Companies over Spike in Prices," *Wall Street Journal*, August 9, 1990, p. A12.

4. Figures based on estimates from House Budget Committee, *Fiscal Year 1991 Budget Agreement: Summary Materials*, October 27, 1990, pp. 25–32.

5. Japan Institute for Social and Economic Affairs, *Japan 1991: An International Comparison*, 1st ed. (Tokyo: Keizai Koho Center, October 31, 1990), p. 79. Figures are based on 1990 exchange rate of 134.40 yen to the dollar. International Monetary Fund, *International Financial Statistics Yearbook, 1991* (IMF, 1991), p. 461.

6. Robert W. Crandall, "Sustained Economic Growth or Sustainable Development?" Brookings Institution, November 30, 1993, p. 18.

7. The decision of planners in Los Angeles to build a twenty-two-mile subway line in one of the world's least densely settled urban centers may seem bizarre, but federal funds will pay for half the project's costs. Alternatives, such as restoring street trolley lines, would have required a much larger local contribution. William Hamilton, "An Underground Railroad to Lure West Coast's Slaves of the Freeway," *Washington Post*, January 31, 1993, p. A4.

8. These housing programs helped build about one-quarter of all new single-family homes after the war.

9. The overwhelming majority of Americans who drive to work park for free. Jessica Mathews, "The Myth of the American Car Cult," *Washington Post*, March 31, 1991, p. B7.

10. "In the Washington, D.C. area," writes one critic, "an employer can provide a parking space as a fringe benefit for an employee at a cost of about $8 a day, about $2,000 a year, without the recipient paying any federal tax on the benefit. To provide the same employee with an extra $2,000 of take-home salary, an employer would have to spend about $4,400 a year (including federal, state, and local taxes, pension contributions and other benefits)." James J. MacKenzie, Roger C. Dower, and Donald D. T. Chen, *The Going Rate: What It Really Costs to Drive* (Washington: World Resources Institute, June 1992), pp. 10–11.

11. In many areas, an end to free parking could have a potentially striking effect on driving. Several studies in California found dramatic increases in ride sharing and transit use following decisions by employers to cease offering subsi-

dized parking. See Michael Cameron, *Transportation Efficiency: Tackling Southern California's Air Pollution and Congestion* (Washington: Environmental Defense Fund, March 1991), pp. 27–28.

12. One of the many interesting innovations of the 1992 energy act was a little-noticed provision to increase tax-exempt allowances for transit vouchers, farecards, or tokens from $21 a month to $60. The simple change had been sought for eight years by Senator Daniel P. Moynihan of New York. Stephen C. Fehr, "Congress Enacts $60 Transit Subsidy for Employees," *Washington Post,* October 10, 1992, p. B8. Despite the change, automotive commuters still receive a much larger implicit tax benefit than do transit riders. The annual cash equivalent value of tax-free job-site parking spaces in Los Angeles, for instance, has been estimated to run as high as $1,072, or nearly $90 a month. Cameron, *Transportation Efficiency,* p. 28.

13. Cameron, *Transportation Efficiency,* p. 29.

14. Road Information Program, *1993 State Highway Funding Methods* (Washington: RIP, June 1993), p. 8.

15. We borrow the "visions" phrase from President Clinton's "comprehensive economic plan" submitted to Congress in February 1993. *A Vision of Change for America,* H. Doc. 103–49, 103 Cong. 1 sess. (February 17, 1993).

16. From 1970 to 1988, total population grew by 41.1 million in the United States, compared with 21.1 million in the thirteen west European nations and 18.3 million in Japan.

17. Government of Japan, Prime Minister's Office, *The National Land Agency* (Tokyo, 1993), pp. 1–6. With so much of Japan's productive capacity concentrated in the Tokyo region, congestion has reached the point of interfering with some of Japan's most vaunted industrial practices (just-in-time inventory management, for example).

18. We do not mean to imply that suburbanization is just a postwar American phenomenon. The dispersal of jobs and population from central cities had much earlier origins and, in varying degrees, has characterized the growth of metropolitan areas in most industrialized countries. See, for instance, Peter Mieszkowski and Edwin S. Mills, "The Causes of Metropolitan Suburbanization," *Journal of Economic Perspectives,* vol. 7 (Summer 1993), pp. 135–47. The rapidity of recent suburban development in the United States has been staggering, however. U.S. population density in urbanized areas in 1960 averaged 3,290 persons per square mile. Despite intense demographic growth, by 1980 the density figure had declined by a third, to 2,177 persons per square mile. Ira S. Lowry, "Planning for Urban Sprawl," Transportation Research Board, *A Look Ahead: Year 2020,* Special Report 220 (Washington: National Research Council, 1988), p. 291. More than 80 percent of all office floorspace in America's suburbs, for instance, has been built since 1970. Nationwide, the share of total office space outside central cities rose from 25 percent in 1970 to 57 percent by 1984. Robert Cervero, *Suburban Gridlock* (Rutgers, N.J.: Center for Urban Policy Research, 1986), p. 1, and, more generally, Thomas M. Stanback, Jr., *The New Suburbanization: Challenge to the Central City* (Westview Press, 1991), chaps. 1, 6.

19. See, more generally, Anthony Downs, *New Visions for Metropolitan America* (Brookings, 1994), chap. 5. Contrary to an implicit assumption of much

"new federalist" theory, empowering local jurisdictions (as most states legislatures do) does not necessarily imply less government interference in markets. See Clint Bolick, *Grassroots Tyranny: The Limits of Federalism* (Washington: Cato Institute, 1993).

20. These are not the only states that have adopted various land-use statutes. In general, however, the programs elsewhere have been much more limited. For an up-to-date survey, see John M. DeGrove, *The New Frontier for Land Policy: Planning and Growth Management in the States* (Cambridge, Mass.: Lincoln Institute of Land Policy, 1992). Also on recent developments, see William Fulton, "In Land-Use Planning, A Second Revolution Shifts Control to the States," *Governing*, vol. 2 (March 1989), pp. 40–45.

21. Under the state of Oregon's comprehensive growth management program, the Portland metropolitan area established a relatively concentrated "urban growth boundary" that managed to constrict virtually all new subdivision applications and residential units within the boundary. In rapidly growing Washington County, which contains many of Portland's suburbs, only 4 percent of the residential permits approved were for sites outside the boundary through much of the 1980s. Following a "metro housing rule" requiring ten housing units per acre, the Portland plan succeeded in reducing lot sizes from an average of almost 13,000 square feet to an average of approximately 8,000 square feet. See Robert L. Liberty, "Oregon's Comprehensive Growth Management Program: An Implementation Review and Lessons for Other States," *Environmental Law Reporter*, vol. 22 (June 1992), pp. 10377–79. Local planners and environmentalists claim these policies have influenced travel behavior. Transit ridership to downtown Portland has increased by 50 percent since 1972; transit now accounts for more than 40 percent of the work trips to the much-revitalized downtown. Keith A. Bartholomew, *A Tale of Two Cities* (Portland: 1,000 Friends of Oregon, 1993), p. 4.

22. The 1973 Oregon law (unnamed by the state's legislature) established urban "containment" as a state policy goal. A distinctive feature of Oregon's pioneering program is the enforcement power conferred on a Land Conservation and Development Commission (LCDC). After 1983, the state LCDC acquired authority to override local zoning ordinances and to require local governments to issue building permits at higher densities. The agency can also withhold distribution of certain state tax revenues to recalcitrant local governments. Liberty, "Oregon's Comprehensive Growth Management Program," p. 10371.

23. "In California, Stricter Rules," *New York Times*, July 15, 1991, p. D5.

24. In 1920, local governments bore 83.2 percent of the costs of public education, compared to 16.5 percent by the states and 0.3 percent by Washington. By 1976, the states were shouldering almost as much of the costs as the locals, 43.9 percent and 47.4 percent, respectively. The federal share had risen to 8.8 percent. National Center for Education Statistics, *Digest of Education Statistics, 1977–78* (Washington, 1978), p. 67. As of 1990, the states accounted for 47.2 percent; local governments, 46.6 percent; and Washington, 6.1 percent. National Center for Education Statistics, *Digest of Education Statistics* (Washington: NCES, 1992), p. 151.

25. In the New York State legislature, for example, the two suburban counties of Long Island, Nassau and Suffolk counties, now elect as many representatives

as do New York City's boroughs of Manhattan and Brooklyn. Robert Cervero, *Suburban Gridlock* (Rutgers, N.J.: Center for Urban Policy Research, 1986), p. 223.

26. The Twin Cities structure of suprametropolitan revenue sharing and land-use planning was established by the Minnesota legislature in 1967. On the history and results of this project, see Arthur Naftalin and John Brandl, *The Twin Cities Regional Strategy* (St. Paul: Metropolitan Council of Governments of the Twin Cities Area, November 1980), and Arthur Naftalin, *Making One Community out of Many: Perspectives on the Metropolitan Council of the Twin Cities Area* (St. Paul: Metropolitan Council of Governments of the Twin Cities Area, September 1986).

27. See Edward M. Gramlich, "The 1991 State and Local Fiscal Crisis," *Brookings Papers on Economic Activity*, 2:1991, pp. 249–75.

28. For an argument in favor of a different division of labor in the provision of social insurance programs, see Alice M. Rivlin, *Reviving the American Dream: The Economy, the States, and the Federal Government* (Brookings, 1992), chap. 9.

29. In California, for example, regional air quality improvement agencies implementing the Clean Air Act have become increasingly concerned with the link between land-use issues and traffic flows. Also, the 1991 Intermodal Surface Transportation Efficiency Act requires every urban area of more than 50,000 inhabitants to establish a metropolitanwide organization charged, inter alia, with examining the role of land-use planning in relieving congestion.

30. President Clinton's campaign called for spending an additional $60 billion over four years on various infrastructural investments. The oft-cited lag in highway expenditures was questionable. Is spending supposed to remain forever at (or above) the levels that prevailed during the peak period of the great national investment in the interstate system? See, in general, Heywood T. Sanders, "What Infrastructure Crisis?" *Public Interest*, no. 110 (Winter 1993), pp. 3–18. On the investment "gap," and the uncertain relationship between infrastructural investment and productivity growth, see Clifford Winston and Barry Bosworth, "Public Infrastructure," in Henry J. Aaron and Charles L. Schultze, eds., *Setting Domestic Priorities: What Can Government Do?* (Brookings, 1992), pp. 267–93.

31. The ISTEA designated $6.5 billion, or 5.7 percent, of highway funding for "demonstration projects." This represented a fivefold increase over spending on such projects authorized in the 1987 Surface Transportation Act. See Winston and Bosworth, "Public Infrastructure," p. 287. Traffic management systems, such as congestion-pricing plans, represent a tiny share of demonstration projects. The argument here, however, is less about the relative amounts of funding (the experimental pricing mechanisms are often relatively low-cost) than about whether conventional transportation spending should continue to take precedence over them.

32. For a comprehensive proposal to price highway facilities more efficiently, see Kenneth A. Small, Clifford Winston, and Carol A. Evans, *Road Work: A New Highway Pricing and Investment Policy* (Brookings, 1989). See also Elmer W. Johnson, *Avoiding the Collision of Cities and Cars: Urban Transportation Policy for the Twenty-First Century* (Chicago: American Academy of Arts and Sciences, 1993), pp. 15–25. New developments in electronics and computer technology are

now poised to transform the potential uses of price rationing in transportation. Electronic identification of vehicles could eliminate antiquated toll booths in favor of much more supple and time-sensitive congestion-fee systems.

33. Department of Energy, *National Energy Strategy: Powerful Ideas for America*, 1st ed. (GPO, February 1991), pp. 64–70.

34. "Historic Partnership Forged with Auto Makers Aims for 3-Fold Increases in Fuel Efficiency in as Soon as Ten Years," the White House, Office of the Press Secretary, September 29, 1993, p. 1.

35. Indeed, two Japanese companies, Honda and Mitsubishi, seem well on their way. In road tests as early as 1991, Honda Civics equipped with new VTEC-E 1.5 liter engines achieved 86 miles to the gallon when operating at constant speeds of 37 miles per hour. David E. Sanger, "Fuel Efficiency: New Japan Coup?" *New York Times*, July 31, 1991, pp. D1, D7; also Doron P. Levin, "A Fuel-Efficient Grab for Power," *New York Times*, September 20, 1991, pp. D1, D3.

36. The European complaint before the GATT alleged that CAFE unfairly favored large, integrated, full-line manufacturers and worked to the disadvantage of limited-line producers that concentrate on the high end of the automobile market, as several of Europe's car makers do. The complaint also alleged discrimination between imported products and like domestic products, and that a disproportionate amount of CAFE penalty payments were paid by foreign car manufacturers, a violation of GATT's article III:2. Quite apart from this trade dispute, there appear to be perverse effects of CAFE on aspects of America's own trade performance. See Thomas Gale Moore, "A Hidden Culprit in Auto Imports," *Wall Street Journal*, January 14, 1992, p. A15.

37. The average fuel-economy ratings of imported passenger cars have exceeded the ratings for the domestic fleets every year since the inception of CAFE. As late as 1985, the gap remained wide, with imports averaging 31.5 mpg and the domestics averaging 26.3 mpg. The disparity has since narrowed, largely because of a general deterioration in the import average, but also in part because of reclassifications described here. Department of Transportation, *Summary of Fuel Economy Performance* (Washington, September 1992).

38. U.S. reliance on imported oil has risen for three straight years, setting a record (49.5 percent of consumption) in 1993. "U.S. Reliance on Oil Imports Sets a Record in '93," *Washington Post*, January 20, 1994, p. D10.

Notes to Appendix A

1. David L. Greene, "Vehicle Use and Fuel Economy: How Big Is the 'Rebound' Effect?" *Energy Journal*, vol. 13, no. 1 (1992), pp. 117–43. The definition of light-duty vehicles is passenger cars and light trucks with two axles and four wheels. These vehicles include all standard pickup trucks, vans, and multipurpose vehicles, as well as passenger cars driven by individuals for personal use. Of course, a substantial fraction of the light trucks are also used for commercial purposes, but the available data do not permit segregation of commercial from personal uses.

2. Estimating fuel consumption and miles traveled by passenger cars and light

trucks is very difficult. The Federal Highway Administration estimates these magnitudes from fragmentary state reports and a variety of other indexes with at best uncertain statistical precision.

3. The least-squares regression is estimated using a second-order serial-correlation correction. Following Greene, we use data for all passenger cars and two-axle, four-wheel trucks. Data on VMT and mpg are obtained from the Federal Highway Administration, *Highway Statistics* (Department of Transportation, various issues). Because light-truck data are available only since 1966, we also confine our results to the years after 1965. The real price of motor fuel is the CPI-U for motor fuel divided by the CPI-U for all items. Real GDP and CPI data are from the *Economic Report of the President*, various issues.

4. The gas-rationing dummy variables are combined into a single variable in Dermot Gately, "The U.S. Demand for Highway Travel and Motor Fuel," *Energy Journal*, vol. 11 (July 1990), pp. 59–73.

5. These data are drawn from J. Dillard Murrell, Karl H. Hellman, and Robert M. Heavenrich, "Light-Duty Automotive Technology and Fuel Economy Trends through 1993" (Ann Arbor, Mich.: Environmental Protection Agency, May 1993).

6. Our measures of the real price of fuel and steel are the CPI-U motor-fuel index and a weighted average of transaction prices of sheet and bar steel, each deflated by the overall CPI-U.

7. The current real price of fuel is dominated by the *CAFER* variable over much of the period. During the 1968–83 period, however, before CAFE was important, fuel prices have a much stronger and more significant effect. Thereafter, as *CAFER* rose and real fuel prices fall, the average weight of vehicles remains relatively low as producers are forced to raise the prices on larger cars or reduce the prices of smaller ones to meet the CAFE standard.

8. Performance was maintained by a drop in vehicle weight and an increase in engine efficiency as measured by horsepower per cubic inch.

9. Murrell, Hellman, and Heavenrich, "Light-Duty Automotive Technology."

10. All variables are obtained from *Consumer Reports*, various issues. The fuel efficiency is a harmonically weighted average of city and highway mpg as measured by Consumers Union. Weight is the curb weight of the car tested; displacement is the size of the engine tested.

11. The price of fuel did not begin rising substantially until late 1973, when the 1974 models had been introduced. In fact, it required another two years for technical fuel efficiency in new passenger-car models to respond to these prices.

12. The omitted size classes are subcompact and compact. When either is included, it does not assume a statistically significant coefficient.

Notes to Appendix B

1. Data for light trucks are available only since 1966; therefore, all estimates for light-duty vehicles are only for 1966–91 or some subset thereof.

2. One might argue that the inclusion of mpg in an ordinary least-squares

model is invalid because MPG is itself endogenous. That is, MPG responds to fuel prices. However, when the equation is estimated by two-stage least squares with the lagged real price of steel and a time trend as instruments for MPG, the results do not change. Thus, we report the Almon-lag results without the inclusion of MPG. The values of p_1 and p_2 reported in table B-1 are the Cochrane-Orcutt corrections for serial correlation.

3. Carol A. Dahl, "Gasoline Demand Survey," *Energy Journal*, vol. 7 (January 1986), p. 73.

4. The 1966–92 period is used because data on VMT before 1966 are not consistent with those for 1966 onward.

5. The average new-car fuel efficiency is derived from EPA's tests, whose protocol has changed over the 1968–91 period. These data are tabulated by J. Dillard Murrell, Karl H. Hellman, and Robert M. Heavenrich, "Light-Duty Automotive Technology and Fuel Economy Trends through 1993" (Ann Arbor, Mich.: Environmental Protection Agency, May 1993).

The average fuel efficiency of all cars on the road is derived from Federal Highway Administration estimates of total passenger-car miles and total fuel consumption by passenger cars. The estimation methodology employed by the states reporting to FHWA varies across states and over time. Unfortunately, these are the only time-series data available for all cars on the road.

6. The t-statistics for the lagged fuel prices are for the Almon-lag formulation.

7. David L. Greene, "CAFE or Price? An Analysis of the Effects of Federal Fuel Economy Regulation and Gasoline Price on New Car MPG, 1978–89," *Energy Journal*, vol. 11 (July 1990), pp. 37–57.

Index

Air quality standards: of EC, 57–58; gasoline tax impact on, 5, 115; U.S. violation of, 5, 6
Air travel, 3, 62
Alaska, 77
Alexander, Bill, 88, 89
American Automobile Association, 17, 70, 107
American Petroleum Institute, 66
Automotive industry: CAFE credits for, 30, 32, 45, 123; CAFE response by, 28–29, 30, 32; congressional regulation of, 1–2, 22–23, 87–88, 92, 98–99; domestic/import standards for, 24, 30, 32, 122–23; environmental standards for, 57–58; and foreign competition, 27; fuel efficiency improvements by, 14, 37–39, 137; fuel-price elasticities of, 46–48; mpg ratings for, 31; weight/acceleration price increase, 39–40. See also Chrysler Corporation; Ford Motor Company; General Motors Corporation
Automotive vehicles: air quality impact of, 5; CAFE standards for, 23, 29, 92; Energy Department projections for, 4; fuel efficiency of, 37–39, 43, 46–47, 49–50, 87; luxury, 30, 32; mass ownership of, 63–64; mpg determinants for, 136–37, 138–39; per capita, 9; percentage of new, 8; price determinants of, 40, 131–33; retail sales of (1972–92), 29; safety of, 40–41; size/weight characteristics of, 24, 26, 28, 35, 36, 37, 39–40; stock composition changes, 8, 29; VMT determinants for, 135; and VMT increases, 6, 7, 8

Balanced Budget Act of 1985, 100
Basic Law (Germany), 76
Baucus, Max, 105
Boren, David L., 105
Breaux, John B., 105
Btu tax, 66, 86–87, 105, 106
Budget 1991, 102–04
Budget 1994, 104–07
Budgets. See Fiscal policy
Bush administration: 1991 budget, 102–04; fuel economy standards, 24; gas tax proposal, 71, 86; new technology proposal, 121; Operation Desert Storm, 6

CAFE. See Corporate Average Fuel Economy
California, 119
Canada: energy tax policy, 73, 74, 77, 78, 79; gasoline price/tax rates, 60, 61
Carbon dioxide, 5, 34
Carbon monoxide, 5
Carter administration, 88, 93
Catalytic converters, 57, 58
Charles River Associates, 33–34
Chernick, Howard, 50–51, 52, 53
Chrysler Corporation, 27, 30, 47–48, 65, 137
Churchill, Winston, 70
Clark, Joe, 82
Clean Air Act of 1970, 92
Clean Air Act of 1990, 58
Clean air standards. See Air quality standards
Clinton, Bill: Btu tax, 66, 86–87, 105, 106; 1994 budget, 91, 104–07; CAFE sup-